Keith C. Brown, CFA
University of Texas, Austin
Donald J. Smith
Boston University

AF693727

Interest Rate and Currency Swaps: A Tutorial

The Research Foundation of
The Institute of Chartered Financial Analysts

Research Foundation Publications

Analysts' Earnings Forecast Accuracy in Japan and the United States
by Robert M. Conroy, Robert S. Harris, and Young S. Park

Active Currency Management
by Murali Ramaswami

Bankruptcy Prediction Using Artificial Neural Systems
by Robert E. Dorsey, Robert O. Edmister, and John D. Johnson

Canadian Stocks, Bonds, Bills, and Inflation: 1950–1987
by James E. Hatch and Robert E. White

Closed-Form Duration Measures and Strategy Applications
by Nelson J. Lacey and Sanjay K. Nawalkha

Corporate Bond Rating Drift: An Examination of Credit Quality Rating Changes Over Time
by Edward I. Altman and Duen Li Kao

Corporate Governance and Firm Performance
by Jonathan M. Karpoff, M. Wayne Marr, Jr., and Morris G. Danielson

Default Risk, Mortality Rates, and the Performance of Corporate Bonds
by Edward I. Altman

Durations of Nondefault-Free Securities
by Gerald O. Bierwag and George G. Kaufman

Earnings Forecasts and Share Price Reversals
by Werner F.M. De Bondt

The Effect of Illiquidity on Bond Price Data: Some Symptoms and Remedies
by Oded Sarig and Arthur Warga

Equity Trading Costs
by Hans R. Stoll

Ethics, Fairness, Efficiency, and Financial Markets
by Hersh Shefrin and Meir Statman

Ethics in the Investment Profession: A Survey
by E. Theodore Veit, CFA, and Michael R. Murphy, CFA

Ethics in the Investment Profession: An International Survey
by H. Kent Baker, CFA, E. Theodore Veit, CFA, and Michael R. Murphy, CFA

The Founders of Modern Finance: Their Prize-Winning Concepts and 1990 Nobel Lectures

Franchise Value and the Price/Earnings Ratio
by Martin L. Leibowitz and Stanley Kogelman

Fundamental Considerations in Cross-Border Investment: The European View
by Bruno Solnik

Global Asset Management and Performance Attribution
by Denis S. Karnosky, and Brian D. Singer, CFA

Initial Public Offerings: The Role of Venture Capitalists
by Joseph T. Lim and Anthony Saunders

Managed Futures and Their Role in Investment Portfolios
by Don M. Chance, CFA

The Modern Role of Bond Covenants
by Ileen B. Malitz

A New Method for Valuing Treasury Bond Futures Options
by Ehud I. Ronn and Robert R. Bliss, Jr.

A New Perspective on Asset Allocation
by Martin L. Leibowitz

Options and Futures: A Tutorial
by Roger G. Clarke

The Poison Pill Anti-Takeover Defense: The Price of Strategic Deterrence
by Robert F. Bruner

A Practitioner's Guide to Factor Models

Predictable Time-Varying Components of International Asset Returns
by Bruno Solnik

Program Trading and Systematic Risk
by A.J. Senchack, Jr., and John D. Martin

The Role of Risk Tolerance in the Asset Allocation Process: A New Perspective
by W.V. Harlow III, CFA, and Keith C. Brown, CFA

Selecting Superior Securities
by Marc R. Reinganum

Stock Market Structure, Volatility, and Volume
by Hans R. Stoll and Robert E. Whaley

Time Diversification Revisited
by William Reichenstein, CFA, and Dovalee Dorsett

Interest Rate and Currency Swaps: A Tutorial

© 1995 The Research Foundation of the Institute of Chartered Financial Analysts

All rights reserved. No part of this publication may be reproduced, stored in a retrieval system, or transmitted, in any form or by any means, electronic, mechanical, photocopying, recording, or otherwise, without the prior written permission of the copyright holder.

This publication is designed to provide accurate and authoritative information in regard to the subject matter covered. It is sold with the understanding that the publisher is not engaged in rendering legal, accounting, or other professional service. If legal advice or other expert assistance is required, the services of a competent professional should be sought.

ISBN 0-943205-32-8

Printed in the United States of America

September 1995

Mission

The Research Foundation's mission is to identify, fund, and publish research that is relevant to the CFA® Body of Knowledge and useful for AIMR member investment practitioners and investors.

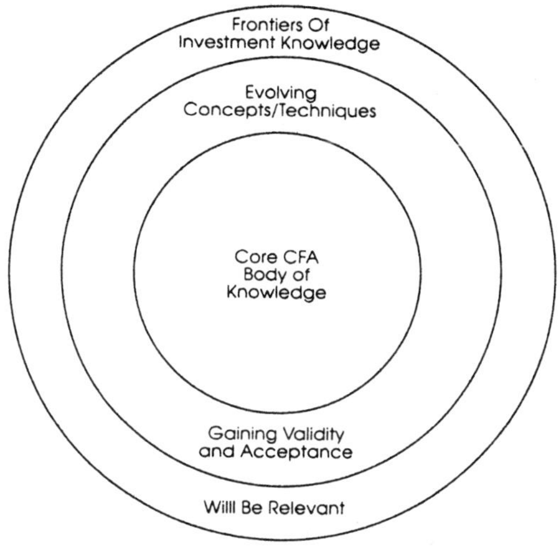

The Research Foundation of
The Institute of Chartered Financial Analysts
P.O. Box 3668
Charlottesville, Virginia 22903
U.S.A.
Telephone: 804/980-3644
Fax: 804/980-3634

Table of Contents

Acknowledgments

This project began in 1986 when, as full-time consultants to Manufacturers Hanover Trust Company, we first recognized the impact interest rate and currency swaps were having on corporate finance and institutional investment. We have been fortunate to have had opportunities to follow closely the development of these markets and to work with a number of market professionals. We owe a great debt of gratitude to our many colleagues at Manufacturers Hanover, Chemical Bank, and Texas Commerce Bank. In particular, we would like to thank Barbara Luttich, Gary Hickerson, and Mike Fitzgerald, as well as Tom McCaskill, Tom Kennedy, Tom Geggatt, and Eileen Green, who provided the platform for developing much of the material contained in this volume.

We would also like to thank Gary Gastineau for his support and guidance in the formative stages of this project. In fact, his invaluable *Dictionary of Financial Risk Management* provided us with a considerable amount of the motivation needed to create the glossary that appears at the end of the tutorial.

Lastly, we would like to thank the Research Foundation of the Institute of Chartered Financial Analysts for its solicitation and generous funding of our work. We appreciate the efforts of Katy Sherrerd and her staff in helping to bring this project to fruition and for recognizing the important role that swap contracting plays in today's financial markets.

Keith C. Brown, CFA
Donald J. Smith

Foreword

Derivatives tend to provoke some colorful emotions among people who don't know much about them. Some turn white with fear, others red with anger (witness the reactions of the citizens of Orange County, California). In practice, a little knowledge goes a long way toward tempering these reactions.

This tutorial provides more than a little knowledge about two particularly useful forms of derivatives—interest rate and currency swaps. Both are widely used by corporations and investors for risk-management purposes in a world in which the volatility of both interest rates and exchange rates has increased markedly. The number of interest rate swap contracts in 1993 was seven times the number in 1987; the number of currency swaps was five times as great. Surely, these numbers alone are testimony to the need for such instruments. In financial products, as in others, demand does indeed elicit innovation and supply.

Keith Brown and Don Smith, with this tutorial, have created an invaluable resource for those wishing—or needing—to know more about swaps. The authors steer readers gently through the complexities of and possible variations on these instruments, providing step-by-step instructions and "real-life" examples of how to use them. The exercises (and solutions) after each chapter permit readers to learn by doing, as well as by reading. Another feature readers will find useful is a comprehensive current bibliography of other books, journal articles, and papers relating to the subject of swaps.

The Research Foundation is pleased to present this second entry in its tutorial series. We believe it is a useful addition to the literature on swaps and, like the instruments themselves, meets a real demand for such products in the field of derivatives. The authors should be commended for the thoroughness and comprehensiveness of this work.

Katrina F. Sherrerd, CFA
Executive Director
Research Foundation of the
Institute of Chartered Financial Analysts

Chapter 1. Overview of the Swap Market

Many innovative financial products have appeared (and disappeared) during the past couple of decades. With the benefit of hindsight, it is now clear that one of the most important and lasting innovations developed in this era is the over-the-counter swap contract. The interest rate and currency swap markets have become enormous in the sheer number and size of transactions and participants. Perhaps the most telling statement of impact is that swaps have attained "commodity status." These days, financial analysts routinely consider the effects of "swapping" into or out of a particular interest rate or currency exposure. Although our primary focus is on interest rate and currency swaps, we show that the same contract design can be used to manage equity and commodity price risks as well.

Broken down to its essential nature, a swap contract is quite straightforward. Two *counterparties* agree to a periodic exchange of cash flows for a set length of time based on a specified amount of principal. Both cash flows in an interest rate swap are denominated in the same currency; in a currency swap (sometimes called a cross-currency swap), the cash flows are expressed in different monetary units. In either type of contract, one of the cash flow streams typically is based on a fixed interest rate set at the inception of the deal, and the other is referenced to an index that varies over time. A standard, or "plain vanilla," interest rate swap is an exchange of a fixed interest rate for LIBOR (the London Interbank Offered Rate). Each settlement period, the two rates are compared and the difference (times the transaction's *notional principal*) is paid by one counterparty to the other. A typical currency swap is an exchange of a fixed interest rate, say 8 percent in Canadian dollars, for U.S. dollar LIBOR. An important difference is that an interest rate swap does not involve an exchange of principal (hence the term "notional" principal), whereas actual principal amounts are usually traded at the inception and maturity of a currency swap.

Historical Development of the Swap Market

Swap contracting as we know it today is a fairly recent phenomenon. The first swap agreement was negotiated in 1981 by Salomon Brothers on behalf of the World Bank and IBM and involved an exchange of cash flows denominated in Swiss francs and deutschemarks. The first standard fixed-for-floating interest rate swap in the United States was executed in 1982 with the Student Loan Marketing Association ("Sallie Mae") as a counterparty.

These transactions raise two questions: First, given that firms have borrowed money from one another (thereby creating interest rates) and have traded across national borders in different currencies (thereby creating foreign exchange rates) for hundreds of years, why have we had interest rate and currency swaps for only a short period of time? Second, why did the interest rate swap, which is the simpler of the two contracts by virtue of having no foreign exchange component, develop after the currency swap?

The defining factor behind the timing of the development of the swap markets is summarized in a single word: *volatility*. In particular, what matters is the volatility of interest rates (particularly in the United States) and exchange rates. Two recent events significantly reshaped the volatility of these two variables. The first was the suspension in August 1971 of the Bretton Woods worldwide system of maintaining fixed exchange rates linked to a gold standard. Thereafter, exchange rates throughout the world were effectively allowed to float to market-determined levels (albeit with frequent central bank intervention). The second catalyzing event occurred in October 1979, when the U.S. Federal Reserve Board of Governors, led by its chairman Paul Volcker, in an attempt to reduce the inflation rate, elected to change its operating target to focus on bank reserve growth rates rather than the level of short-term interest rates.

The effect of each of these events on rate volatility is displayed rather emphatically in Figure 1.1. The top panel shows how the first difference (i.e., the current minus the previous rate) of the monthly series of Japanese yen/U.S. dollar exchange rates has evolved since January 1960. The most striking feature is the virtual break in the constancy of the pattern that occurred in the latter part of 1971, following the breakdown of the Bretton Woods agreement. The lower panel illustrates how the Federal Reserve's policy change increased the volatility of the ten-year, constant-maturity U.S. Treasury series in late 1979. When these charts are taken together, the answers to the questions about the evolution of the swap markets become evident. First, although corporations always had been exposed to interest and exchange rates, the financial instruments to hedge those risks only became available when volatility reached a level at which market making would be profitable. Second, volatility in the markets for foreign exchange increased well before the volatility of domestic interest rates increased.

By any standard of measurement, the growth of the swap markets that was spurred by these events has been remarkable. Table 1.1 presents annual statistics on total dollar volume and number of contracts for interest rate and currency swaps. Also reported is average size of an outstanding contract in each market. Several aspects of these data are revealing. First, from 1987 (the first year for which this information was gathered in a systematic manner) to 1993, outstanding principal in the entire swap industry increased from less than \$1 trillion to more than \$7 trillion. This growth is especially striking given that the volume prior to 1981 was effectively zero. Second, interest rate swap activity is substantially greater than that for currency swaps. In 1993, for instance, total notional principal of interest rate swaps was seven times that for currency swaps. Third, the rate of expansion in the two markets over this time frame differs; the outstanding principal of interest rate agreements grew at an average annual rate of 44.36 percent compared with 30.43 percent for currency contracts. Finally, although the size of the typical currency swap deal appears to have fluctuated around the \$27 million mark for some time, interest rate swap transactions have been getting steadily larger in scale.

The primary users of swap agreements are corporate and institutional managers seeking to hedge their underlying operating statement and balance sheet exposures to adverse movements in interest rates or foreign exchange rates. In fact, according to a 1991 survey of firms' chief financial officers by *Institutional Investor*, three-quarters of the firms with revenues of at least \$3 billion had used swaps at some point. Cited motivations for using swaps included a corporate treasurer trying to keep the funding cost of a floating-rate debt issue from getting too high, another treasurer protecting the home-currency revenue generated by product sold overseas, an insurance company executive attempting to align the interest rate sensitivities of the firm's assets and liabilities, and a portfolio manager trying to execute a tactical asset allocation strategy in a cost-effective way. Notice that these motivations do not involve the pursuit of financial arbitrage. This omission is notable because many swaps in the early years of the market aimed to lower the end user's cost of borrowed funds by attaching the swap to a newly issued

Figure 1.1 Volatility in the Exchange Rate and Interest Rate Markets

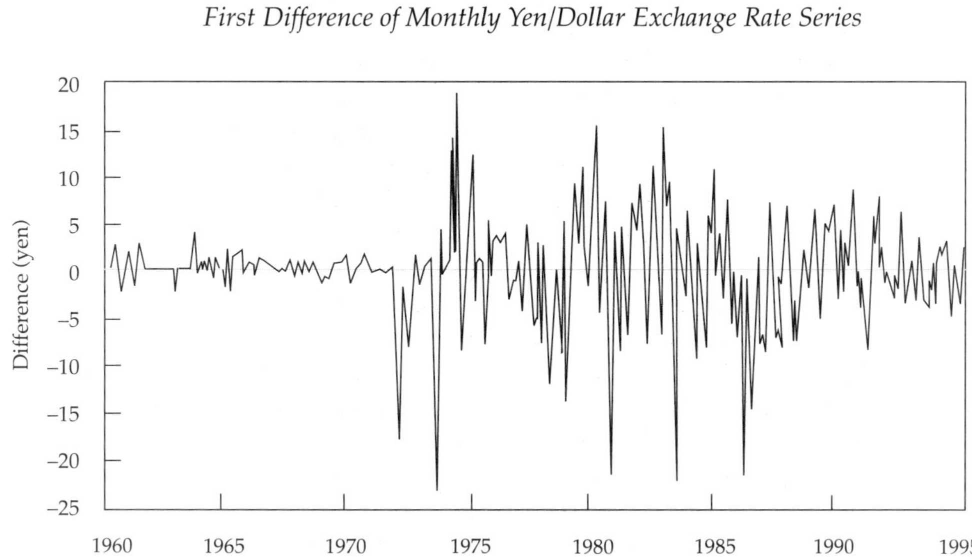

Data Source: Federal Reserve System.

bond. The swap market, however, could not have grown as large and as rapidly as it has if it had to rely largely on continuing inefficiency in the capital market, an inefficiency that permits the new-issue arbitrage opportunity.

A key element to the swap market's success has been the flexibility of the contract itself. Because each swap is negotiated in the over-the-counter market, there is no limit on the terms or conditions that can be written into the contract, assuming that the two parties find them mutually agreeable. The essential variables in a swap contract include the level of the fixed rate, the manner in which the variable reference rate is to be determined, the scale of the transaction (i.e., the notional principal), the currency of the cash flows, the dates of the settlement payments, and the events that define default. Although plain vanilla terms of agreement have emerged, unconventional "structured" swaps also can be transacted. This feature distinguishes swaps from exchange-traded futures contracts, which

Table 1.1 Growth of the Interest Rate and Currency Swap Markets

Year-End	Total Notional Principal (USD equivalent, in millions)	Total Contracts	Average Contract Size ($millions)
Interest Rate Swaps			
1987	$ 682,888	34,127	$20.01
1988	1,010,203	49,560	20.38
1989	1,539,320	75,223	20.46
1990	2,311,544	102,349	22.58
1991	3,065,065	127,690	24.00
1992	3,850,806	151,545	25.41
1993	6,177,352	236,126	26.16
Currency Swaps			
1987	$ 182,807	6,612	$27.65
1988	316,821	10,271	30.85
1989	434,849	15,285	28.45
1990	577,535	22,717	25.42
1991	807,166	31,035	26.01
1992	860,387	32,841	26.20
1993	899,618	32,606	27.59

Note: The currency swap total is adjusted for double-counting of contracts.
Source: The International Swaps and Derivatives Association.

have standardized terms. In fact, one of the main reasons for the extraordinary development of the swap market has been the extent to which the inherent flexibility of the contract allows corporate risk managers to customize solutions to their hedging needs.

Over-the-counter swaps differ from exchange-traded futures contracts in another fundamental way. The daily mark-to-market valuation and settlement procedures of a futures exchange limit credit risk dramatically. Given that gains and losses are realized daily, no unrealized value builds up over the lifetime of the futures contract as it does on a swap. Thus, a swap contract is necessarily a risky instrument in that default by the counterparty could lead to significant economic loss (although the amount of notional principal can be a very deceptive measure of the extent of risk). Both counterparties to the swap bear this credit risk. Moreover, swaps have tended to be unsecured obligations, although in recent years, a growing trend toward collateralized arrangements has developed.

These two aspects of interest rate and currency swaps—customization and credit risk—explain why commercial banks have played such a major role in the development of the market. At first, banks acted as brokers to the market, putting the corporate *end users* together and collecting an arrangement fee. Banks eventually stepped in as intermediaries to the transactions and served as the counterparties to the end users. This arrangement facilitated growth of the swap market because commercial banks, more than any other institution in the economy, have the human and financial capital to assess and manage credit risk. Moreover, many money-center banks saw swaps as a natural replacement to the business they were losing as their best corporate customers accessed capital markets to raise funds directly instead of indirectly via bank loans, a phenomenon dubbed "disintermediation." Over-the-counter derivatives, such as swaps, offered a means of "reintermediation" between commercial banks and corporations. Table 1.2 lists the biggest swap and derivatives houses worldwide. Note that commercial banks are not just market makers; they also tend to be heavy end users of swap contracts to manage their own balance sheet exposures.

Another interpretation of the role of commercial banks in the swap market is as an intermediary between the futures industry and corporate risk managers. Many swap contracts compete directly with exchange-traded futures, as in the case of a plain vanilla interest rate swap exchanging a fixed rate for LIBOR versus a strip of Eurodollar futures contracts. Because the swap can be customized to the specific needs of the end user, in particular with regard to the exact settlement dates, it can minimize the basis risk that remains even after executing the hedge. Many corporate end users prefer a more exact hedge undertaken with a bank counterparty rather than structuring the hedge itself with futures contracts, even if it costs a little more and entails bearing the bank's credit risk. The bank, in turn, can lay off the risk it assumes when entering the swap with the corporation by using the futures contracts themselves. In effect, the bank intermediary acquires a futures position with its attendant daily mark-to-market set-

Table 1.2 Outstanding Notional Principal of Leading Derivatives Dealers, 1993

Financial Institution	Total Notional Principal ($billions)
Chemical Bank	$2,416
Bankers Trust	1,982
Citicorp	1,981
J.P. Morgan	1,660
Union Bank of Switzerland	1,452
Swiss Bank	1,352
Société Générale	1,209
Mitsubishi Bank	1,182
Crédit Lyonnais	1,110
Chase Manhattan	1,042
Crédit Suisse	1,017
Salomon	967
BankAmerica	964
Banque Indosuez	945
Merrill Lynch	918
Goldman Sachs	752
Barclays	751
Paibas	742
National Westminster	577
Royal Bank of Canada	554

Note: German and most Japanese banks do not disclose derivative position sizes.
Source: Fortune, March 7, 1994.

tlement procedures and passes it on to the corporation as a contract that settles up only periodically. In fact, the growth of trading activity in futures contracts has been just as dramatic as that of the swap market in recent years, which indicates that the over-the-counter swap market and futures exchanges complement one another as much as they compete.

An important institutional presence in the swap market is the International Swaps and Derivatives Association (ISDA). This organization, which was originally known as the International Swap Dealers Association, is an industry trade group that provides its members with many services, ranging from periodic surveys of trends in the market to advocacy on regulatory issues. Easily the most important contribution ISDA has made to the growth of the industry was to create a set of standardized terminology and conditions that has governed virtually every market transaction since 1987. Specifically, ISDA developed (and continues to update) *Master Agreement* documents for interest rate and currency swaps that spell out precisely, among other aspects, the language of the deal, how agreements need to be confirmed, what happens in the event of a counterparty default, and how the parties to the transaction should treat the swap for tax purposes.

Interest Rate Swaps: Basic Product Design and Market Conventions

At first glance, swap market terminology can be a confusing blend of banking, capital market, and futures market vocabulary. Several conventions, however, have emerged to standardize the language necessary to negotiate and understand swap transactions. Figure 1.2 illustrates several of these conventions for a plain vanilla, U.S.-dollar-denominated interest rate swap agreement. The two counterparties have arranged to make periodic exchanges of cash flows based on a common notional principal and two separate interest rates, one that remains fixed for the life of the agreement and one that is reset (i.e., "floats") according to changing market conditions. The two parties to the transaction are referred to as the *pay-fixed* (Counterparty A) and *receive-fixed* (Counterparty B) sides of the deal.

Figure 1.2 Swap Market Pricing Mechanics

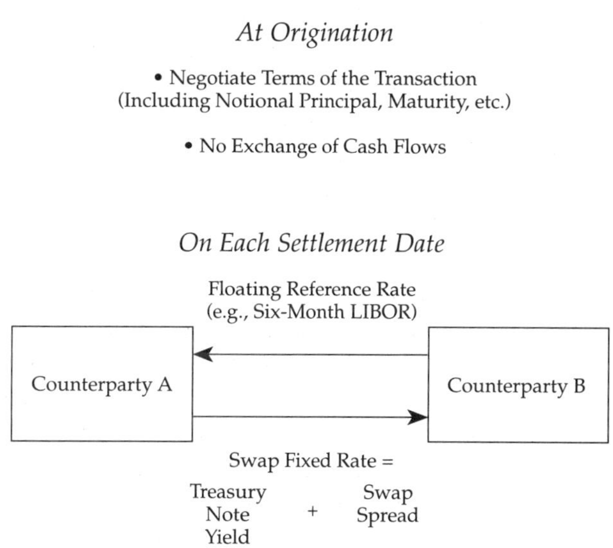

No exchange of cash flows takes place at origination of the swap.

The fixed-rate payer is sometimes said to have "bought" the swap or, equivalently, taken the long position, which would then leave the fixed-rate receiver as the "seller," or short position. In fact, nothing is actually bought or sold, because at inception, the swap is neither an asset nor a liability. Each party has entered a zero-sum contract that might, and probably will, take on positive value to one side; if it does, the other side will have a corresponding amount of negative value. The expressions "buy" and "sell" arise from interpreting the floating reference rate as the commodity that the two counterparties are trading; the swap's fixed rate is the price for this recurring transaction. That is, Counterparty B can be viewed as having agreed to sell the reference rate on each settlement date for the fixed rate agreed upon at the outset.

Notice also that the floating-rate side of the transaction is quoted *flat*; any modification to the price of the swap typically is negotiated as an adjustment to the fixed rate. For example, a market maker might set a lower pay-fixed rate when transacting with a weaker counterparty than with a stronger one; the receive-fixed side is LIBOR flat in each case. The reference rate on the swap can be any mutually agreeable index (e.g., LIBOR, the prime rate, a commercial paper index, or the average of certificate of deposit rates). Nevertheless, a recent ISDA survey reported that about 90 percent of the U.S.-dollar-based contracts used either three- or six-month LIBOR as the floating rate.

Another important convention shown in Figure 1.2 is that the fixed-rate side of the contract is broken down into two components: a Treasury note yield and a *swap spread.* The particular Treasury note yield selected depends on the maturity, or *tenor,* of the swap. The usual practice is to use the yield of the on-the-run (i.e., the most recently issued) security maturing closest to the swap's final settlement date. A convenient facet of these conventions is that the market maker's quoted price for the agreement is reduced to the swap spread, because all market participants can monitor the current Treasury yield. In fact, a market maker usually quotes two swap spreads—the bid side when it pays the fixed rate and the offer side when it receives the fixed rate.

Table 1.3 lists a representative set of quoted fixed rates on swaps based on six-month LIBOR. Two aspects of this table are noteworthy. First, as the swap maturity lengthens, the absolute level of the swap spread tends to rise. This phenomenon suggests that the swap spread has a separate term structure from the usual maturity term structure built into the Treasury yield curve. Second, across the entire list of swap maturities—which is representative of the tenors commonly available in the market—the bid–ask differential on the swap spread quote never exceeds 4 basis points. This differential represents the market maker's profit margin on a pair of "matched" deals (i.e., simultaneously executed pay-fixed and receive-fixed transactions having the same notional principal and settlement dates), so apparently the plain vanilla segment of the swap market is quite competitive. These bid–ask spreads were much wider in the formative years of the swap market. Figure 1.3 illustrates a matched pair of five-year agreements using these quotes, with Counterparty C now serving the role of the second corporate end user.

Several important standards govern the process for calculating the periodic settlement payments. The most important is that settlements are made on a net basis; that is, although Figures 1.2 and 1.3 suggest that two cash flows will change hands each settlement period on

Table 1.3 Representative Quotes for Plain Vanilla Interest Rate Swaps Based on Six-Month LIBOR

Swap Maturity (years)	Treasury Yield (%)	Bid Swap Spread (bps)	Ask Swap Spread (bps)	Effective Fixed Swap Rate (%)
2	6.60	24	27	6.84–6.87
3	6.87	27	30	7.14–7.17
4	7.13	29	32	7.42–7.45
5	7.28	25	28	7.53–7.56
7	7.42	35	39	7.77–7.81
10	7.60	35	38	7.95–7.98
15	7.80	56	60	8.36–8.40

Source: Chemical Securities, Inc.

Figure 1.3 A Matched Pair of Five-Year Swap Transactions

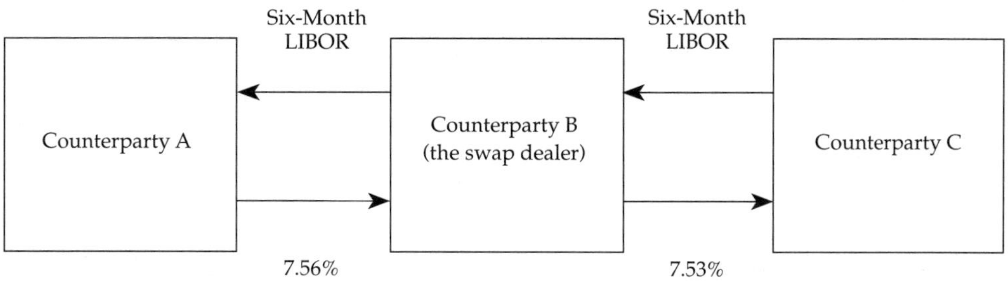

each deal, in reality, the counterparty owing the larger of the two amounts will simply pay the difference. Second, the fixed and floating rates specified in the swap agreement might not be directly comparable. For instance, the fixed rate typically is a semiannually compounded rate quoted on a bond basis (consistent with a quoted Treasury yield). The day-count convention for the swap fixed rate used for partial-year cash flows typically is either "actual/365" or "30/360." In contrast, U.S. dollar LIBOR is a money-market rate based on a 360-day year; its partial-year cash flows are calculated on an "actual/360" basis. Assuming an actual/365 day count for the fixed-rate payment, the formulas for the settlement calculations under these conditions are as follows:

$$(\text{Fixed-rate payment})_t = (\text{Swap fixed rate}) \times \left(\frac{\text{Number of days}}{365}\right) \times (\text{Notional principal})$$

and

$$(\text{Floating-rate payment})_t = (\text{Reference rate})_{t-1} \times \left(\frac{\text{Number of days}}{360}\right) \times (\text{Notional principal}),$$

where the subscript denotes the settlement period date. Notice three important features of these equations. First, the principal involved in the interest rate swap transaction is never exchanged; it is notional (or hypothetical) in the sense that it is used only as a scale factor to translate a percentage rate into a cash amount. Second, the fixed-rate payment might vary from one period to another if the settlement periods themselves have different numbers of days. Note, however, that fixed-rate payments based on a 30/360 day count will not vary at all. Finally, the reference rate used to settle at date t is actually determined one period in arrears (i.e., at date $t - 1$). This convention, which matches the usual practice for determining interest payments in the floating-rate note and bank loan markets, ensures that both cash flows will always be known one full settlement period in advance. With these definitions, the net settlement obligation is defined in a straightforward manner as the difference between the fixed-rate and floating-rate payments.

Table 1.4 demonstrates the settlement date cash flows from the perspective of the fixed-rate payer in the five-year swap illustrated in Figure 1.3. Specifically, assume that after the initial agreement was negotiated, the terms of the transaction were confirmed as follows:

- Origination date: September 30, 1994
- Maturity date: September 30, 1999
- Notional principal: U.S. $30 million
- Fixed-rate payer: Counterparty A
- Swap fixed rate: 7.56 percent (semiannual, actual/365 bond basis)
- Fixed-rate receiver: Counterparty B (the swap dealer)
- Floating rate: Six-month LIBOR (money-market basis)
- Settlement dates: September 30th and March 30th of each year
- LIBOR determination: Determined in advance, paid in arrears

The third column of Table 1.4 lists an assumed path that the six-month spot LIBOR follows over the course of the contract. As the fixed-rate

Table 1.4 Settlement Cash Flows for the Fixed Payer on a Five-Year Interest Rate Swap

Settlement Date	Number of Days	Assumed Current LIBOR	Fixed-Rate Payment (Counterparty A)	Floating-Rate Receipt (Counterparty B)	Counterparty A's Net Payment (Receipt)
9/30/94	—	5.50%	—	—	—
3/30/95	181	5.75	$1,124,679	$ 829,583	$ 295,096
9/30/95	184	6.50	1,143,321	881,667	261,654
3/30/96	182	6.75	1,130,893	985,833	145,060
9/30/96	184	7.50	1,143,321	1,035,000	108,321
3/30/97	181	7.75	1,124,679	1,131,250	(6,571)
9/30/97	184	8.25	1,143,321	1,188,333	(45,013)
3/30/98	181	7.50	1,124,679	1,244,375	(119,696)
9/30/98	184	7.25	1,143,321	1,150,000	(6,679)
3/30/99	181	7.75	1,124,679	1,093,542	31,138
9/30/99	184	8.00	1,143,321	1,188,333	(45,013)

payer, Counterparty A makes (receives) the net settlement payment whenever the day-count-adjusted level of LIBOR is less than (exceeds) the swap fixed rate of 7.56 percent. This net settlement amount is shown in the last column of the table as the difference between the counterparties' cash flows.

Currency Swaps: Basic Product Design and Market Conventions

Two factors make the cross-currency swap agreement a more difficult transaction to analyze than the single-currency agreement considered above. First, because the associated cash flows are denominated in different monetary units, the principal amounts are usually exchanged at the origination and maturity dates of the contract. Second, because two currencies are involved, the interest rates defining the transaction can be expressed on either a fixed-rate or a floating-rate basis in either or both currencies. Assuming that the U.S. dollar is one of the currencies involved in the deal, this leaves the following four possibilities: (1) a fixed rate in the foreign currency versus a fixed rate in U.S. dollars, (2) a fixed rate in the foreign currency versus a floating rate in U.S. dollars, (3) a floating rate in the foreign currency versus a fixed rate in U.S. dollars, or (4) a floating rate in the foreign currency versus a floating rate in U.S. dollars. Although all of these formats are used in practice, the predominant quotation convention in the market is the second; that is, a plain vanilla currency swap is assumed to exchange a fixed rate in the foreign currency for U.S. dollar LIBOR. This structure is shown in Figure 1.4.

Notice in this diagram that two distinct types of exchanges take place: principal on both origination and maturity, and coupon interest on all of the settlement dates. Customarily, both principal exchanges are executed at the spot foreign exchange (FX) rate prevailing at the initiation date, regardless of subsequent market FX rates. Furthermore, as in the interest rate swap, the floating-rate side of the coupon exchanges in the standard currency swap is usually quoted flat. Thus, the dollar cash flow paid by Counterparty E on each settlement date is determined by multiplying the relevant LIBOR (which would once again have been determined at the previous settlement date) by the U.S. dollar principal amount, adjusted by the day-count factor. The periodic cash flow that Counterparty D is obligated to pay is simply the product of the quoted fixed rate and the foreign-currency-based principal amount. Because the cash flows differ in denomination, currency swaps do not settle on a net basis.

Table 1.5 lists a representative set of quotes for various maturities and the main international currencies. For comparative purposes, quotes for plain vanilla U.S. dollar interest rate swaps are presented in the last row of the table. These rates represent the fixed foreign interest rates that a market maker would receive for payment

Figure 1.4 A Basic Currency Swap Transaction

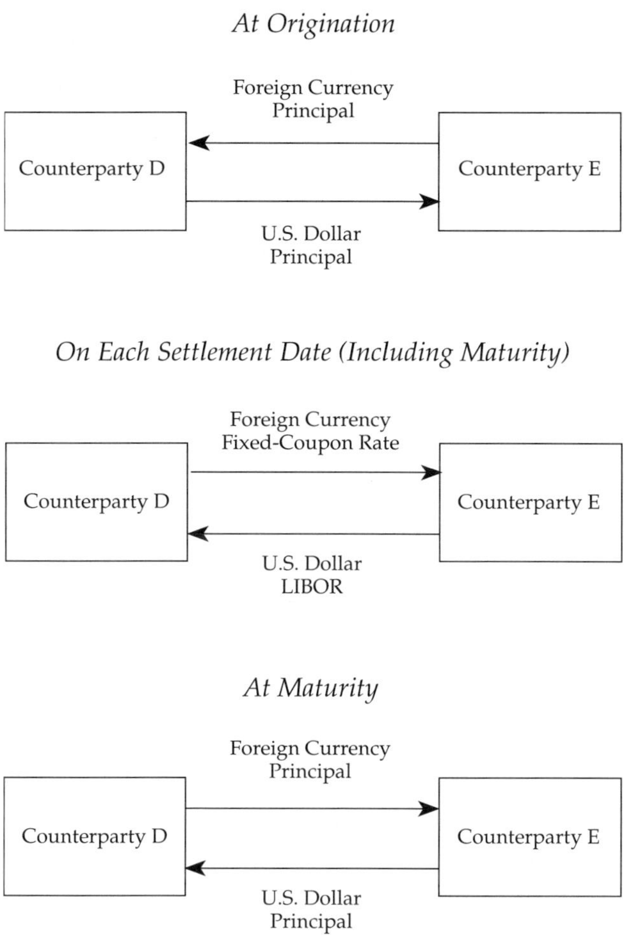

Table 1.5 Representative Quotes for Plain Vanilla Currency Swaps Based on Six-Month U.S. Dollar LIBOR for Two-, Three-, and Four-Year Maturities

Currency	2 Years	3 Years	4 Years
Yen	3.27%	3.78%	4.12%
Sterling	8.13	8.55	8.65
Swiss franc	5.07	5.24	5.38
Deutschemark	6.43	6.92	7.21
U.S. dollar	7.79	7.97	8.08

Source: Chemical Securities, Inc.

of U.S. dollar LIBOR. For instance, on a four-year contract, a corporate counterparty would have to pay the currency swap dealer 4.12 percent in Japanese yen (times the principal in yen) to receive U.S. dollar LIBOR (times the principal in dollars). Notice that in each market, the swap yield curve is upward sloping.

To see how these rate conventions translate into cash flows, suppose Counterparty D has agreed to pay the dealer (Counterparty E) 8.65 percent on the four-year sterling swap. Assume further that the transaction has the following characteristics:

- Origination date: November 15, 1994
- Maturity date: November 15, 1998
- Notional principal: GBP 20 million and USD 34.4 million
- Fixed-rate payer: Counterparty D
- Swap fixed rate: 8.65 percent in pounds sterling (semiannual bond basis)
- Fixed-rate receiver: Counterparty E (the swap dealer)
- Floating rate: Six-month LIBOR in U.S. dollars (money-market basis)
- Settlement dates: November 15th and May 15th of each year
- LIBOR determination: Determined in advance, paid in arrears

The initial and ultimate principal exchanges are based on the dollar/pound spot exchange rate of USD 1.72/GBP that is assumed to have prevailed at the swap origination date. With the preceding customs, the pound-denominated coupon settlement payments are computed as [0.0865 × (Number of days/365) × GBP 20 million], and the dollar-based cash flows are determined by [LIBOR × (Number of days/360) × USD 34.4 million]. These amounts are shown in Table 1.6 from the perspective of Counterparty D (i.e., the fixed-rate payer).

Although the plain vanilla form of a currency swap is of the fixed foreign currency/floating dollar variety, that is not always the most useful way to package cash flows in order to satisfy a corporate end user. For instance, what if Counterparty D in the previous example had wanted to receive a fixed rate in U.S. dollars, instead of LIBOR, in exchange for fixed sterling payments? Fortunately, the standard fixed/floating currency swap can easily be repackaged by combining it with a floating/fixed U.S. dollar interest rate swap. This objective can be accomplished by negotiating the following two transactions with the swap market maker:

Table 1.6 Settlement Cash Flows for the Fixed-Payer on a Four-Year, British Pound Sterling Currency Swap

Settlement Date	Number of Days	Assumed Current LIBOR	Fixed-Rate Payment (millions)	Floating-Rate Receipt (millions)
Initial Exchange of Principal				
11/15/94	—	5.75%	USD 34.400	GBP 20.000
Coupon Exchanges				
5/15/95	181	6.00	GBP 0.858	USD 0.994
11/15/95	184	6.25	0.872	1.055
5/15/96	182	6.70	0.863	1.087
11/15/96	184	7.25	0.872	1.178
5/15/97	181	7.00	0.858	1.254
11/15/97	184	6.75	0.872	1.187
5/15/98	181	5.50	0.858	1.167
Final Coupon and Principal Exchange				
11/15/98	184	5.75	GBP 0.872 and GBP 20.000	USD 0.967 and USD 34.400

- Receive dollar LIBOR in exchange for paying the sterling given rate of 8.65 percent, and
- pay dollar LIBOR in exchange for receiving a dollar fixed rate, assumed to be 8.04 percent.

Because the second of these swaps involves only dollar-based cash flows, physical exchange of principal is required only for the first transaction. Figure 1.5 illustrates the sequence of cash flow exchanges that will occur on the settlement dates.

As a practical matter, if both of these transactions were executed simultaneously with the same market maker, the corporate end user (Counterparty D) would not undertake two separate transactions. Rather, to minimize the requisite documentation and bookkeeping, the swap intermediary in this case would undoubtedly offer the counterparty a direct, blended quote of "receive U.S. dollar 8.04 percent, pay sterling 8.65 percent," leaving LIBOR out altogether. Moreover, using U.S. dollar LIBOR as the base facilitates computation of the full range of fixed/fixed nondollar swaps—for instance, a fixed rate in Swiss francs versus a fixed rate in deutschemarks. These fixed/fixed swaps were once known as CIRCUS swaps, which stood for "combined interest rate and currency swaps."

Recent Trends in the Use of Swap Contracts

In recent years, swap contracting has expanded into new markets, as well as into new versions of the basic product. For instance, it is now possible to trade both interest rate and currency swaps that are denominated in more than 18 different currencies. New nonplain vanilla swap designs and related products include

- *Off-market swaps*, which set the fixed rate to be something other than the prevailing "at-market" level in order to create an initial payment at the origination of the agreement;
- *Varying notional principal swaps*, in which the size of the deal either expands or contracts from one settlement date to the next according to a predetermined schedule;
- *Indexed amortizing rate swaps*, in which the notional principal varies in response to changes in some market index (such as the level of LIBOR) during the agreement;
- *Entry and exit options on swaps* (known as *swaptions*), which give the holder the right, but not the obligation, to get either into or out of a swap at prearranged terms;

Figure 1.5 Creating a U.S. Dollar, British Pound Sterling Fixed/Fixed Currency Swap (Settlement Date Payments)

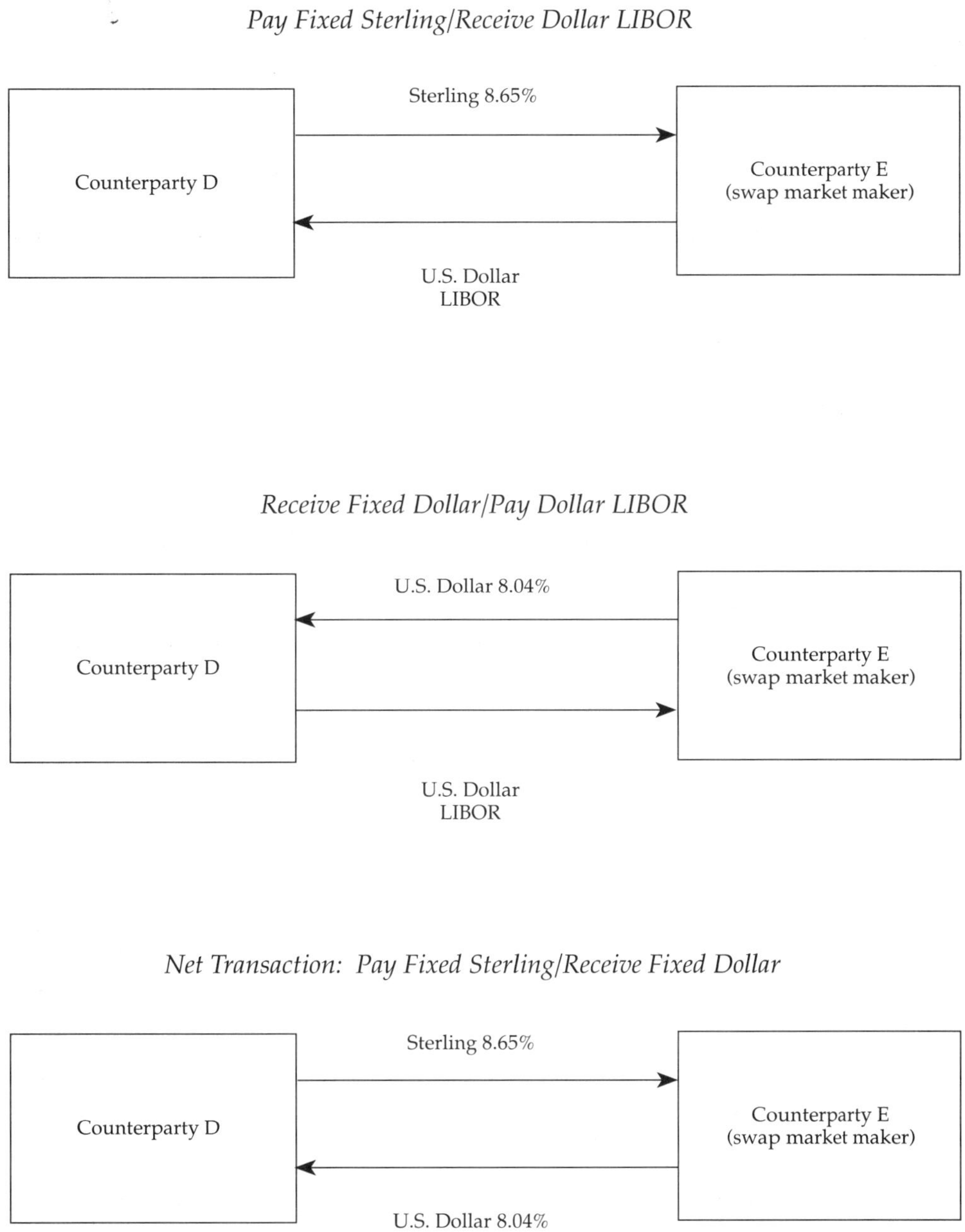

- *Basis swaps*, calling for the exchange of two different floating rates (e.g., LIBOR vs. prime);
- *"Diff" swaps*, which can be thought of as cross-currency basis swaps in that the cash flows are linked to floating rates in different countries but are denominated in the same base currency;
- *Cap* and *floor agreements*, which are the respective option analogs to the pay-fixed and receive-fixed sides of the swap contract itself;
- *Collars, corridors,* and *participation agreements*, which are combinations of caps and floors; and
- *Equity* and *commodity swaps*, which define one of the cash flows of the swap in terms of the return to an equity (e.g., Standard & Poor's 500) or a commodity (e.g., West Texas Intermediate Oil) index.

We will discuss these innovations in subsequent chapters.

To get a better idea of the range of the swap industry, consider Table 1.7, which is based on a recent ISDA market survey. The table shows the total outstanding notional principal for both interest rate and currency swaps of all varieties at year-end 1993. Also shown are the percentages of the various total outstanding volumes represented by each currency. These figures, which are listed in rank order by currency for interest rate swap contracts, show clearly that although U.S. dollar transactions are easily the largest single presence in either product market, they are far from dominant. Indeed, roughly two-thirds of the deals in each group are negotiated in a nondollar currency. In particular, about one in five transactions across the two markets is denominated in Japanese yen, with another 20 percent coming from a combination of deals done in Swiss francs, German deutschemarks, or British pounds. In fact, if the U.S.-dollar- and Japanese-yen-based activity were removed, the vast majority of swap activity in the world would be centered on the currencies of the Western European countries, including the European Currency Unit basket. Transactions in Canadian dollars and in currencies of Pacific Rim countries (Australia, New Zealand, and Hong Kong) account for a relatively small part of these markets.

Growth in the market for over-the-counter interest rate option products has paralleled that of the swap industry. Table 1.8 summarizes an ISDA report on the use of caps, floors, combination agreements (i.e., collars, corridors, and participations), and swaptions as of year-end 1992. The display lists the number of contracts transacted (both long and short), as well as the total notional principal of dollar-denominated agreements. Perhaps most notable is the small size of the interest rate option market relative to the swap market itself. Recall from Table 1.1 that total interest rate swap volume for 1992 was in excess of \$3.85 trillion with 151,545 contracts traded; the dollar-denominated portion of the market exceeded \$1.76 trillion in 52,258 contracts. In this light, the market for over-the-

Table 1.7 Swap Activity by Currency as of Year-End 1993

	Interest Rate Swaps		Currency Swaps	
Currency	Dollar Equivalent (millions)	Percent of Total	Dollar Equivalent (millions)	Percent of Total
U.S. dollar	\$2,457,043	39.78%	\$ 640,081	35.58%
Japanese yen	1,247,444	20.19	317,590	17.65
Deutschemark	629,724	10.19	139,377	7.75
French franc	456,371	7.39	45,754	2.54
British sterling	437,138	7.08	88,285	4.91
Swiss franc	182,207	2.95	146,544	8.14
Italian lira	162,042	2.62	45,439	2.53
Euro currency unit	133,133	2.16	73,510	4.09
Australian dollar	131,130	2.12	92,693	5.15
Canadian dollar	126,309	2.04	70,666	3.93
Dutch guilder	52,052	0.84	19,494	1.08
Spanish peseta	42,115	0.68	33,995	1.89
Swedish krona	32,049	0.52	34,403	1.91
Belgium franc	31,102	0.50	13,586	0.76
Hong Kong dollar	9,467	0.15	4,172	0.23
Danish krone	9,110	0.15	6,509	0.36
New Zealand dollar	6,209	0.10	4,871	0.27
Other currencies	32,707	0.53	22,266	1.24
Total	\$6,177,352		\$1,799,235	

Note: The currency swap total is unadjusted for double-counting of contracts.
Source: International Swaps and Derivatives Association.

Table 1.8 Cap, Floor, Combination, and Swaption Activity as of Year-End 1992

Activity	Caps	Floors	Combination Options	Swaptions	Total
Transaction Volume					
Number of contracts bought	3,176	840	211	3,594	12,821
Number of contracts sold	14,439	5,200	169	3,153	22,961
Total	17,615	6,040	380	6,747	30,782
U.S. Dollar Notional Principal (millions)					
Long positions	$ 81,450	$25,341	$ 3,932	$16,193	$126,916
Short positions	150,446	36,904	9,789	15,139	212,278
Total	$231,896	$62,245	$13,721	$31,332	$339,194

Note: Positions have been adjusted for double-counting of contracts.
Source: International Swaps and Derivatives Association.

counter interest rate option products was roughly one-tenth the size of the whole interest rate swap market, and the total number of option contracts traded represented only about one-fifth of the volume in swaps. Notice also that cap agreements, which protect the contract's holder against rising interest rates, were more popular than floor contracts (which pay off when rates fall), measured in either dollar or contract volume. Although the distribution of long and short positions is largely a function of interest rate expectations that prevailed at the time, the prevalence of caps is consistent with the notion that these contracts are used extensively by liability managers seeking protection against increases in their borrowing costs.

Exercises

Exercise 1.1: With the interest rate swap quotations shown in Table 1.3, use a box-and-arrow diagram to illustrate a matched set of seven-year, plain vanilla interest swap transactions from a dealer's point of view (i.e., the simultaneous acquisition of pay-fixed and receive-fixed transactions having the same notional principal and settlement dates). Also, calculate the swap dealer's profit on each settlement date, assuming a notional principal of \$25 million and, for simplicity, settlement dates that are exactly 182.5 days apart.

Solution: With bid and offer fixed rates for the seven-year deals quoted at 7.77 percent and 7.81 percent, respectively, the transaction can be illustrated as in Figure E-1.1. Notice that, barring default by one of the corporate counterparties, the dealer is not concerned with the actual level of LIBOR on any settlement date. If LIBOR is greater (less) than 7.81 percent, the dealer will make (receive) the net settlement payment to Firm X but receive (make) a payment from Firm Y when LIBOR is greater (less) than 7.77 percent. Thus, on every settlement date, the dealer will receive the difference between the bid and offer fixed rates prorated to the appropriate number of days in the settlement period and scaled to the notional principal amount. In this case, the calculation is given by

$$(0.0781 - 0.0777) \times \left(\frac{182.5}{365}\right) \times (\$25{,}000{,}000) = \$5{,}000.$$

Thus, the dealer will receive \$5,000 every six months for the next seven years from this pair of transactions.

Figure E-1.1 A Matched Set of Seven-Year Swaps

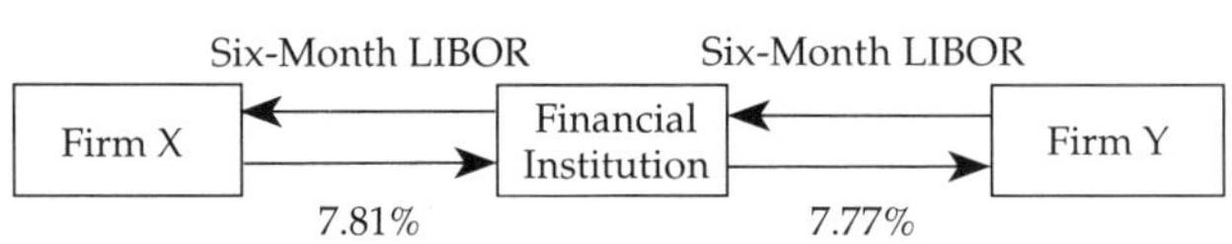

Exercise 1.2: Using the interest rate swap quotations listed in Table 1.3, calculate the swap cash flows from the standpoint of the fixed-rate receiver on a three-year swap with a notional principal of \$40 million. (Assume the relevant part of the settlement date pattern and the realized LIBOR path shown in Table 1.4 for the five-year agreement. Also, calculate fixed-rate payments on an actual/365 day-count convention.)

Solution: Given that no principal is exchanged at the origination of a plain vanilla interest rate swap on September 30, 1994, the first settlement will take place on March 30, 1995. As the fixed-rate receiver, the counterparty in question will calculate the following gross cash flows on this date:

$$\text{Floating-rate payment} = (0.0550) \times \left(\frac{181}{360}\right) \times (\$40{,}000{,}000) = \$1{,}106{,}111$$

and

$$\text{Fixed-rate receipt} = (0.0714) \times \left(\frac{181}{365}\right) \times (\$40{,}000{,}000) = \$1{,}416{,}263.$$

Thus, the net receipt due the receive-fixed counterparty is \$310,152 (i.e., \$1,416,263 − \$1,106,111). Notice that the value for six-month LIBOR used in the floating-rate calculation is determined by the September 30, 1994, value of that rate; the swap fixed rate is 7.14 percent, the bid side of the dealer's three-year quote. The complete list of settlement cash flows is given in Table E-1.1.

Table E-1.1 Settlement Cash Flows, Fixed-Rate Receiver

Settlement Date	Number of Days	Assumed Current LIBOR	Fixed-Rate Receipt	Floating-Rate Payment	Fixed-Rate Receiver's Net Receipt (Payment)
9/30/94	—	5.50%	—	—	—
3/30/95	181	5.75	\$1,416,263	\$1,106,111	\$ 310,152
9/30/95	184	6.50	1,439,737	1,175,556	264,181
3/30/96	182	6.75	1,424,088	1,314,444	109,643
9/30/96	184	7.50	1,439,737	1,380,000	59,737
3/30/97	181	7.75	1,416,263	1,508,333	(92,070)
9/30/97	184	8.25	1,439,737	1,584,444	(144,707)

Exercise 1.3: As a swap dealer, you have just been contacted by a prospective corporate counterparty who wishes to do a three-year "fixed/fixed" yen/sterling currency swap. In particular, the corporation needs to pay a fixed interest rate in Japanese yen and to receive a fixed rate in British pounds. Your current spot FX and three-year currency swap quotes (versus six-month U.S. dollar LIBOR) are as follows:

	Japanese Yen	*British Pound*
Spot Exchange Rate	JPY 127.47/USD	USD 1.82/GBP
Currency Swap Bid	4.85%	9.83%
Offer	4.92%	9.93%

These quotes imply that you would be willing to pay 4.85 percent in yen to receive U.S. dollar LIBOR, but you would need to receive 4.92 percent in yen when paying LIBOR. Your bid–offer spread is 7 basis points in yen. Note that the bid–offer spread is higher in sterling because each basis point is not worth as much, given that sterling would be at a forward discount to yen.

(a) Describe the sequence of transactions necessary to construct this swap from the counterparty's perspective, including your quotes for both of the fixed rates.

(b) Construct a table similar to Table 1.6 summarizing the cash flow exchanges on each exchange date, again adopting the end-user's viewpoint. In this analysis, assume that the deal is to be scaled to a transaction size of USD 25 million and that the number of days in the settlement payments alternates between 182 and 183, starting with 183 days between the origination date and the first settlement date.

Solution: First of all, recognize that at the current exchange rates, USD 25 million translates into JPY 3,186,750,000 (the product of USD 25,000,000 and JPY 127.47/USD) and GBP 13,736,264 (USD 25,000,000 divided by USD 1.82/GBP). These become the principal amounts governing the transaction. Then:

(a) The desired swap could be accomplished by combining the following currency swaps:

- Pay 4.92 percent Japanese yen, receive U.S. dollar LIBOR, and

- receive 9.83 percent British sterling, pay U.S. dollar LIBOR.

The result is a pay 4.92 percent yen, receive 9.83 percent sterling swap, which represents your offer swap rate in yen and your bid rate in sterling.

(b) After swapping principal amounts at the origination date, the cash flow exchanges on first settlement date from the counterparty's standpoint are calculated as follows:

$$\text{Yen payment} = (0.0492) \times \left(\frac{183}{365}\right) \times (\text{JPY } 3{,}186{,}750{,}000) = \text{JPY } 78{,}608{,}828$$

and

$$\text{Pound receipt} = (0.0983) \times \left(\frac{183}{365}\right) \times (\text{GBP } 13{,}736{,}264) = \text{GBP } 686{,}390.$$

The full set of cash exchanges, which will be known at the inception of the deal, is shown in Table E-1.2.

Table E-1.2 Cash Flow Exchanges, Counterparty

Settlement Date	Days in Settlement	Payments (millions)	Receipts (millions)
Initial	—	GBP 13.736	JPY 3,186.75
1	183	JPY 78.61	GBP 0.69
2	182	78.18	0.68
3	183	78.61	0.69
4	182	78.18	0.68
5	183	78.61	0.69
Final	182	JPY 3,186.75 and JPY 78.18	GBP 13.736 and GBP 0.68

Exercise 1.4: Suppose that on September 30, 1994, the treasurer for Company X wishes to restructure the coupon payments of one of her outstanding debt issues. The bond in question is scheduled to pay semiannual interest on September 30th and March 30th each year until September 30, 1999, and has a coupon rate of 8 percent with a face value of $35 million. On the same day, the treasurer for Company Y wants to restructure the interest payments on his $50 million, four-year, floating-rate note having a coupon reset each September 30th and March 30th to a reference rate of LIBOR flat. The maturity of this floating-rate bond is September 30, 1998.

(a) Using the representative plain vanilla interest rate swap quotes in Table 1.3, describe how both treasurers, working with a market maker, can use a swap agreement to alter synthetically their current cash flow obligations. Specifically, assume that Company X wishes to wind up with floating-rate exposure and Company Y desires fixed-rate debt.

(b) Assuming that the market maker negotiates these swap transactions simultaneously, will they represent a matched book? If not, describe two remaining sources of market exposure that the dealer still faces.

Solution: Although the timing of the coupon payments for the two companies is comparable, the terms of the swaps they seek are not. Specifically, Company X needs a five-year, receive-fixed swap for a notional principal of $35 million and Company Y desires a four-year, pay-fixed, $50 million deal.

(a) Company X could synthetically alter its fixed-rate payments by entering into a receive-fixed swap, accepting the market maker's five-year bid quote of 7.53 percent. The transaction is shown in Figure E-1.2.

Figure E-1.2 Company X's Synthetic Debt Conversion

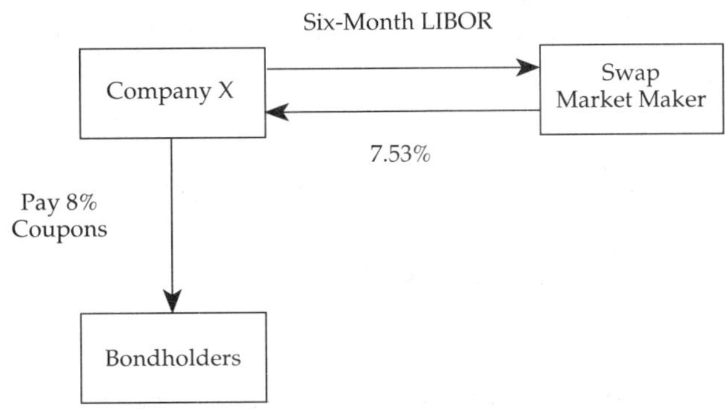

To calculate the resulting synthetic floating rate that Company X will be obligated to pay, recall that in the U.S. dollar market, LIBOR is quoted on a 360-day basis, but the swap fixed rate, which is linked to Treasury yields, is on a 365-day basis. Adjusting for this discrepancy so that the net cost of funds is expressed on a money-market basis, we have

Fixed-rate debt coupon payment	= (8.00%) × (360/365)	= 7.89%
Swap:		
LIBOR payment		= LIBOR
Fixed receipt	= (7.53%) × (360/365)	= (7.43%)
Net cost of funds		= LIBOR + 0.46%.

The treasurer at Company X can expect her semiannual interest cost to be 46 basis points higher than the level of six-month LIBOR set one period in arrears. Similarly, taking the offered side of the four-year market, the pay-fixed swap necessary to convert Company Y's floating-rate debt and the resulting synthetic fixed-rate funding cost (on a 365-day basis) is shown in Figure E-1.3. The result is a net funding cost for Company Y of [(LIBOR) × (365/360)] + (7.45%) − [(LIBOR) × (365/360)] = 7.45%.

Figure E-1.3 Company Y's Synthetic Debt Conversion

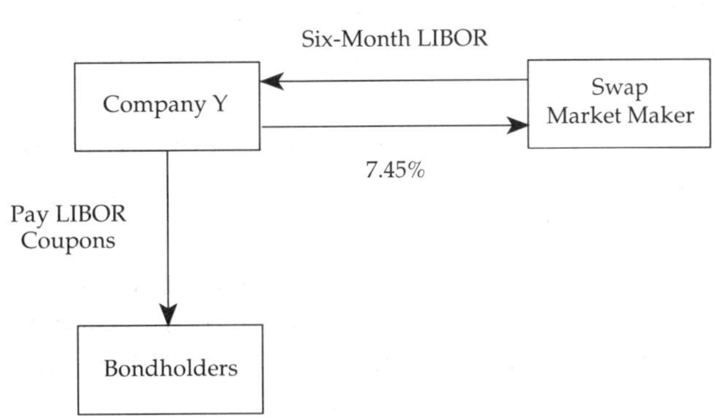

(b) Although this arrangement may appear to be a matched set of transactions, the market maker has two distinct interest rate exposures. First, the swaps are different in maturity by one year, so the dealer is left with an unhedged commitment to pay the fixed rate of 7.53 percent to Company X in Year 5. If LIBOR during this period is less than 7.53 percent, the dealer will have to make a net settlement payment with no compensating cash inflow on the other side. Second, during the four years common to both swaps, the contracts are written for different notional principal amounts. One way to see the problem this arrangement creates is to split the $50 million swap with Company Y into: (1) a $35 million swap to match the transaction with Company X and (2) an unhedged residual deal of $15 million. If LIBOR exceeds 7.45 percent during the first four years, the market maker would have to pay out on this unmatched portion with no offsetting inflow. Figure E-1.4 depicts these two exposures.

Figure E-1.4 Market Maker's Swap Exposures

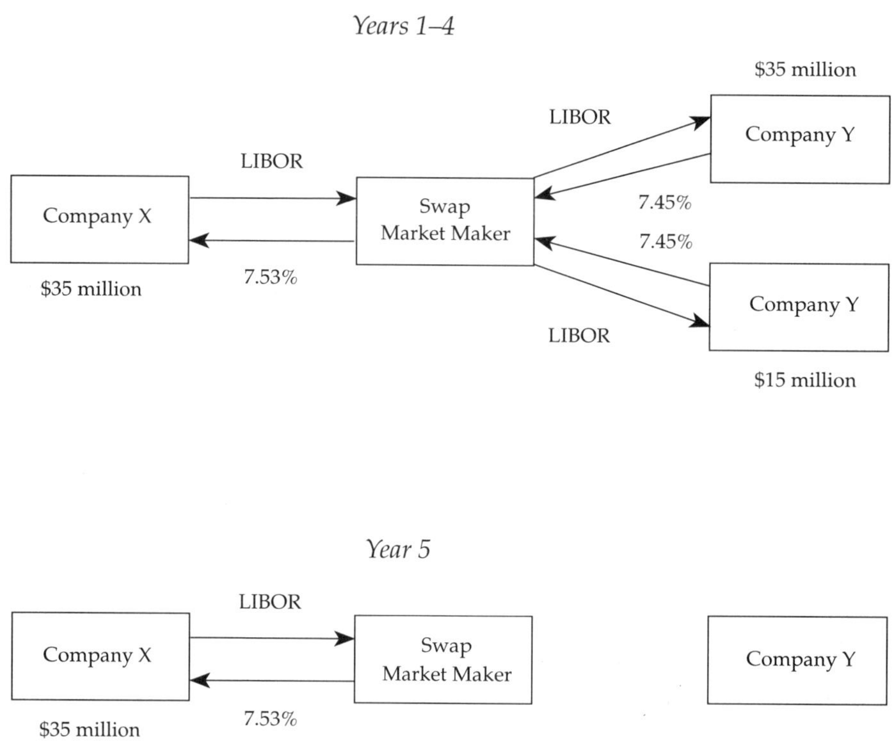

Chapter 2. Economic Interpretations of a Swap Contract

Although interest rate and currency swaps are inherently simple financial contracts specifying a periodic exchange of cash flows, they can be interpreted several ways: as a pair of capital market transactions, as a sequence of forward contracts, and as a pair of options contracts. These interpretations demonstrate that swaps serve to integrate financial markets by connecting the cash, futures, and options markets for fixed-income securities.

A Swap as a Pair of Capital Market Transactions

Consider a plain vanilla interest rate swap in which a firm receives a fixed rate of 8 percent for five years and pays six-month LIBOR. Settlement is on a net basis in arrears, and the notional principal is $100 million. LIBOR is determined at the start of each period according to the method spelled out in the documentation (e.g., which banks will be surveyed and how their offered rates will be averaged). Then, at the end of the period, the firm pays its counterparty the difference between LIBOR and 8 percent (times 0.5, times $100 million) if LIBOR exceeds 8 percent and receives the difference if LIBOR is less than 8 percent. (This calculation assumes, for simplicity, that the day-count convention on both the fixed rate and LIBOR is 30/360. Therefore, the adjustment to the rate differential is 0.5 regardless of the actual number of days in the semiannual period.) The sequence of settlement cash flows on the swap contract will be the same, barring default, as if the firm (1) had issued a $100 million, five-year floating-rate note (FRN) that pays LIBOR flat each period, in arrears, and (2) used those funds to purchase a five-year, $100 million fixed-rate note that has a coupon rate of 8 percent (paid semiannually at a rate of 4 percent per period).

FRNs first appeared in the financial marketplace in the 1970s in response to rising interest rates brought on by higher levels of inflation. In general, FRNs pay a coupon referenced to a money-market rate such as LIBOR plus (or minus) a margin that reflects the credit quality of the issuer, its degree of marketability, and its tax status. The idea is that because the coupon payment will adjust each period to reflect fully current market conditions, price changes will be quite limited compared with fixed-rate bonds of equivalent maturity. In fact, the market price would be expected to be par value at the time the coupon is reset and to differ from par only if the margin is no longer sufficient (e.g., if the issuer has been downgraded or the liquidity of the security has eroded). The FRN considered here can be viewed as a sequence of six-month

Eurodollar time deposits that pay a coupon rate set at LIBOR flat.

The combination of buying a fixed-rate note funded by issuing an FRN is illustrated in Figure 2.1. Notice that the cash inflows (above the time line) and outflows (below the time line) for the principal at origination and at maturity are assumed to offset each other fully in the two capital market transactions. The remaining coupon payments are the same as an interest rate swap exchanging 8 percent fixed for floating-rate LIBOR. The floating flows are portrayed as a sequence of shaded boxes of varying sizes, and the fixed-rate flows are all the same size. Note that the initial floating flow is in fact fixed, because it is set at the current level of LIBOR, which is observed in the spot market for Eurodollar time deposits. Therefore, the initial settlement exchange is known in advance, but the remainder will depend on future levels of LIBOR. Given that the market prices of the FRN and the fixed-rate note are equal, the swap coupon of 8 percent must be the "at-market" rate. If the prices of the fixed- and floating-rate notes differ, implying an initial net payment from one counterparty to the other, the swap rate would be an "off-market" transaction.

Figure 2.1 once again highlights the fact that a plain vanilla interest rate swap entails neither an initial exchange of principal nor any at maturity. Such an exchange would not add any value, only additional credit risk. Recall, however, that currency swaps do involve exchange of principal. Consider a firm that receives a fixed rate of 8 percent based on a principal of $100 million in U.S. dollars and pays a fixed rate of 10 percent

Figure 2.1 Interpreting a Plain Vanilla Receive-Fixed Interest Rate Swap as a Pair of Capital Market Transactions

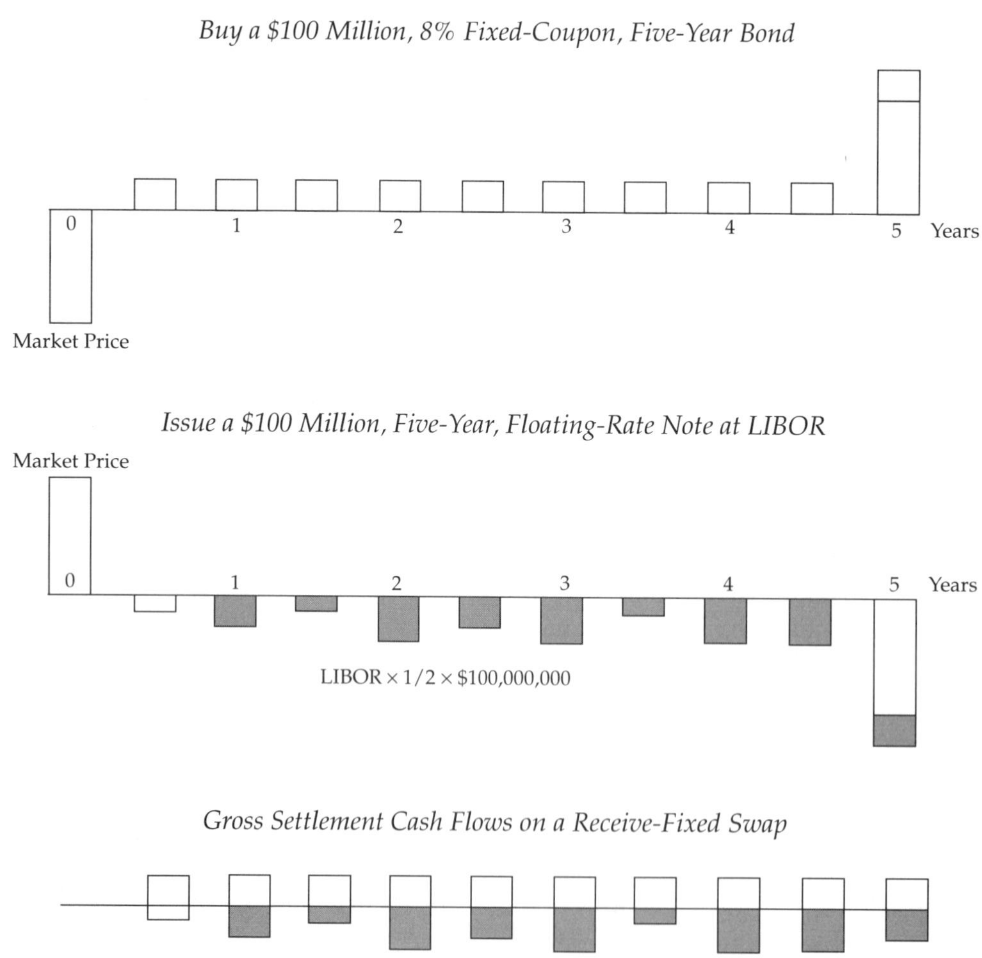

based on 160 million deutschemarks. This swap would have an initial exchange and later a re-exchange of principal, typically using the initial spot market rate (here assumed to be DEM 1.60/USD) for both transactions. This swap can be interpreted as the purchase of the fixed-rate dollar note funded by issuing the deutschemark note and selling the initial deutschemark proceeds for dollars in the spot FX market. These hypothetical transactions are depicted in Figure 2.2. Note that the coupon payments are assumed to be annual, following the convention in the Eurobond market of paying coupon interest only once a year.

Figure 2.2 Capital Market Interpretation of a Currency Swap

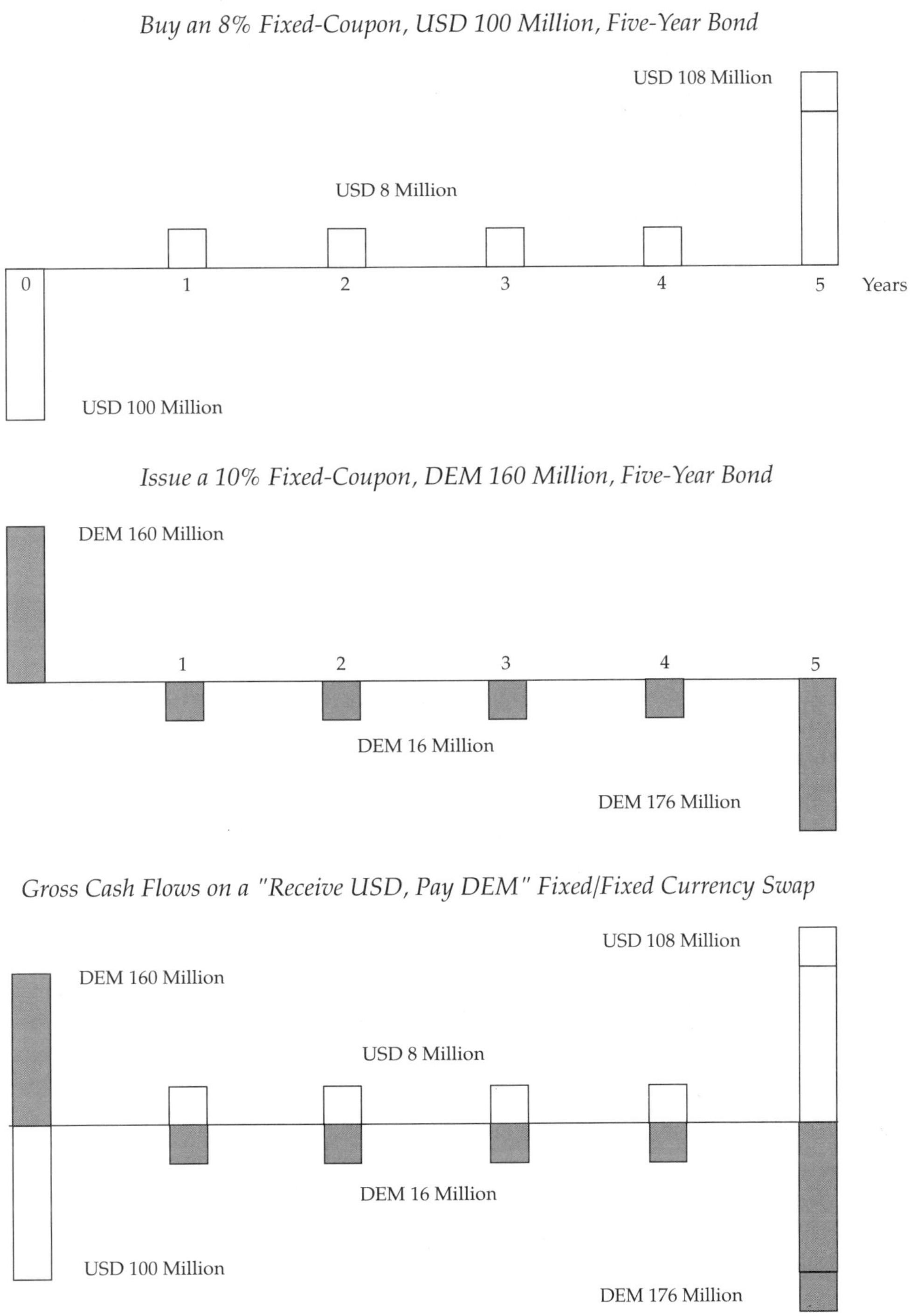

These two examples raise an interesting question: If the cash flows on a swap contract can be fully replicated by capital market transactions, why does a swap market need to exist? The answer is found not so much in theory as in practice—swaps turn out to be a particularly efficient way to transform the nature of assets and liabilities. That the same transformation could be done by buying one type of bond and selling another is an important theoretical concept but not an alternative likely to make the short list of a corporate treasurer facing an actual risk-management problem.

Using a combination of capital market instruments presents an obvious practical problem: buying and selling bonds that have the exact same payment dates. A swap contract avoids this problem and also has some other unambiguous advantages.

- *Lower transaction costs*: Issuing debt can be expensive because of the costs of underwriting and registration, whereas swaps trade at rather tight bid–offer spreads (5–10 basis points or less). Moreover, a swap can be unwound much more quickly and at less expense than buying back publicly issued debt.
- *Less credit risk*: A swap is an *executory* contract, meaning that one need perform only if the counterparty performs. That reduces the credit risk to the difference in the present value of the lost receipts and the present value of the payments that no longer would have to be made. The default on a bond would not entail that offset, so the ultimate loss could be as much as the present value of the lost coupons, as well as the lost principal.
- *No change in debt–equity ratios*: The swap is an *off-balance-sheet* instrument, whereas the issuance of a bond raises leverage ratios even if the bond that is issued merely finances the purchase of an equally valued bond.
- *Anonymity*: A swap allows a firm to reposition its balance sheet quickly and quietly, without alerting its competitors to its strategy (at least within a reporting period).

The interpretation of a swap as a combination of bonds is particularly useful in calculating its *mark-to-market* (MTM) value. Usually, the value of a swap is determined from the fixed rate on a *replacement* swap having the same terms (such as the remaining time to maturity and the credit risk of the counterparty) as the original agreement. Consider, for example, the status of the swap illustrated in the bottom panel of Figure 2.1, assuming that a year has passed and the current market fixed rate on a new four-year, receive-fixed interest rate swap is 7 percent. The swap would have a positive MTM value to the firm because it has a contract to receive an "above-market" fixed rate of 8 percent for payment of LIBOR. This calculation is a straightforward exercise in bond mathematics: What is the present value of the annuity represented by the eight remaining 4 percent periodic cash flows, compared with an annuity of 3.5 percent, now that the discount rate has fallen to 3.5 percent per period? This solution is as follows:

Swap MTM value =

$$\left[\sum_{t=1}^{8} \frac{\$4{,}000{,}000}{(1 + 0.0350)^t} - \sum_{t=1}^{8} \frac{\$3{,}500{,}000}{(1 + 0.0350)^t}\right]$$

$$= \$3{,}436{,}978.$$

The swap, which started out at a value of zero, has become an asset to the fixed-rate receiver with an MTM value of $3,436,978.[1]

Now suppose that trading volume in the swap market is dramatically reduced for some reason. In such a case, realistic market quotations on replacement swaps might be difficult to obtain. Nevertheless, the MTM value of the receive-fixed swap could be estimated as the difference between the market value of the hypothetical fixed-rate bond less the value of the FRN. As long as there is trading in bonds having similar coupon rates, maturities, and credit ratings as the counterparties to the swap, a reasonable

[1] Swap dealers typically mark the swap portfolio to the midpoint of the bid–offer spread, thereby using the same rate to value either a pay-fixed or receive-fixed position. When calculating loss on event of default of the counterparty, however, the dealer would use the market bid rate on a receive-fixed swap that has gone into default and the offer rate on a pay-fixed swap.

approximation to the MTM value can be obtained. Even in the best of circumstances, however, the values from the replacement swap and from the bond market should differ because of differences in the treatment of swaps and bonds in bankruptcy.

Another application of the capital market interpretation to an interest rate swap is to calculate the sensitivity of the MTM value to changes in swap fixed rates, as summarized by the swap's *duration* statistic.[2] The duration of the receive-fixed swap in the example above can be estimated as the duration of the 8 percent, five-year note held long minus the implied duration of the FRN that was issued. The implied duration of an FRN is the remaining time in the coupon period expressed as a fraction of a year, which follows from interpreting duration as an elasticity. Immediately before the rate reset date, the percentage change in the price would be zero for any percentage change in the interest rate, because the FRN is assumed to reset to par value. After reset, the note is equivalent to a time deposit having a maturity equal to the time until the next reset date. Suppose that the counterparties to our swap are both Aaa-rated firms and that the 8 percent, fixed-rate note and the FRN at LIBOR flat are priced in the market at par value. Under these circumstances, the duration of the fixed-rate bond would be calculated as 4.2 years and the implied duration of the FRN as 0.5 years, so the implied duration of the swap is 3.7 years.

The duration statistic for the swap (or, better, the *modified duration* whereby the Macaulay duration is divided by 1 plus the periodic yield) could be used to ascertain the impact of the contract on the firm's overall exposure to interest rate risk, as measured by the gap between the duration of assets and liabilities. In general, entering a plain vanilla interest rate swap has one of the following effects: (1) Receiving the fixed rate on a swap shortens the duration of liabilities (or lengthens the duration of assets) in order to gain when market rates fall (i.e., a receive-fixed swap has a positive implied duration), or (2) paying the fixed rate on a swap lengthens the duration of liabilities (or shortens the duration of assets) in order to gain when market rates rise (i.e., a pay-fixed swap has a negative implied duration statistic).

The notion of duration is much more difficult to extend to a currency swap than to an interest rate swap because more than one yield is involved. The MTM value on a plain vanilla interest rate swap depends fundamentally on just one variable—the fixed rate on the replacement swap. The MTM value on a currency swap depends on three variables—the interest rate in each of the two currencies and the spot market exchange rate. Consider again the receive-USD/pay-DEM currency swap outlined earlier. The MTM value after a year would be the present value of the dollar inflows less the present value of the deutschemark outflows converted to dollars at the spot market exchange rate. Those present values can be obtained from the domestic bond market in each currency, based on yields to maturity for bonds having the same coupon rates, remaining term to maturity, and credit ratings of the counterparties. A summary statistic such as duration, however, is generally not applicable because of the less-than-perfect correlation between interest rates in different currencies.

A Swap as a Series of Forward Contracts

Now consider a two-year quarterly settlement swap whereby a firm pays a fixed rate of 6 percent and receives three-month LIBOR. Even though the actual settlements will be on a net basis, the gross inflows and outflows can be pictured as in Figure 2.3. The swap appears to be a sequence of three-month forward contracts,

[2] The duration statistic of a bond can be interpreted several ways: the price elasticity given a change in the yield to maturity, the weighted average time to maturity whereby the weights are the shares of market value represented by each cash flow, a zero-coupon-bond-equivalent risk factor (in that a ten-year coupon bond having a duration of eight years would have almost the same price sensitivity as an eight-year, zero-coupon bond). Key limitations of the commonly used Macaulay duration statistic, named for Frederick Macaulay, who first developed it in 1938, are the underlying assumption of a parallel shift to a flat yield curve and interaction between the level of interest rates and credit risk premiums. Nonetheless, it is a widely used summary statistic for the impact of interest rate changes on asset valuations. See the appendix for a more detailed discussion.

Figure 2.3 Cash Flows on Quarterly Settlement, Pay-Fixed Interest Rate Swap

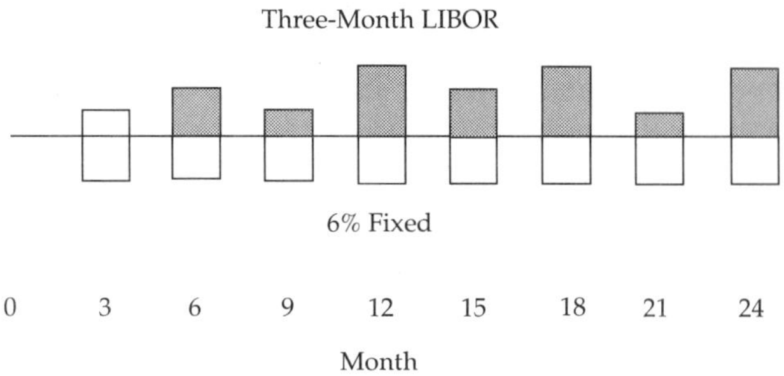

each one an exchange of 6 percent for three-month LIBOR (times 1/4, times the notional principal). In the market for interest rate risk-management products, such contracts are called forward rate agreements (FRAs). An FRA is merely a one-date swap, and a swap can be viewed as a series of FRAs.

The FRA's name indicates the time frame of the reference rate: A 3 × 6 FRA means a contract on three-month LIBOR, three months forward; a 12 × 18 FRA means a contract on six-month LIBOR, one year forward. FRA market makers quote a bid–offer spread on a rate basis. For example, suppose that the FRA rates for three-month LIBOR shown in Table 2.1 prevail in the market at date zero, with current LIBOR assumed to be 4.50 percent. On a 3 × 6 FRA, the market maker is prepared to pay a fixed rate of 4.81 percent for receipt of three-month LIBOR and to receive a fixed rate of 4.85 percent for payment of LIBOR. In either case, no payment will take place until LIBOR is revealed in Month 3. Net settlement can then be made in arrears at Month 6 or in advance at Month 3. If in arrears, the settlement flow will be calculated just like on an interest rate swap by multiplying the rate differential by the fraction of the year spanned by the transaction (e.g., 1/4 for a three-month contract) and by the notional principal. The in-advance settlement amount is calculated as the present value of the in-arrears amount, using the prorated level of the realized LIBOR as the discount rate.

Table 2.1. Indicative Bid–Offer Quotes on Three-Month Forward Rate Agreements

Period	Bid	Offer
3 × 6	4.81%	4.85%
6 × 9	5.20	5.24
9 × 12	5.64	5.68
12 × 15	6.37	6.41
15 × 18	6.78	6.82
18 × 21	7.10	7.14
21 × 24	7.36	7.40

Suppose that the market maker buys a 3 × 6 FRA from Company ABC at its bid rate of 4.81 percent and, at the same time, sells a 3 × 6 FRA to Company XYZ at its offer rate of 4.85 percent, each for a notional principal of $10 million. As in the swap market, "buy" and "sell" are awkward yet commonly used words when describing FRA transactions. Given that the FRA has an initial value of zero and therefore is neither an asset nor a liability, it cannot be bought or sold; instead, one simply enters a contract that subsequently may have a positive or negative value. Nevertheless, recalling that LIBOR can be interpreted as the "commodity," the fixed rate is then the price paid or received in exchange for LIBOR. The transactions are displayed in Figure 2.4.

Now suppose that three-month LIBOR is 5.00 percent on the rate determination date in Month 3. If the contract specified settlement in arrears at Month 6, ABC would be obligated to pay the market maker $4,750, calculated as 5.00 percent less 4.81 percent, times 1/4 (assuming that there are 90 days between Months 3 and 6 and that LIBOR is quoted on a 360-day basis), times $10 million. If settled in advance, the Month 3 payment would be

$$\$4{,}750 \div \left[1 + \frac{90 \times 0.0500}{360}\right] = \$4{,}691.36.$$

Similarly, the payment from the market maker to XYZ would be $3,750.00 in Month 6 or $3,703.70 in Month 3. The market maker is fully

Figure 2.4 3 × 6 FRAs Transacted at the Market Maker's Bid and Offer Rates

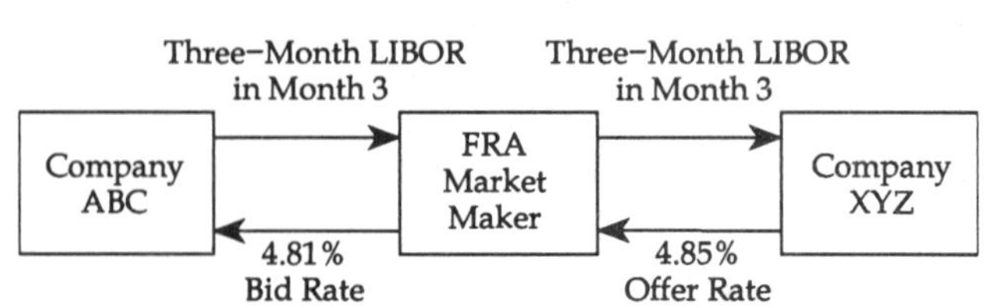

hedged from interest rate risk by having matched FRAs; its spread of 4 basis points compensates it for the inevitable credit risk and its transaction costs.

Now reconsider the firm that entered the two-year, pay-fixed swap at 6 percent. In lieu of the swap, the firm could have bought a sequence of FRAs—the 3 × 6, 6 × 9, and so forth. From Table 2.1, the rates on those FRAs are the market maker's offers—4.85 percent, 5.24 percent, 5.68 percent, and so on out to the 21 × 24 at 7.40 percent. The key point is that compared with the interest rate swap, the sequence of FRAs would have a known, but different, fixed rate for each period. A plain vanilla swap not only has a known fixed rate but also that rate is the same for each settlement period. Because LIBOR is the same for either alternative, the fixed rate on the swap must be some sort of average of the FRA rates. Chapter 4 will demonstrate that the swap fixed rate is indeed such an average in the sense that the present values of the cash flows represented by the various FRA rates and the single swap rate must be equal in a market free from arbitrage opportunities.

The significance of this interpretation is that a swap now can be viewed as a series of off-market FRAs whenever the swap yield curve is not completely flat. Suppose the time path of FRAs is upward sloping, as in the example above. Each individual "on-market" FRA would have an initial value of zero. Likewise, the interest rate swap has an initial value of zero, but some of its individual settlement dates, as off-market FRAs, have positive, and others negative, initial values. With this yield curve scenario, the first few settlement dates on the pay-fixed swap will have negative value because the firm is paying an above-market fixed rate for receipt of LIBOR. The last few swap payment dates will then have positive values compared with the on-market FRAs because the firm is paying a below-market fixed rate.

This interpretation demonstrates that the credit risk inherent in a swap agreement results from its structural design of applying the same fixed rate to all settlement periods, as well as from the random nature of interest rates. Assume for a moment that LIBOR follows a path that is completely anticipated by the market and that those anticipations track the time path of the FRAs. Settlement payments (and the buildup of value that creates credit risk) would be zero on a series of on-market FRAs but not on a plain vanilla interest rate swap. The payer of the fixed rate in an upwardly sloped yield curve environment takes on more default risk than the counterparty because the fixed-rate payer would have outflows at first and then anticipate later inflows in return.

Why does the plain vanilla variety of swap contract have the same fixed rate each period instead of the sequence of fixed rates corresponding to the series of comparable FRAs? The answer lies in the history of swaps, however brief that history may be. The first wave of interest rate swaps in the early 1980s comprised mostly new-issue arbitrage transactions. The swaps were attached to newly launched bonds to create synthetic instruments at what were deemed to be lower "all-in" costs of funds than were available by directly issuing the desired type of liability. Inasmuch as this was done typically with a traditional fixed-income bond, the swap was designed to provide a fixed payment each period to offset exactly the coupon flow on the bond. More recently, swaps have been used widely in financial restructurings that might need a known, but not necessarily constant, fixed rate for each future time period. Had that been the primary application in the early years, the plain vanilla swap instrument of today might have come to be described as a sequence of on-market rather than off-market FRAs.

To see how this "series of forward contracts" interpretation applies to currency swaps, return to the deal portrayed in Figure 2.2. The firm receives dollars based on an 8 percent interest rate and a principal of USD 100 million and pays deutschemarks based on a 10 percent interest rate and a principal of DEM 160 million. Looking at each settlement date in isolation, the entire currency swap appears to be a portfolio of FX forward contracts—an initial spot market FX trade at the going rate of DEM 1.60/USD, then four FX forwards each at DEM 2.00/USD, and finally in Year 5, a much larger FX forward at DEM 1.6296/USD. Notice that the last transaction is a weighted average of the coupon and the principal exchanges; that is, $1.6296 = (8/108 \times 2.00) + (100/108 \times 1.60)$.

A fixed/fixed currency swap such as this one

can also be described as a series of off-market FX forward contracts (except when the interest rate differential between the currencies is zero). To see this requires the series of on-market FX forward rates. These rates can be obtained from the interest rate parity condition whereby the forward exchange rate equals the spot rate times the ratio of (1 plus) the yields in each currency. Suppose that the yield curves in dollars and deutschemarks are flat at 8 percent and 10 percent, respectively. Then the FX forward rates consistent with interest rate parity can be obtained from the following equation:

$$(\text{Forward DEM/USD}) = (\text{Spot DEM/USD}) \times \left(\frac{1 + 0.10}{1 + 0.08}\right)^t$$

for $t = 1, 2, 3, 4$, and 5. The numerical values of those on-market FX forward rates are given in the last column of Table 2.2.

The firm that is buying dollars via the currency swap and paying deutschemarks has unfavorable trades on the first four dates and then a favorable one on the fifth. The firm is paying 2 deutschemarks for every dollar on the swap contract, but only 1.6296 to 1.7219 deutschemarks per dollar would have been needed in the explicit FX forward market. Balancing that, however, is the final purchase at DEM 1.6296/USD on the full amount, including the principal, whereas the on-market FX forward would have been at DEM 1.7537/USD. The dollar receipts would be the same; the difference is in the amount and timing of the deutschemark payments. Notice the present value of the deutschemark outflows would be equivalent for both the currency swap and the series of FX forwards. The credit risk, however, would not be identical. Because of its structural design of applying the same off-market rate to each coupon exchange, the currency swap has more credit risk than would the series of FX forwards. This firm's counterparty has a favorable trade on each of the first four dates, trades that it would not likely default on (as long as the dollar is worth fewer than 2 deutschemarks). As with interest rate swaps, this particular design can be traced to the early years of the swap market, when currency swaps were used in new-issue arbitrages based on coupon-bearing bonds.

Table 2.2 Forward Rates Implied by Interest Rate Parity and the Currency Swap

Date of Exchange (year)	USD Amount (millions)	Implicit Off-Market FX Forwards (DEM/USD)	Interest Rate Parity FX Forwards (DEM/USD)
1	$ 8	2.0000	1.6296
2	8	2.0000	1.6598
3	8	2.0000	1.6905
4	8	2.0000	1.7219
5	108	1.6296	1.7537

A Swap as a Pair of Option Contracts

A well-known result in options pricing theory is *put–call-forward parity*, the proposition that a combination of buying a call option and writing a put option on the same commodity for the same strike price and expiration date is equivalent to a long forward position. The forward price is assumed to be the same as the mutual strike price on the options, and the delivery date is assumed to match the expiration date. The equivalence is in terms of the ultimate payoff. If the market price for the commodity at the time of delivery exceeds the preagreed purchase price, the gain on the forward contract is the same as on the in-the-money call option. Likewise, if the market price is below the contractual price, the loss on the forward equals the loss on the in-the-money put option that has been written. (Note that the expressions "in the money" and "out of the money" refer to the perspective of the option holder; the writer of an option loses when the contract is in the money to its owner.)

An analogous proposition is *cap–floor-swap parity*, a result that is not really all that surprising given that an interest rate swap has already been interpreted as a series of forward contracts. Interest rate cap and floor agreements are multiperiod interest rate option contracts, each contract corresponding to a different settlement period. A cap agreement is a series of cash settlement interest rate options, typically based on LIBOR. The writer of the cap, in return for an option premium that is usually paid at origination, is obliged to pay the difference between

LIBOR and the strike, or cap, rate (times the fraction of the year, times the notional principal), whenever that difference is positive. The writer of a floor agreement makes settlement payments only when LIBOR is below the floor rate. No payment is made if LIBOR is above the floor or below the cap. As with FRAs, settlement can be either in advance or in arrears, although the latter is more common given that these contracts are typically used to hedge exposure to floating-rate bank loans and notes (which themselves typically settle in arrears).

Before interpreting an interest rate swap as a combination of caps and floors, it is useful to describe these multiperiod option contracts in more detail. For example, consider a three-year, semiannual settlement, 8 percent cap on six-month U.S. dollar LIBOR. The buyer of the cap pays the writer an up-front premium, quoted as a percentage of the notional principal, say, 120 basis points.[3] If the notional principal is $100 million, the cost of the cap is $1.2 million. Suppose that settlement dates are on the 15th of May and November of each year and that LIBOR on one particular May 15th is 9.125 percent. The holder of the cap will receive settlement in arrears that November in the amount of $575,000, calculated as (9.125 percent − 8 percent) × (184/360) × $100 million, assuming an actual/360 day-count basis.

The payoff relationships for caps and floors can be pictured using traditional, option-style diagrams. Figure 2.5 portrays an 8 percent cap and a 4 percent floor on LIBOR. Notice that the payoff on the cap takes the same form as a typical call option on a commodity and the floor takes the form of a put option. Indeed, following the convention in which LIBOR is the commodity, caps are referred to as "calls on LIBOR" and floors as "puts on LIBOR." Alternatively, a cap agreement on LIBOR is a series of put options on an underlying Eurodollar time deposit. In effect, the owner of the option has the right, but

Figure 2.5 Payoff Diagrams for Buying and Writing an Interest Rate Cap and Floor

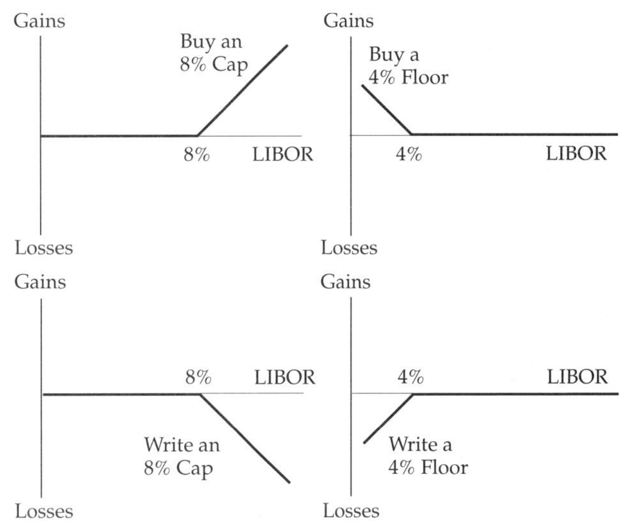

not the obligation, to sell to the writer a time deposit having a coupon rate equal to the cap strike rate in the amount of the notional principal of the contract. The owner "exercises" that option if current LIBOR exceeds the cap rate, thus selling a relatively low-coupon deposit at par value. The proceeds of that sale can then be used to buy a time deposit that earns the higher, market rate. The gain on those hypothetical transactions is equivalent to the payoff on the cap agreement. Whether one interprets a cap as a call on LIBOR or a put on a time deposit (and, similarly, a floor as a put on LIBOR or a call on a time deposit) is purely a matter of semantic preference.

An interest rate *collar* is a combination of a cap and a floor, a long position in one and a short position in the other. To buy a 4–8 percent collar on LIBOR is to buy an 8 percent cap and to write a 4 percent floor. On a given settlement date, the buyer will receive cash payments when LIBOR exceeds 8 percent, make payments when LIBOR is below 4 percent, and neither receive nor pay if LIBOR is at or between 4 percent and 8 percent. Often the motive for a firm to buy a collar is to reduce the initial cost of acquiring the protection from higher levels of LIBOR, because the up-front receipt from writing the floor can be used to offset the cost of buying the cap.

A special case of an interest rate collar occurs when the premiums on the cap and the floor are

[3] In practice, interest rate caps and floors are quoted by market makers on a volatility basis, for instance, 18.5 percent bid and 19.5 percent offered. That measure of volatility (stated as a standard deviation), plus the strike rate, the current term structure of interest rates, and the time frame for the contract, are then entered into an option pricing model to obtain the actual amount of the premium.

equal and therefore fully offset each other. For example, suppose that the premium on a three-year, 4 percent floor is 120 basis points, matching the premium on the 8 percent cap. The combination is known as a "zero-cost" or "zero-premium" collar. A more accurate, but surely less marketable, name would be a "rate-contingent, deferred-cost" collar. The idea is that a cap agreement alone has a known, fully prepaid cost for the upside interest rate insurance. The zero-cost collar, however, has an uncertain cost—uncertain with respect to both timing and amount—for the same amount of interest rate insurance. If LIBOR were to remain at a sufficiently low level over the lifetime of the contract, the ultimate cost of the zero-cost collar could far exceed the cost of the cap.

A firm's choice between a swap, cap, and collar to manage interest rate risk will depend on a number of factors, including accounting and tax treatment of the various derivatives, initial cost and free cash flow, the firm's risk tolerance, and the firm's view on the average future level for LIBOR. The last factor, the rate view, is summarized in Figure 2.6. Assume that the firm has interest rate exposure from having issued an FRN on which it pays LIBOR + 0.25 percent. Suppose further that the firm's revenue from operations is uncorrelated with actual and expected inflation, as well as with short-term interest rates. Therefore, higher levels of LIBOR could cause financial distress. Notice that for similar degrees of upside protection, the firm might prefer (1) the cap, if LIBOR is expected to be low, on balance; (2) the collar, if LIBOR is expected to be in a middle range; or (3) the pay-fixed swap, if LIBOR is expected to be high. Ironically, a risk manager's decisions inevitably express a view on market rates, even if the motive for acquiring the risk-management product is lack of confidence in the view itself.

The amortized cost of the cap agreement is indicated in Figure 2.6 by the vertical distance between the cost of funds for the FRN alone and the "capped" FRN. The simplest method of spreading the up-front premium over the contract's lifetime, and also the method most commonly used to date for tax and accounting purposes, is straight-line amortization. If the premium on a three-year cap is 120 basis points, the amortized cost would be 40 basis points a year. This, however, neglects the financing cost of the multiyear insurance. Suppose that the three-year, fixed-rate cost of funds is 6.25 percent (assuming semiannual interest payments). Then the amortized cost inclusive of financing would be 44.5 basis points, calculated as a six-period annuity in which the rate per period is 3.125 percent and multiplied by 2 to annualize the cost per period.

Straight-line amortization of the premium, whether the financing cost is included or not, neglects the time decay of a typical option. In particular, the third year of the cap should be

Figure 2.6 Comparing the Funding Cost of Hedging with a Cap, Collar, and Swap

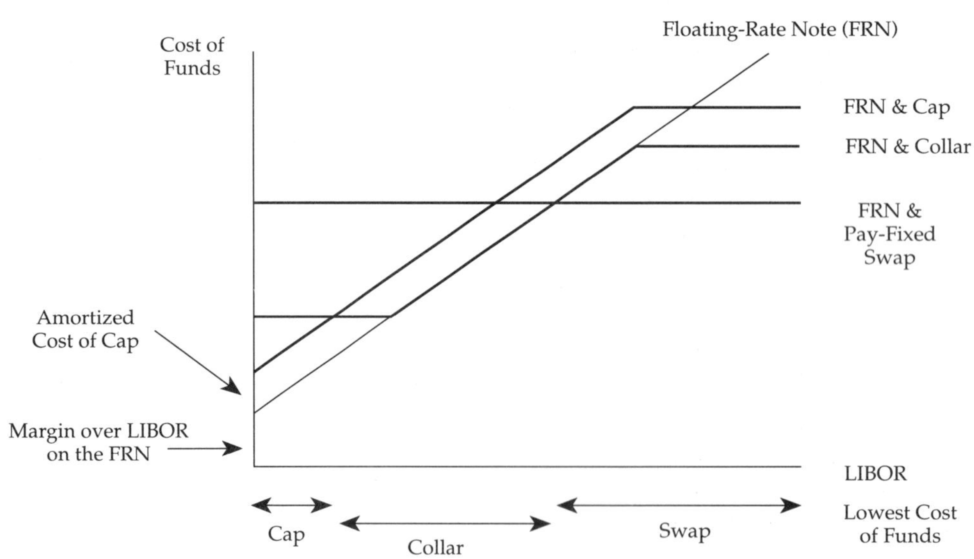

more expensive than the second year. Calculating the annual incremental cost of a multiyear option requires a valuation model. Suppose that a one-year, 8 percent cap on six-month LIBOR would cost only 15 basis points. If LIBOR is initially below 8 percent, the option holder will definitely not receive any payment in six months. So, the entire value of the one-year, out-of-the-money cap depends on the next level of LIBOR. If a two-year, 8 percent cap costs 55 basis points, the imputed cost for the second year would be 40 basis points. Therefore, the incremental cost for the third year would be 65 basis points.[4]

Now let us return to the interpretation of an interest rate swap as a combination of a cap and a floor. Actually, an interest rate swap is just a special case of an interest rate collar. Consider again the 4–8 percent, zero-cost collar on LIBOR that was constructed from buying the 8 percent cap and writing the 4 percent floor. Now tighten the collar by lowering the cap rate down to 7 percent. The up-front premium must go up—an insurance policy providing protection whenever LIBOR exceeds 7 percent has to cost more than a policy that pays off only when LIBOR gets above 8 percent. Suppose that premium is 200 basis points (times the notional principal). To attain a zero initial cost, the floor that is written must generate 200 basis points in premium as well. That condition will require a higher floor rate—a contract whereby the writer makes settlement payments whenever LIBOR is less than 5 percent will certainly be worth more than one with a strike rate of 4 percent. Keep tightening the collar, and at some strike rate common to both the cap and the floor, say 6 percent, the combination will be zero-cost. That point, illustrated in Figure 2.7, will be the at-market pay-fixed swap fixed rate.

Figure 2.7 An Illustration of Cap–Floor-Swap Parity

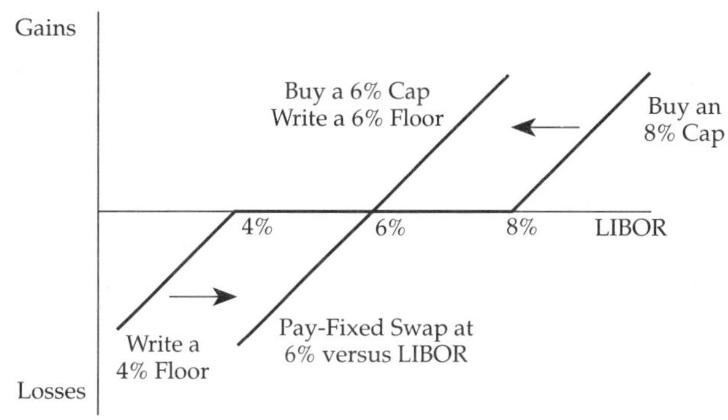

To summarize, buying a 6 percent cap and writing a 6 percent floor on LIBOR is equivalent in terms of settlement cash flows to an interest rate swap paying a fixed rate of 6 percent and receiving LIBOR. When LIBOR is above 6 percent, the net settlement receipt on the swap is the same as the receipt on the in-the-money cap that is owned. When LIBOR is below 6 percent, the net settlement payment on the swap is the same as the payment on the in-the-money floor that has been written. Similarly, writing a cap and buying a floor at the same strike rate is the same as a receive-fixed interest rate swap. Note that the cap–floor combination at the same strike always has the same payoffs as a swap contract. If this common strike rate is not set equal to the market swap rate, however, it will be equivalent to an off-market swap. When the combination also nets to a zero initial cost, the common strike rate matches the at-market swap coupon.

Swap-cap–floor parity can be used to test the internal consistency of credit risk and valuation models for swaps vis-a-vis options contracts. For example, because selling a cap and buying a floor at the same strike rate can offer the same cash flows as a receive-fixed swap, the projected credit risk on the swap must be comparable to

[4] The Emerging Issues Task Force (EITF) of the Financial Accounting Standards Board (FASB) has been working on the problem of amortizing the up-front premium on a multiyear option contract. At the time of this writing, the EITF appears likely to recommend moving to option-based methods for amortization. The problem is an intriguing one: How much of the total cost of the 8 percent, three-year cap should be assigned to the initial year? So far, we have seen three possible answers—40 basis points, 44.5 basis points, and 15 basis points. Another candidate is 65 basis points! Suppose that financial market conditions (specifically, the term structures of interest rates and implied volatilities) remain unchanged for a year. Because of time decay, the value of the now two-year cap agreement will decline from 120 to 55 basis points. The issue then is when to assign the 65-basis-point time premium. We will not suggest an answer, only advise readers to stay current with the accounting literature because a steady stream of important rulings is likely as FASB catches up to developments in risk management and derivatives.

the credit risk on the floor agreement. (Note that a firm bears the counterparty's credit risk on bought options and not on written options because only in the former case is the firm relying on the other party's future performance.) Any difference in the assigned credit risk between the swap and the option combination would have to be explained by some difference in documentation and legal rulings and precedents. Another implication of this parity relationship is that option pricing models, which have attained a considerable level of theoretical sophistication, can be used in the valuation of swap contracts.

Whenever a firm analyzes an interest rate swap contract, it should work through the alternatives of structuring the transaction as a cap/floor package with the same counterparty or splitting the transaction into its component options and booking those separately with different counterparties. It should ask whether one structure has any advantages over the other in terms of taxation, accounting, and pricing. The two alternatives generate the same net settlement cash flows, but that does not always translate to the same after-tax funding cost or the same bottom-line accounting results.

Interpreting an Off-Market Interest Rate Swap

Suppose the at-market terms on three-year, semiannual settlement interest rate swaps require a firm to pay a fixed rate of 6 percent for receipt of six-month LIBOR. If the firm instead is willing to pay a fixed rate of 8 percent on what would be an off-market swap, it clearly should receive something in return. For example, assume that the firm is seeking to transform a fixed-rate bond holding bearing a coupon rate of 8 percent to a synthetic floating-rate asset, because its view is that short-term rates will be rising higher and faster than generally anticipated by market participants, perhaps even leading to an inverted yield curve. One strategy, of course, would be simply to sell the bond and invest its proceeds in FRNs. Suppose, however, that the firm is unwilling for some reason to divest itself of the bond and instead wants to restructure its asset portfolio using derivatives.

If the firm entered an at-market 6 percent pay-fixed swap, its all-in synthetic floating rate would be LIBOR plus 2 percent over the tenor of the swap; the 2 percent is the difference between the 8 percent received on the underlying bond and the 6 percent paid on the swap. If the firm chose the off-market, 8 percent, pay-fixed swap, its synthetic floating rate would be LIBOR flat, supplemented by a lump-sum receipt at the initiation of the swap. Notice that this strategy effectively "monetizes" the unrealized appreciation of the underlying bond, converting that appreciation to cash without having to sell the bond. The difference in results is illustrated in Figure 2.8, in which the shaded boxes represent the off-market adjustments to the plain vanilla agreement.

In general, the payer of an above-market fixed rate receives an up-front payment; the payer of a below-market fixed rate makes the initial payment. Calculating the amount of the lump-sum initial receipt on the off-market swap is straightforward in theory but more difficult in practice. It will be the present value of a 2 percent annuity (times the notional principal, adjusted for the day-count basis). The valuation issue is to select the discount rate (or rates) used in determining the present value. Suppose that 6.25 percent is the firm's three-year, fixed-rate cost of funds for a semiannual payment, fully amortizing bank loan. Calculated as the present value of a six-period annuity of 1 percent per period discounted at 3.125 percent per six-month period, we have

$$\sum_{t=1}^{6} \frac{0.01}{(1 + 0.03125)^t} = 0.05395,$$

or 5.395 percent of the swap's notional principal. Finally, notice that there is no particular reason to expect that the swap fixed rate is the firm's own fixed-rate cost of funds, given that the swap is set against LIBOR flat and the firm might not be able to issue a par-value FRN at that level.

Another conceptual problem is how to account properly for the lump-sum receipt. Notice that the off-market swap in the lower panel of Figure 2.8 appears to be a combination of an on-market swap, which would have an initial economic value of zero, and a loan contract. The lump-sum receipt would be the proceeds of the

Figure 2.8 Settlement Flows for an At-Market and Off-Market Interest Rate Swap

Plain Vanilla, Pay-Fixed Swap at the Market Rate of 6%

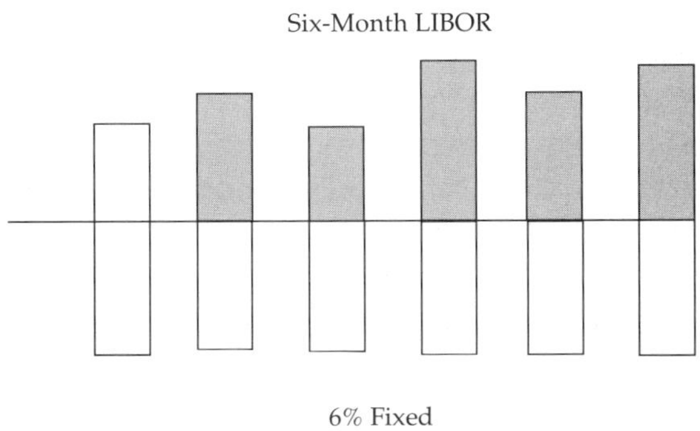

Off-Market, Pay-Fixed Swap at the Rate of 8%

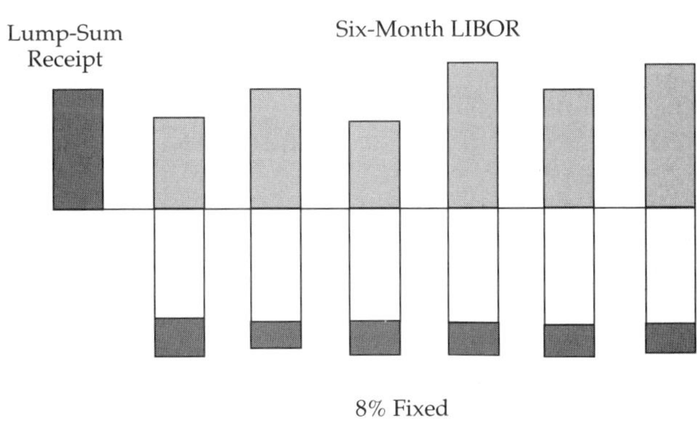

loan; the series of incremental fixed payments in excess of 6 percent represents the level-payment, fully amortized repayment schedule, including both principal redemption and interest. Viewed in this way, the debit to cash corresponding to the initial receipt is balanced by the credit to a loan liability. That loan would be written down each year by the portion of the 2 percent that is principal; the remainder would be interest expense.

The various interpretations of a swap contact can shed some additional light on the accounting for an off-market swap. First, consider the capital market interpretation. An on-market swap is analogous to owning an FRN that pays LIBOR and issuing an equally valued, fixed-rate note that pays a fixed coupon rate of 6 percent. The off-market swap is interpreted as owning the same FRN at LIBOR but issuing a more highly valued fixed-rate note bearing the 8 percent coupon rate. The difference in the initial market values of the FRN and the 8 percent bond is the cash the fixed payer receives on the off-market swap, which is pictured in the upper panel of Figure 2.9.

This capital market interpretation suggests that the up-front cash received could be accounted for in the same manner as the premium on a newly issued, high-coupon bond. Upon entering the off-market swap, the fixed payer would debit cash and credit some liability account on the balance sheet (call it the *swap premium*). That premium would be amortized over the life of the swap as a deduction to interest expense. This approach attains essentially the same result as the loan approach. The amount of the initial lump-sum payment is spread out over the swap's lifetime as an offset

Figure 2.9 Interpreting an Off-Market Interest Rate Swap

A Capital Market Interpretation

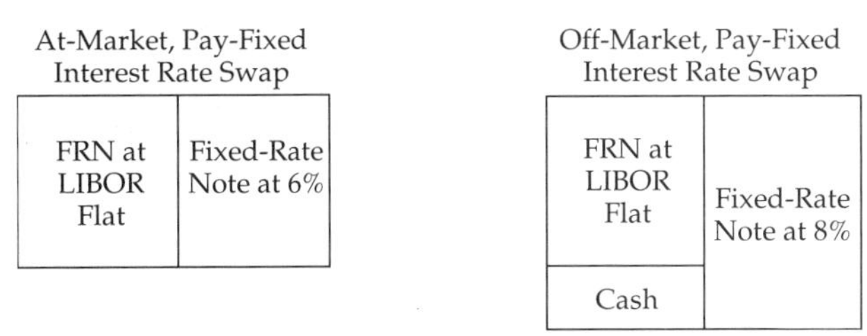

An Options Interpretation

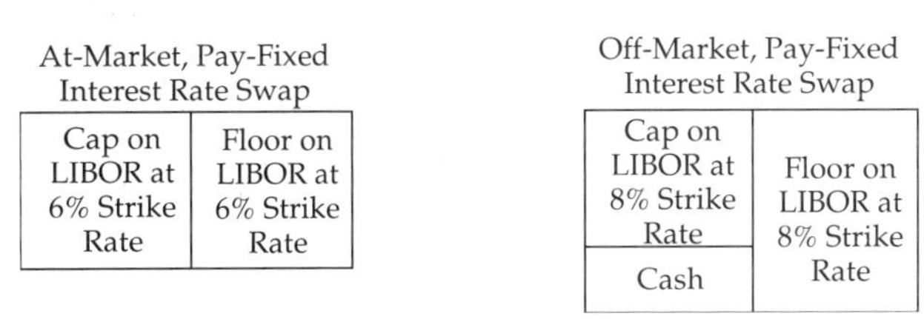

to the amount of interest paid. What can matter is how the loan or swap premium is amortized—on a straight-line or compound-interest basis. The difference is especially important for tax purposes.

Second, consider the interpretation of the swap as a pair of options. The on-market, pay-fixed at 6 percent swap is equivalent to buying a 6 percent interest rate cap on LIBOR and writing a 6 percent floor. The premiums on the cap and floor must be equal because the combination generates a swap with no initial payment. The off-market swap, however, at a fixed rate of 8 percent is equivalent to buying a less expensive 8 percent cap and writing a more expensive 8 percent floor. Raising the strike rate on an interest rate cap lowers its cost; raising the strike rate on a floor increases its cost. The net outcome is an initial receipt of cash corresponding to the difference in premiums. This approach is illustrated in the lower panel of Figure 2.9. Notice that the initial cash received for agreeing to pay the above-market fixed rate should be the same in both panels—5.395 percent of the notional principal in this example. That is, the difference in the values of the bonds and the values of the options is the same, regardless of the volatility assumptions used to value the caps and the floors.

This interpretation suggests that the up-front cash received could be accounted for in the same manner as the premiums on caps and floors that compose the swap. In general, the premium is amortized over the lifetime of the option, typically on a straight-line basis, although as discussed previously, recently there has been a movement to amortize over time according to the incremental value for each year that is derived from an option pricing model. Also, a major difference in the accounting for purchased and written options is that the former may qualify for accrual (hedge) accounting and the latter must be marked to market. Nevertheless, suppose that both premiums on the long position in the cap and the short position in the floor are amortized in the same manner. Then the net difference in the two is the amount credited to interest income (because the premium on the floor that is written exceeds the premium on the cap that is bought). This approach also is essentially the same as the loan method because an increase to interest income has the same ultimate effect as a reduction in interest expense.

The key point is that the various interpretations of an off-market interest rate swap unambiguously imply that the initial cash receipt to the payer of the above-market rate should be amortized over the lifetime of the contract. Nevertheless, for a time in the 1980s, Internal Revenue Service (IRS) regulations required the fixed-rate payer to book the initial cash receipt as income in the initial accounting period. This requirement led to a number of tax-driven, off-market swap deals, usually to inject some "income" into the balance sheet to capture the value of tax-loss carryforwards (or foreign tax credits) that were about to expire worthless because of the lack of taxable income. The IRS eventually ruled in 1989 that the lump-sum, up-front proceeds on an exchange contract such as a swap must be amortized over the life of the swap. Later, in 1991, the IRS further clarified its position to rule that initial proceeds that are *material* (say, greater than 40 percent of the notional principal) must be booked using the loan approach. Smaller sizes of initial proceeds (say, 10–40 percent) must be amortized, while even smaller amounts (say, less than 10 percent) can be fully booked as interest income.

Summary of Economic Interpretations of Swap Contracts

Our objective in interpreting a plain vanilla swap in various ways is to demonstrate that swap contracts help integrate financial markets. An interest rate or currency swap can be easily described as a pair of capital market transactions, each having a different coupon-reset frequency or a different currency denomination (or both). Although this interpretation misses the treatment of swaps in bankruptcy, it does provide a few useful applications. The capital market approach indicates how swaps can be valued using bond prices, quite a practical concept if trading in the swap market were to slow appreciably or was not active to begin with, as in the case of an emerging market. This approach also indicates how to place a duration value on a swap, even when the swap is initially neither an asset nor a liability to its end user.

The forward market interpretation is useful in understanding some of the aspects of credit risk on a swap. When the term structure of interest rates is not flat, and when interest rate differentials across currencies are not zero, interest rate and currency swaps can be described as off-market series of forward contracts. That concept introduces an asymmetry of risk exposure between the two counterparties. Typically, a sequence of actual forwards will have less credit risk because of the structural design of assigning a single fixed rate to all settlement periods on a plain vanilla swap.

The options market interpretation is an extension to the well-known put–call-forward parity condition. With swaps, the result is that paying a fixed rate on a swap is the same as buying a cap and writing a floor. In the same manner, receiving a fixed rate is the same as selling a cap and buying a floor. This connection is very useful from an analytic perspective because all of the power of option pricing models can be applied to swap contracts.

These interpretations can be used to get some insight into the valuation of a nonplain vanilla swap such as an off-market interest rate swap. Paying an above-market fixed rate is shown to be the same in terms of cash flows as buying an FRN at LIBOR flat and funding the purchase by issuing a high-coupon bond having a market price higher than the FRN. The same can be said for buying an out-of-the-money interest rate cap and writing an in-the-money floor agreement. The initial proceeds of the off-market swap would be the same as the difference between the market values of the FRN and fixed-rate note and between the embedded cap that is owned and the floor that is written. The same patterns would hold for receiving the fixed rate on a swap, which is comparable to buying a fixed-rate bond and issuing the FRN or buying a floor and writing a cap at the same strike rate.

Exercises

Exercise 2.1: Suppose that you work in the back office derivatives operations of a regional commercial bank. Each day, the scheduled cash flows on a number of transactions need to be finalized as the reference rate is determined. Your job is to confirm the calculations, advise the counterparties of their scheduled receipts or payments, and pass that information on to the bank's accounting and cash-management departments. The calculations are usually done by computer, but yours is down for the day. Assume that the current date is March 15th and the three-month LIBOR is determined to be 6.125 percent (it was set two business days prior). Note that there are 92 days between March 15th and June 15th. Work out the obligations on the following transactions:

(a) A 3×6 FRA with Company ABC: The bank pays a fixed rate of 5.87 percent and receives three-month LIBOR on a notional principal of $7.8 million. Both rates are on an actual/360 day-count basis, and settlement is in arrears.

(b) A 3×6 FRA with Company DEF: The bank receives a fixed rate of 5.91 percent and pays three-month LIBOR on a notional principal of $12 million. Both rates are on an actual/360 day-count basis and settlement is in advance.

(c) A quarterly settlement interest rate swap with Company GHI: The bank receives a fixed rate of 6.77 percent and pays three-month LIBOR on a notional principal of $20 million. The fixed rate is on a 30/360 basis, the floating rate is on an actual/360 basis, and settlement is in arrears.

(d) A quarterly settlement interest rate cap sold to Company ABC on three-month LIBOR at a strike rate of 6 percent for a notional principal of $15 million. The strike rate is on an actual/360 basis, and settlement is in arrears.

(e) A quarterly settlement interest rate floor sold to pension fund XYZ on three-month LIBOR at a strike rate of 6 percent for a notional principal of $50 million. The strike rate is on an actual/360 basis, and settlement is in arrears.

Solution:

(a) The bank is scheduled to receive $5,083.00 from ABC on June 15th.

$$(0.06125 - 0.0587) \times \frac{92}{360} \times \$7{,}800{,}000 = \$5{,}083.00.$$

(b) The bank is scheduled to pay $6,491.72 to DEF on March 15th.

$$(0.06125 - 0.0591) \times \frac{92}{360} \times \$12{,}000{,}000 = \$6{,}593.33$$

$$\$6{,}593.33 \times \left[\frac{1}{1 + (92 \times 0.06125)/360}\right] = \$6{,}491.72.$$

(c) The bank is scheduled to receive $25,444.44 from GHI on June 15th.

$$\left[\left(0.0677 \times \frac{90}{360}\right) - \left(0.06125 \times \frac{92}{360}\right)\right] \times \$20{,}000{,}000 = \$25{,}444.44.$$

(d) The bank is scheduled to pay $4,791.67 to ABC on June 15th.

$$(0.06125 - 0.0600) \times \frac{92}{360} \times \$15{,}000{,}000 = \$4{,}791.67.$$

(e) No payment. The interest rate floor is out of the money because LIBOR is greater than the floor strike rate.

Banks often put their derivatives transactions in a master agreement that provides for *settlement netting* to minimize credit risk. For example, if the FRA and interest rate cap transactions with ABC are under one master agreement, the bank would be scheduled to receive the net amount of the two settlement flows. Because the bank receives \$5,083.00 on (a) and pays \$4,791.67 on (d), the net payment from ABC to the bank would be \$291.33 on June 15th.

Exercise 2.2: Suppose that the grid shown in Table E-2.1 represents movements in the swap yield curve over a five-year time period. The percentages are the fixed rates on annual settlement swaps against one-year LIBOR. For example, the fixed rate on a three-year swap entered in Year 1 would be 6.41 percent. A three-year swap transacted in Year 2 will have a higher fixed rate, namely 7.78 percent.

Calculate the sequence of mark-to-market values on a five-year swap that is entered in Year 1. Follow this swap to its maturity, calculating its market value for each year. Use the swap fixed rate as the discount factor in present value calculations and assume a notional principal of \$25 million.

Table E-2.1 Movements in the Swap Yield Curve

Tenor (years)	Year 1	Year 2	Year 3	Year 4	Year 5
One	5.10%	6.75%	8.50%	7.35%	6.75%
Two	5.82	7.23	8.21	7.70	7.41
Three	6.41	7.78	8.50	8.41	7.90
Four	6.87	8.10	8.66	8.90	8.31
Five	7.20	8.19	8.74	9.25	8.66

Solution: The key point is that the replacement swap for each year is the one with a maturity that matches the remaining tenor on the swap being valued.

Year 1: MTM Value = 0

$$\text{Year 2: MTM Value} = \sum_{t=1}^{4} \frac{(0.0810 - 0.0720) \times \$25 \text{ million}}{(1.0810)^t} = \$743{,}573$$

$$\text{Year 3: MTM Value} = \sum_{t=1}^{3} \frac{(0.0850 - 0.0720) \times \$25 \text{ million}}{(1.0850)^t} = \$830{,}057$$

$$\text{Year 4: MTM Value} = \sum_{t=1}^{2} \frac{(0.0770 - 0.0720) \times \$25 \text{ million}}{(1.0770)^t} = \$223{,}828$$

$$\text{Year 5: MTM Value} = \frac{(0.0720 - 0.0675) \times \$25 \text{ million}}{1.0675} = -\$105{,}386.$$

Notice that the MTM value reached a maximum in the third year. This pattern is typical because two offsetting factors are at work: (1) The longer the swap has been in existence, the greater the likely difference between the current market rate and the

Figure E-2.1 Converting a Dollar Bond with a Currency Swap

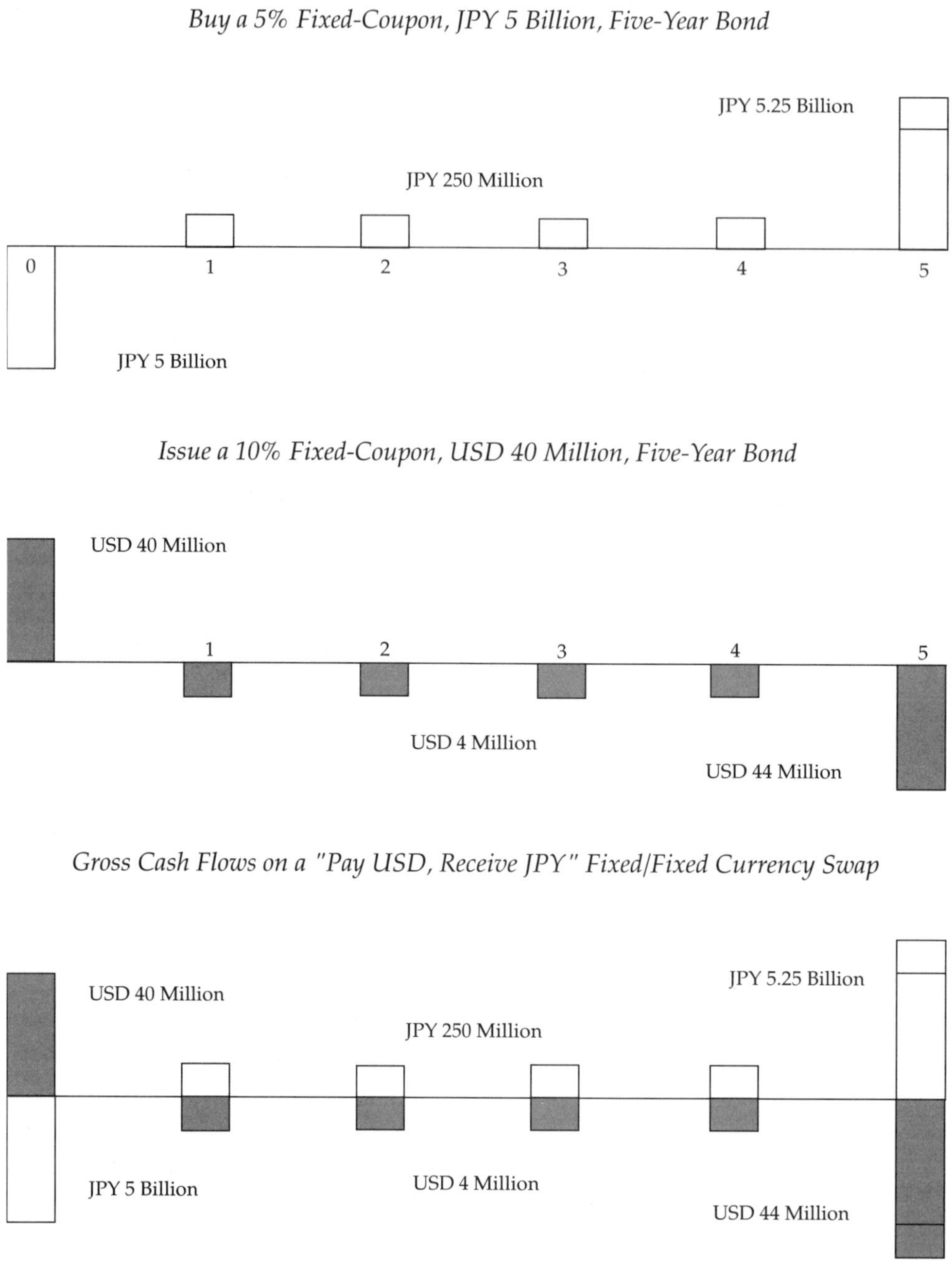

fixed rate on the swap, and (2) the longer the swap has been in existence, the fewer the number of remaining settlement dates. The former factor tends to increase, and the latter to decrease, the MTM value of the swap. Also note that when the swap has a positive value, such as during the first four years, the firm is concerned with the credit risk of the counterparty. If the counterparty were to default, that MTM value would be the amount of loss at that point.

Exercise 2.3: As the treasurer of a Japanese automobile manufacturer, you are concerned about the foreign exchange exposure associated with the dollar-based revenues the firm generates by selling cars in the United States. One way to hedge this balance sheet exposure is to incur an offsetting amount of dollar-denominated liabilities. Accordingly, you are considering converting one of your yen-denominated bonds into fixed-rate, synthetic, dollar-denominated debt with a fixed/fixed currency swap.

The issue that you are thinking of converting has a five-year maturity with a 5 percent coupon paid annually in arrears. The face value of the note is JPY 5 billion. A discussion with a swap market maker reveals that a fixed rate of 5 percent in yen could be swapped for a fixed rate of 10 percent in U.S. dollars. Also, the rate at which the principal flows would be exchanged at origination and maturity is the current FX spot rate of JPY 125/USD.

(a) Describe how the currency swap that you will require can be interpreted as a pair of bond transactions. Indicate specifically which bond would be bought and which would be sold.

(b) Calculate the five-year sequence of forward exchange rates implicit in this currency swap transaction, as well as the analogous series of forward rates implied by the interest rate parity condition.

Solution: The currency swap needed is one in which the manufacturer will receive yen and pay dollars. Moreover, the currency swap will be an exchange of fixed rates. At the current exchange rate, JPY 5 billion is equivalent to USD 40 million (JPY 5 billion ÷ JPY 125/USD), and the annual coupon exchanges would be for JPY 250 million and USD 4 million.

(a) The five-year capital market transactions replicating the swap would be

- Buy a yen-denominated bond with a 5 percent coupon and face value of JPY 5 billion, and
- sell a dollar-denominated bond with a 10 percent coupon and face value of USD 40 million.

The result of these approaches is shown graphically in Figure E-2.1. Notice that when this swap is coupled with the existing short position in the five-year yen bond, the net effect will be to convert the yen-denominated obligation into dollar-denominated debt.

(b) The spot and forward exchange rates built into the currency swap are as shown in Table E-2.2. The exchanges in Years 1 through 4 are calculated as JPY 250 million divided by USD 4 million; the fifth-year transaction is a composite of USD 4 million at JPY 62.5/USD and USD 40 million at JPY 125/USD. The given rate of JPY 119.318/USD is the weighted average: JPY 62.5 (4/44) + JPY 125 (40/44).

Table E-2.2 FX Forward Implied by Interest Rate Parity

Year	Transaction Type	Rate (JPY/USD)
0	Spot FX trade	125.000
1	One-year FX forward	62.500
2	Two-year FX forward	62.500
3	Three-year FX forward	62.500
4	Four-year FX forward	62.500
5	Five-year FX forward	119.318

The forward rates implied by interest rate parity are the following:

Spot FX Trade = JPY 125/USD

$$\text{One-year FX forward} = (\text{JPY } 125/\text{USD}) \times \left[\frac{(1 + 0.05)}{(1 + 0.10)}\right] = \text{JPY } 119.318/\text{USD}$$

$$\text{Two-year FX forward} = (\text{JPY } 125/\text{USD}) \times \left[\left(\frac{(1 + 0.05)}{(1 + 0.10)}\right)^2\right] = \text{JPY } 113.895/\text{USD}$$

$$\text{Three-year FX forward} = (\text{JPY } 125/\text{USD}) \times \left[\left(\frac{(1 + 0.05)}{(1 + 0.10)}\right)^3\right] = \text{JPY } 108.718/\text{USD}$$

$$\text{Four-year FX forward} = (\text{JPY } 125/\text{USD}) \times \left[\left(\frac{(1 + 0.05)}{(1 + 0.10)}\right)^4\right] = \text{JPY } 103.776/\text{USD}$$

$$\text{Five-year FX forward} = (\text{JPY } 125/\text{USD}) \times \left[\left(\frac{(1 + 0.05)}{(1 + 0.10)}\right)^5\right] = \text{JPY } 99.059/\text{USD}.$$

Thus, from your point of view, as the payer of U.S. dollars and receiver of Japanese yen on the swap, you will be getting: (1) the spot exchange rate at Year 0, (2) a favorable exchange rate in Years 1 through 4, and (3) an unfavorable exchange at Year 5.

Exercise 2.4: The treasurer of a British brewery is planning to enter an at-market, plain vanilla, three-year, quarterly settlement interest rate swap to pay a fixed rate of 8 percent and to receive three-month sterling LIBOR. First, he decides to check various cap–floor combinations to see if any might be preferable. A market maker in British pound sterling over-the-counter options presents the treasurer with the following price list (in basis points) for three-year, quarterly settlement caps and floors:

	Interest Rate Caps		*Interest Rate Floors*	
Strike Rate	*Buy*	*Sell*	*Buy*	*Sell*
7%	582	597	320	335
8	398	413	401	416
9	205	220	502	517

The basis point prices when multiplied by the notional principal give the actual purchase or sale price in pounds sterling. These quotes are from the perspective of the market maker, not the firm. That is, the treasurer could buy a 9 percent cap from the market maker for 220 basis points or sell one for 205 basis points. The strike rates are quoted on a 365-day basis, as is sterling LIBOR.

In financial analysis of this sort, the treasurer assumes that the three-year cost of funds on fully amortizing debt would be about 8.20 percent (for quarterly payments). Should another structure be considered in lieu of the plain vanilla swap?

Solution: The key is to recognize that the combination of buying the cap and writing a floor at the same strike rate generates the same settlement cash flows as a pay-fixed swap. The fixed rate on the swap would equal the strike rate on the cap and floor.

Consider first the 8 percent cap–floor combination. The treasurer could buy the cap for 413 basis points (the market maker's offer) and sell the floor for 401 basis points (the market maker's bid). The net is an up-front outflow of 12 basis points (times the notional principal). Because the 8 percent pay-fixed swap would not entail an initial payment, the 8 percent cap–floor combination can be rejected.

Consider next the 7 percent cap–floor combination. The treasurer could buy the cap for 597 basis points and sell the floor for 320 basis points, resulting in a net up-front outflow of 277 basis points. The fixed rate on the synthetic swap would be 7 percent, however, not 8 percent. The attraction of the cap–floor alternative turns on the trade-off of a present value of 277 basis points versus a three-year annuity of 100 basis points (actually a 12-period annuity of 25 basis points per quarterly period). Using the three-year fixed rate of 8.20 percent, the present value of the savings is 263.57 basis points; that is,

$$\sum_{t=1}^{12} \frac{25}{\left(1 + \frac{0.0820}{4}\right)^t} = 263.57.$$

Because the 263.57 basis points is less than the up-front cost of 277 basis points, the 7 percent cap–floor combination can be rejected as well.

Consider finally the 9 percent cap–floor combination. The treasurer could buy the cap for 220 basis points and sell the floor for 502 basis points, resulting in a net up-front inflow of 282 basis points. The fixed rate on the synthetic swap would be 9 percent. Because the initial receipt exceeds the present value of the higher swap coupon (i.e., 282 > 263.57), this combination should be considered. Is it definitely better? Perhaps so in terms of cash flow and the time value of money, but the treasurer would also have to consider the tax and accounting treatment of the difference in the options premiums to confirm the benefit.

Chapter 3. Swap Applications

In recent years, swap contracts have become an important and popular way for corporations to repackage their asset and liability cash flows. This chapter considers several applications that demonstrate three general reasons for the popularity of swaps. First, swaps are a cost-effective way to transform a firm's existing risk profile. If a company's operating structure leaves it exposed to adverse movements in domestic interest or foreign exchange rates, swaps can be efficient mechanisms for synthetically altering the balance sheet accounts in order to close these sensitivity gaps. Second, swaps are used widely in the process of issuing new securities to obtain a cheaper borrowing cost or enhance investor return. These applications, which often rely on an end user's specific market view or an apparent arbitrage across different financial product markets, represent the essence of what has come to be called *structured finance*. Finally, the swap contract can be an expedient means for a corporate manager to exploit information about the firm that the capital market does not possess (i.e., *asymmetric information*). This role of swaps will be particularly useful when the information in question involves an evaluation of the firm's relative creditworthiness.

Risk-Management Applications

In the quest to achieve a profitable operating structure, a corporation often finds itself with an unintended exposure to financial risk. For instance, a firm whose credit quality forces it to finance long-term asset acquisitions with short-term bank loans must be concerned with rising domestic interest rates. Also, a U.S.-based manufacturer with substantial overseas sales (and hence foreign currency receipts) is exposed to a strengthening U.S. dollar. When a corporation is in such a situation, it must either accept the exposure as part of its general risk-management strategy (i.e., speculation) or attempt to remove the exposure from its balance sheet by hedging. Within the hedging alternative, the company again has two choices: It can formally restructure its balance sheet accounts by, say, refinancing short-term, floating-rate debt with a new long-term, fixed-rate issue; or it can implement the desired change artificially by using swaps as an off-balance-sheet restructuring tool. This section details three examples of how this latter approach works.

Balance Sheet Gap Management. Consider the risk-management problem faced by Company FNC, a financial services corporation whose stylized balance sheet is presented in Table 3.1. Although a substantial amount of the funding for this firm comes from debt on which the coupon resets periodically, the majority of its assets are held in long-term investments. The potential problem with this sensitivity mismatch is that interest rate changes will affect the market value of FNC's assets and liabilities to different degrees; therefore, its net worth is

Table 3.1 Company FNC's Balance Sheet and Asset/Liability Durations

Item	Market Value	Duration (years)
Assets		
Cash (noninterest bearing account)	\$ 100	0.00
5-year term loans, valued at par to yield 10%	400	4.17
10-year amortizing mortgages valued at par to yield 10%	500	4.73
Total	\$1,000	
Liabilities		
5-year, floating-rate note with annual reset to LIBOR (current LIBOR = 8%)	\$ 600	1.00
7-year, zero-coupon bond issued to yield 8%	300	7.00
Total	\$ 900	
Net worth	\$ 100	

Asset and Liability Duration Calculations:

$$D_{\text{asset}} = \left(\frac{100}{1{,}000}\right)(0.00) + \left(\frac{400}{1{,}000}\right)(4.17) + \left(\frac{500}{1{,}000}\right)(4.73) = 4.03 \text{ years}$$

$$D_{\text{liability}} = \left(\frac{600}{900}\right)(1.00) + \left(\frac{300}{900}\right)(7.00) = 3.00 \text{ years}$$

subject to these rate fluctuations. Specifically, as interest rates rise, the value of the company's assets will decline by more than the value of the liabilities, thereby shrinking net worth. Said differently, because the company is "short funded," a rate increase will cause its funding cost to rise before it can reinvest the asset base at a more profitable level.

One approach to measuring this asset/liability sensitivity imbalance that is particularly effective for financial firms is *duration gap*. Duration gap is usually computed as follows:

$$D_{\text{gap}} = D_{\text{asset}} - \left(\frac{\text{Total liabilities}}{\text{Total assets}}\right) \times D_{\text{liability}}.$$

In this calculation, the durations of the asset and liability portfolios from the balance sheet are obtained as weighted averages of the respective accounts, with the relative market values of the individual positions determining the weighting scheme. Also, the duration of the liabilities is scaled by a measure of the firm's leverage, thus adjusting for the fact that any firm with a positive net worth has more assets than liabilities.[1] The asset and liability duration figures calculations for FNC Company are as follows:

$$D_{\text{asset}} = \left(\frac{100}{1{,}000}\right) \times 0.00 + \left(\frac{400}{1{,}000}\right) \times 4.17 + \left(\frac{500}{1{,}000}\right) \times 4.73 = 4.03 \text{ years},$$

and

$$D_{\text{liability}} = \left(\frac{600}{900}\right) \times 1.00 + \left(\frac{300}{900}\right) \times 7.00 = 3.00 \text{ years}.$$

Thus, the duration gap calculation for FNC is

$$D_{\text{gap}} = 4.03 - \left(\frac{900}{1{,}000}\right) \times 3.00 = 1.33 \text{ years}.$$

The fact that FNC Company's duration gap is positive means that it is exposed to rising rates; its net worth is like a long position in a one-year four-month, zero-coupon bond. A negative gap value, which would occur when shorter term assets are financed with longer term liabilities, could be interpreted as equivalent to a short zero-coupon holding of comparable magnitude, thereby exposing the firm to falling rates. A duration gap of zero implies a hedged position in which assets and liabilities are equally responsive to future rate movements.

Unless FNC wants to hold this exposure (and in so doing speculate on falling rates), it will attempt to set its duration gap to zero. One way to accomplish this task would be to restructure

[1] As reviewed in the appendix, the duration statistic is often used in the context of linking percentage changes in interest rates with the resulting *percentage* change in position value. Thus, with different levels of assets and liabilities, simply matching asset and liability durations would still leave the firm exposed on a *dollar* basis. Also, notice that although the maturity of the mortgage portfolio is twice as long as that of the loan portfolio, the two durations are only about a half-year apart because the former cash flow structure amortizes the principal and the latter does not, thereby shifting the weights associated with the payment dates in the duration calculation closer to the present.

its balance sheet by changing the existing accounts. In general, the treasurer for FNC would either have to shorten asset duration, lengthen liability duration, or some combination of the two. Formal balance sheet restructuring, however, is not usually the most sensible approach. Beyond the obvious costs of attempting to buy or sell what may be illiquid instruments, the more compelling reason for this statement can be seen by assuming FNC tries to close its duration gap by selling some of its loan portfolio and holding the proceeds in cash. Recognizing that the average duration for the blended loan portfolios is 4.48 years [calculated as (400/900) × 4.17 + (500/900) × 4.73], the amount needed to be held in cash, w_{cash}, is found by solving

$$D_{\text{gap}} = [(w_{\text{cash}})(0.00) + (1 - w_{\text{cash}})(4.48)] - \left(\frac{900}{1{,}000}\right) \times 3.00 = 0.00 \text{ years},$$

or $w_{\text{cash}} = 40$ percent (of \$1,000). The remaining level of income-producing assets would be only \$600, an amount not even sufficient to service the firm's existing debt. Thus, its interest rate exposure would be solved, but Company FNC would then be operating at a loss, which of course would also reduce its net worth.

The important point of the preceding analysis is that a firm is best served by selecting the balance sheet structure that makes the most sense for the operating efficiency of the organization and then hedging any attendant exposures some other way. To see how FNC could have eliminated its rate exposure synthetically, suppose that the treasurer had decided to convert some of its annual-reset FRN with a five-year, pay-fixed swap. Assuming for simplicity that the swap fixed rate is 8 percent, the portion of the "floater" position equivalent to the swap's notional principal is effectively transformed into an 8 percent, fixed-rate bond. Valued at par, such a bond would have a duration of 4.31 years. Thus, to determine the dollar value of the FRN liability that would have to be swapped, the treasurer needs to solve for the notional principal on the required pay-fixed swap, p_{swp}, in the following formula:

$$D_{\text{gap}} = (4.03) - \left(\frac{900}{1{,}000}\right) \times \left[\left(\frac{600 - p_{\text{swp}}}{900}\right)(1.0) + \left(\frac{p_{\text{swp}}}{900}\right)(4.31) + \left(\frac{300}{900}\right)(7.0)\right] = 0.00 \text{ years},$$

or $p_{\text{swp}} = \$402$.

A clear advantage of the swap-based approach to hedging is that it does not require FNC to liquidate any existing position or create any new one. Another interesting aspect of this synthetic risk-management solution is that if the treasurer had instead wanted to shorten the firm's asset duration, he or she would have used the *same* swap. That is, an *asset swap* designed to convert some of the existing fixed-rate loans to have a floating-rate coupon would also be of the pay-fixed variety. This result is illustrated generally in Figure 3.1.

Using Forward (i.e., Deferred Start) Swaps. Another benefit of using swaps to control financial risks is that they allow the corporation to tailor a solution to its unique view of the world. For example, when confronted by the balance sheet shown in Table 3.1, suppose FNC's managers decide that (1) they are willing to bear the exposure during the first two years of the FRN's life, based on the view that LIBOR would not rise (and might even fall) during that time, but (2) they want to fix their funding cost in Years 3 through 5. Although a formal restructuring of the existing debt issues to effect this blend of speculation and hedging would be prohibitively expensive, it is quite simple to achieve in the swap market. Specifically, FNC would require a three-year, pay-fixed swap that although negotiated today, would not start until the end of Year 2. This sort of arrangement is known as a *forward swap*.

Figure 3.2 shows the net effect of combining a current position in a five-year, annual-reset FRN with a three-year, pay-fixed swap with a two-year deferred start date. The first thing to notice is that the fixed rate on the forward swap (arbitrarily chosen to be 8.50 percent for this example) is not the same as the fixed rate on the five-year swap commencing immediately (8 percent). In general, the rate on the forward swap will differ from that on the plain swap any time the implied floating-rate yield curve is not flat, because the swap fixed rate should be an aver-

Figure 3.1 Closing a Positive Duration Gap Balance Sheet Position Synthetically

Converting a Floating-Rate Liability with a Pay-Fixed Swap

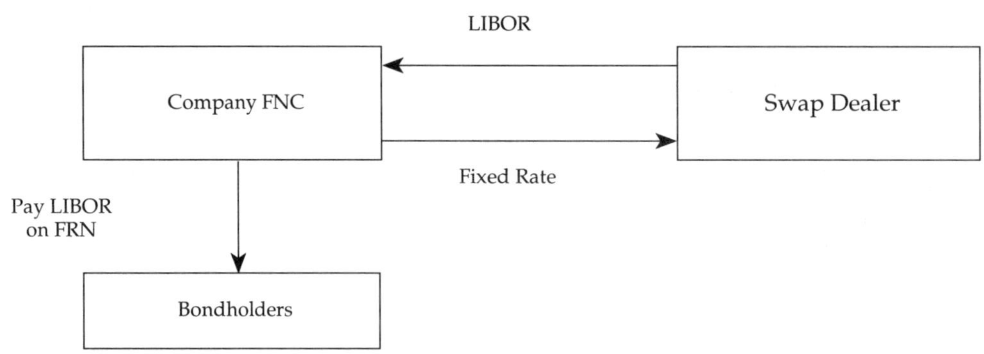

Converting a Fixed-Rate Asset with a Pay-Fixed Swap

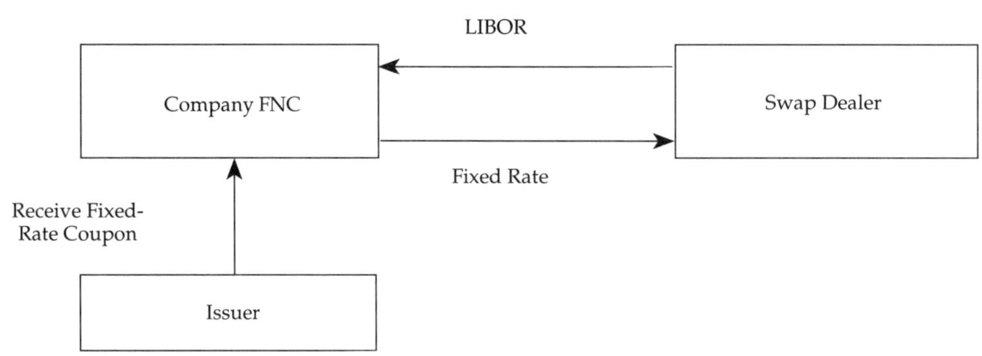

age of the relevant segment of the implied forward rate curve. Thus, in an upward- or downward-sloping yield curve environment, swaps starting at different points in time will have different fixed rates.[2]

The top panel of Figure 3.2 indicates that without the swap in the first two years, FNC retains its positive duration gap and, therefore, is exposed to rising rates. Of course, this risk is exactly the one that the firm's management is willing to assume. The lower panel shows that once the forward swap becomes effective at the beginning of the third year, the company will again be hedged against the adverse economic conditions the management fears. Notice in calculating the duration gap for those three years, we assumed that the fixed rate on a new three-year plain vanilla swap was the same 8.50 percent that prevailed in the forward swap market two years prior. With this assumption, the swapped floater would be valued at par and have a duration of 2.77 years and the zero-coupon liability's duration would be equal to its five-year maturity. Also, assuming no substantive changes in the relative allocations on either side of the balance sheet, the durations for what are now three- and eight-year loan and mortgage

[2] A more formal analysis of how forward swaps should be priced in an efficient market is presented in the next chapter.

Figure 3.2 Converting a Floating-Rate Liability with a Forward Swap

Years 1 and 2

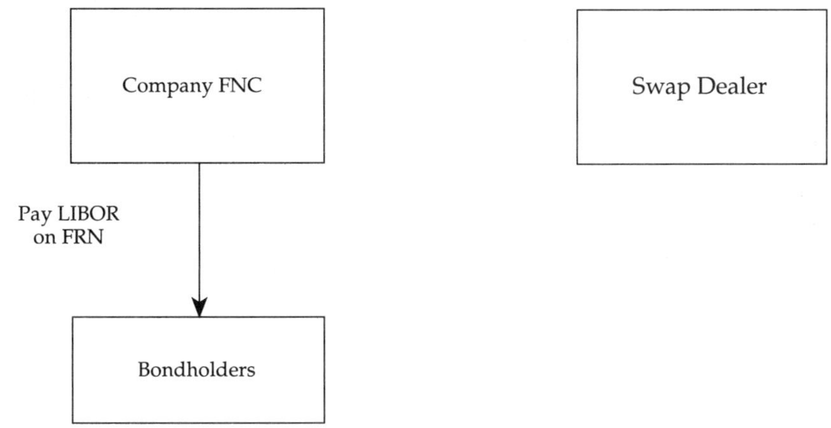

$$\text{Duration Gap} = (4.03) - \left(\frac{900}{1000}\right)(3.00) = 1.33 \text{ years}$$

Interest Rate Exposure: Rising Rates

Years 3 through 5

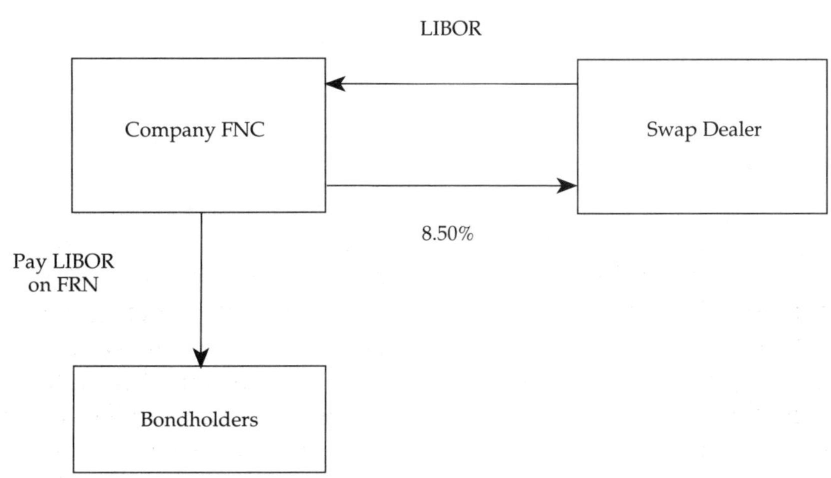

$$\text{Duration Gap} = (2.61) - \left(\frac{900}{1000}\right)\left[\left(\frac{312}{900}\right)(1.0) + \left(\frac{288}{900}\right)(2.77) + \left(\frac{300}{900}\right)(5.0)\right] = 0.00 \text{ years}$$

Interest Rate Exposure: None

portfolios are 2.74 and 3.48, respectively. If, for simplicity, the amortized mortgage principal is held in cash, the asset duration would be 2.61 years (calculated as [(166/1000) × 0] + [(400/1000) × 2.74] + [(434/1000) × 3.48]). Thus, using a procedure similar to that shown in the preceding example, the notional principal on the forward swap would have to be $288 to ensure that the duration gap at the beginning of Year 3 will be zero.

Matching Foreign-Currency-Denominated Assets and Liabilities. Company SND is a Swiss consumer nondurables manufacturer that, to date, has produced and sold its products entirely within Switzerland. As a consequence, all of its accounting statement entries have been denominated in Swiss francs (CHF) with the result that any risk-management problems SND's treasurer faced were attributable largely to fluctuating Swiss interest rates. Recently, however, two changes have taken place. First, SND has begun importing materials needed for its production process from France. SND's new supply contract with the French parts producer runs for three years and will result in SND having an annual French-franc-denominated (FRF) account payable of FRF 5 million. Of course, this foreign currency liability creates a new source of economic risk for SND—namely, the possibility that the Swiss franc will depreciate relative to the French currency thereby making the obligation increasingly expensive in terms of its domestic monetary unit.

The second recent change at SND is that, because of increasingly tight operating margins during the past few years, the treasurer has just received a mandate from senior management to operate the treasury unit as a profit center. That is to say, he will now be allowed to take a limited number of positions implementing his view on future domestic and foreign exchange rate movements. In this context, the treasurer believes the inflation rate in France will be considerably lower than that in Switzerland in the near future and, accordingly, the relative value of the French franc will strengthen compared with the Swiss franc. He recognizes that if this forecast is correct, the firm's recent supply contract will become more expensive (in Swiss francs) as the years pass.

To hedge this new exposure, the treasurer of Company SND can do several things. First, he can try to sell enough of the firm's domestic currency in the FX forward and futures markets to guarantee the acquisition of the requisite French francs for prices fixed in Swiss francs at today's levels. This approach amounts to an attempt to convert the denomination of a future income statement item while otherwise leaving the company's balance sheet untouched. A potential problem with this solution, however, is that liquidity and contract availability in the over-the-counter and exchange-traded FX forward markets may not be sufficient to support such activity.

A second basic approach to hedging that SND could adopt would be to "rebalance" a portion of its asset and liability accounts. Specifically, assume in this case that the company can sell some of its current holdings in Swiss-franc-denominated interest-bearing assets and purchase an equivalent number of French bonds in order to create a three-year French franc revenue stream that would match the FRF 5 million liability. Finally, as the physical conversion of assets suggested by the second hedging scheme is likely to come at the expense of extremely high transaction costs, a third alternative would be to implement this conversion synthetically in the currency swap market.

To see how the synthetic adjustment might be carried out, suppose that Company SND currently holds in its security portfolio a three-year bond priced at a par value of CHF 60 million and paying a fixed annual coupon of 7.50 percent. Under the present conditions in the foreign exchange market, Swiss francs can be converted into French francs at the rate of CHF 0.25/FRF and the 7.50 percent Swiss franc coupon could be swapped for a French franc fixed rate of 6.60 percent in a three-year transaction. With these prices, notice that SND will have to hold only the equivalent of FRF 75.76 million face value in bonds to generate the necessary FRF 5 million cash flow (FRF 75.76 × 0.0660). Thus, the company will have to convert only CHF 18.94 million (or FRF 75.76 million × CHF 0.25/FRF) of its existing bond holding to implement the necessary change. This means that

SND will have used the swap to convert less than a third of its existing Swiss franc holding into the functional equivalent of a French-franc-denominated asset.

The sequence of transactions involved in this conversion, including the accounts payable to the French parts supplier, is illustrated in Figure 3.3. Notice that in making the initial exchange of currencies shown in the upper panel, the company is not yet exposed to a strengthening French franc, because this trade is done at the current spot FX rate. Without the swap on the subsequent dates, however, SND would be forced to pay an increasing amount in Swiss francs to meet the FRF 5 million payable, given the treasurer's view. The currency swap guarantees the treasurer a fixed price for acquiring these cash flows that is known at the inception of the deal.

Figure 3.3 Hedging a Foreign Currency-Denominated Liability with Currency Swaps

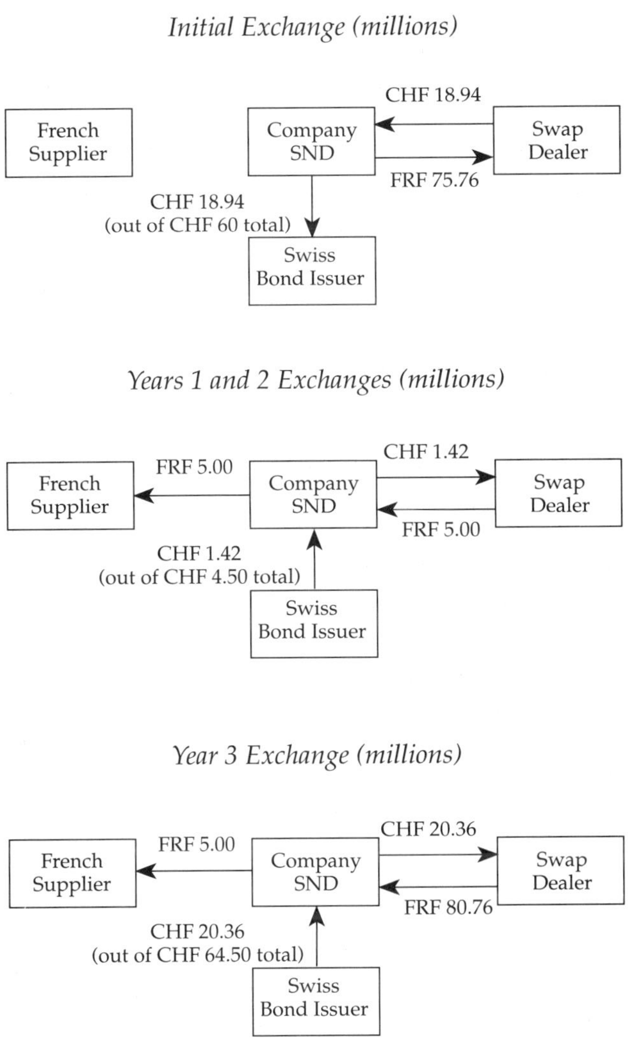

The bottom panel in Figure 3.3 reveals a second advantage of the currency swap. By converting the denomination of the underlying principal along with that of the interest payment that flows through to the supplier, the swap contract also allows the treasurer to speculate on an appreciation in the French franc. That is, at the Year 3 settlement date, his initial FRF 75.76 million principal "investment" will be refunded for the spot price of CHF 18.94. Thus, if the treasurer's view is correct, he will be able to add additional value to SND's manufacturing activities by converting the French currency back to Swiss francs at a profit.

Arbitrage Transactions and Structured Finance

In the context of the swap market, a pure arbitrage transaction occurs when an interest rate or currency swap contract is used to take advantage of pricing inconsistencies across two (or more) different financial markets. In a typical arbitrage scenario, a swap is used to repackage the cash flows of a cheaper security so as to be identical to those of another, more expensive instrument in all material respects (i.e., risk, timing, amount). The arbitrage is then created when a corporation simultaneously buys the less expensive cash flow package and pays for the purchase by issuing the more expensive one. Notice that the widespread existence of such transactions would be inconsistent with the notion of an efficient capital market, which holds that all truly identical sets of cash flows should have the same price. Consequently, for any alleged swap-based arbitrage deal, one of the following statements must be true: Swaps help corporations exploit inefficiencies in the securities industry, or the two cash flow patterns in question are not really identical.

As noted earlier, swap agreements are best seen as a tool for integrating the markets for capital and other derivative products. The swap market never could have reached its current stature by relying on arbitrage applications for its continuing existence; after all, arbitrage is a strategy that "corrects" the pricing discrepancies it seeks to exploit. Thus, a more plausible explanation of price discrepancies than arbitrage is that two apparently comparable cash flow patterns—one "natural" and one transformed with the use of a swap—have important, if subtle, differences that participants in the market recognize when pricing them. Said differently, when evaluating swap-driven deals, it is extremely important to look beneath the surface to see where the hidden risks may lie. This caution can be illustrated by considering nuances of what is regarded as the standard swap story involving *credit risk arbitrage.*

Classical Interest Rate Swap Arbitrage. Suppose that two corporate borrowers each seek five-year funding in the amount of $25 million dollars. The treasurer at Firm AAA, the stronger credit, prefers to issue floating-rate debt because of his belief that short-term interest rates will fall as the Federal Reserve Board eases its monetary policy in an attempt to bolster the sluggish economy. His counterpart at Firm BBB, the weaker credit, prefers issuing fixed-rate debt to match the interest rate insensitivity of the company's net operating revenues. Their respective costs of funds for par-value, semiannual payment fixed- and floating-rate debt issues are as follows:

Firm	*Fixed-Rate Debt Cost*	*Floating-Rate Debt Cost*
AAA	5-year T-bond yield + 25 basis points	LIBOR
BBB	5-year T-bond yield + 85 basis points	LIBOR + 30 basis points
Quality spread	60 basis points	30 basis points

In this example, AAA has an *absolute* advantage in both markets, reflecting its stronger credit standing, but it has a *relative* advantage only in the fixed-rate market, where its spread over the weaker name is worth 60 basis points. Conversely, although Firm BBB pays a higher funding cost in both markets, it has a relative advantage in issuing floating-rate debt, because it is penalized only 30 basis points for its weaker credit standing. This *quality spread* differential creates an apparent opportunity for credit risk arbitrage based on the principle of comparative advantage. Because neither firm enjoys a relative funding advantage in the market in which it wishes to issue debt, each company can benefit from issuing debt in the market in which it does have an advantage and then swapping coupon obligations to obtain the desired funding structure.

To understand these potential gains, suppose that the two treasurers negotiate a swap directly with one another, deciding to split any "arbitrage" gains equally. Accordingly, after Firm AAA issues five-year, fixed-rate debt and Firm BBB issues a five-year FRN, they agree to a swap with the following terms:

- Notional Principal: U.S. $25 million
- Fixed-Rate Payer: Counterparty BBB
- Swap Fixed Rate: $(T + 0.40)\%$ (semiannual actual/365 bond basis)
- Fixed-Rate Receiver: Counterparty AAA
- Floating Rate: 6-month LIBOR (money-market basis)

where T represents the T-bond yield. These bond and swap transactions are shown in Figure 3.4.

The net, synthetic funding cost for each company can be calculated as

AAA's funding cost (money-market basis) =

$$(T + 0.25\%) \times \left(\frac{360}{365}\right) + \left[\text{LIBOR} - (T + 0.40\%) \times \left(\frac{360}{365}\right)\right] = \text{LIBOR} - 0.15\%.$$

BBB's funding cost (actual/365 bond basis) =

$$(\text{LIBOR} + 0.30\%) \times \left(\frac{365}{360}\right) + \left[(T + 0.40\%) - \text{LIBOR} \times \left(\frac{365}{360}\right)\right] = T + 0.70\%.$$

Thus, both counterparties appear to have obtained superior financing by using the swap agreement to take advantage of the 30-basis-point quality spread discrepancy in the fixed- and variable-rate bond markets. By issuing in their respective markets of comparative advantage and then restructuring their coupon obligations with the swap, each firm enjoys a gain in the form of a funding cost that is 15 basis points

Figure 3.4 The Credit Arbitrage Swap Illustrated

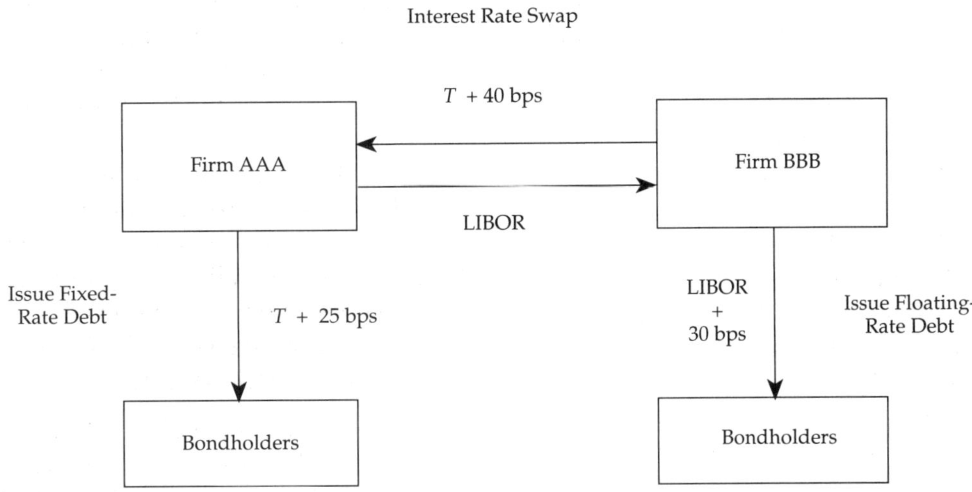

less than through a direct issue in their markets of choice.

Before determining whether these gains represent a legitimate arbitrage situation, another important point must be considered. Notice that Firm AAA has used the swap-driven deal to acquire sub-LIBOR financing when a direct-issue FRN would have required coupons of LIBOR flat. These two structures are not directly comparable, however. To see why, recognize that although Firm AAA's swap-related funding cost depends critically on its counterparty's promise to make the net settlement payment whenever LIBOR is less than $T + 0.40$ percent, the direct-issue cost embeds no such dependency (i.e., Firm AAA does not have to worry about its bondholders defaulting on any promises). What would happen, for instance, if on a settlement date, LIBOR is actually less than $T + 0.40$ percent and Firm BBB defaults on its obligation to make the net settlement payment on the swap? In such a case, Firm AAA's funding cost would be the fixed-rate coupon it issued rather than the LIBOR-based coupon it desired; that its swap counterparty defaults in no way relieves Firm AAA of the obligation to repay its bondholders.

Similarly, Firm BBB's swap-driven funding cost of $T + 0.70$ percent is only truly fixed to the extent that Firm AAA honors its contractual obligations. If AAA should default on a settlement date when LIBOR exceeds $T + 0.40$ percent, BBB would still be forced to pay LIBOR + 0.30 percent under adverse circumstances. In short, then, the funding scheme involving the swap is *riskier* for both counterparties than the respective desired direct issues. Consequently, the swap-related funding cost *should* be lower to account for this increased exposure. Further, although the terms of the swap contract depend largely on the negotiating skills of the two counterparties, it is reasonable to assume that the higher-rated credit will be able to command a larger percentage of the quality spread differential. The critical point is that the existence of arbitrage cannot be evaluated fully until after *all* relevant swap risks—including liquidity, legal, taxation, and accounting, as well as default risk—are regarded in their proper context. We examine these sources of uncertainty more thoroughly in Chapter 5.

Arbitrage with Currency Swaps. Keeping these caveats about credit risk in mind, the preceding arbitrage example can be extended in two ways. First, swaps can be used to transform a company's comparative advantage across different currencies. Second, as we saw earlier, asset swaps can also be used to convert revenue streams in search of a superior investment return.

Suppose that a U.S.-based pension fund is seeking a fixed-rate, seven-year bond investment with a face value of USD 10 million. Assume further that the effective annual yield to maturity on direct-purchase bonds that satisfy the fund's maturity and credit quality policy constraints is 8.00 percent. Because this fund is not restricted from using derivatives or making international investments, the manager thinks that she may be able to increase the net yield by purchasing a foreign-pay bond and swapping the cash flows into dollars.

One specific transaction that she is contemplating is the purchase of a Eurosterling bond issued by a British company. The particular security that she has been offered pays an annual sterling coupon of 9.50 percent and has an otherwise comparable set of characteristics (i.e., duration and default rating). From a swap dealer, she has also obtained the following prices: (1) USD 1.40/GBP for the spot exchange of dollars and pounds, and (2) a bid–offer quote of 9.35–9.42 percent on a seven-year sterling currency swap versus the payment or receipt of 8.00 percent in U.S. dollars. With these terms, a USD 10 million investment would be equivalent to GBP 7.143 million and, accepting the offer side of the dealer's swap quotes, the manager would make annual payments of GBP 0.673 million (calculated as GBP 7.143 × 0.0942) in exchange for receiving USD 0.800 million. The combined cash flows from the swapped Eurosterling bond are shown in Table 3.2.

One way to interpret the apparent arbitrage in this example is to note that the fund manager has been able to exploit the swap market to receive the same USD 800,000 annual coupons she would have gotten with the direct dollar-denominated issue *plus* an additional GBP 6,000. This incremental sterling-denominated sum was the result of the discrepancy between the coupon rate in the Eurobond market (9.50 percent) and the coupon rate in the swap market (9.42 percent). Notice, however, that simply adding this 8-basis-point differential directly onto 8.00 percent in calculating the manager's all-in yield would be incorrect because these two items are denominated in different currencies. Said differently, a basis point in dollars is generally not the same as a basis point expressed in a foreign currency. In this case, 1 basis point in sterling is equal to 0.95 basis points in dollars.[3] Consequently, the effective yield on the swapped Eurosterling issue is 8.076 percent.

Whether the difference between 8.076 percent and the direct-purchase yield of 8.00 percent represents an arbitrage once again is subject to debate. As before, the central issue is whether a swapped bond purchase is truly as good as the direct purchase. In either circumstance, the fund manager will have to worry about default on the part of the issuer, but only in the former case will she also have to worry about her swap counterparty defaulting whenever the pound depreciates in value relative to the dollar. Further, inasmuch as the currency

[3] This value can be derived by discounting a seven-year annuity of 1 basis point in sterling at the rate of 9.50 percent and then reannuitizing that amount in dollars at 8.00 percent. That is, the dollar value of 1 basis point in sterling is the solution to the following equation:

$$\sum_{t=1}^{7} \frac{1}{(1+0.0950)^t} = \sum_{t=1}^{7} \frac{x}{(1+0.0800)^t},$$

or $x = 0.95$.

Table 3.2 Asset Arbitrage with a Currency Swap
(cash flows in millions)

Year	Bond Receipts	Currency Swap: Receipt	Currency Swap: Payment	Net Cash Flow
0	−GBP 7.143	GBP 7.143	USD 10.000	−USD 10.000
1	0.679	0.800	0.673	USD 0.800 + GBP 0.006
2	0.679	0.800	0.673	0.800 + 0.006
3	0.679	0.800	0.673	0.800 + 0.006
4	0.679	0.800	0.673	0.800 + 0.006
5	0.679	0.800	0.673	0.800 + 0.006
6	0.679	0.800	0.673	0.800 + 0.006
7	0.679	0.800	0.673	0.800 + 0.006
	and GBP 7.143	USD 10.000	GBP 7.143	USD 10.000

swap requires a physical exchange of principal, this default exposure is greater than it would have been on a single-currency interest rate swap, in which the principal is notional. If the swap counterparty in this example is also the bond dealer that sold the manager the Eurosterling issue, the dealer will probably be able to hold the bond as collateral, thereby reducing its credit exposure to the pension fund.

Structured Finance Applications. Generally speaking, structured finance can be viewed as a form of financial market intermediation in which the disparate wants and needs of the ultimate sources and uses of capital are mutually satisfied through the creative unbundling and rebundling of cash flows. Of course, derivatives play a special role in the repackaging process, and swaps are a prominent feature of the financial engineer's tool kit. The role that the intermediary plays in these situations is to ensure that the patterns of cash flows the issuer wants to pay can be reorganized to match the pattern of cash flows that the investor wants to receive and, at the same time, to provide sufficient financial incentive for everyone to participate in the deal.

As a straightforward example of this process, suppose that Corporation DEF seeks $50 million in seven-year, fixed-rate funding. Because this firm has several outstanding fixed-rate debt issues in this maturity range, investors have little appetite for any more at the present time. As a consequence, DEF would have to pay a coupon of 9.50 percent on a par-value bond, which is a little high by historical standards, given the company's present credit grade. Several institutional investors, however, have expressed an interest in taking positions in any of three different types of floating-rate structures, each of which pays semiannual interest linked to LIBOR. The coupon resetting formulas for the three FRNs, which are functions of the relative demand for each innovation, are quoted on an actual/360 money-market basis as follows:

- *Traditional FRN:* Six-Month LIBOR + 0.25%
- *Reverse (or "Bull") FRN:* 18.40% − Six-Month LIBOR
- *Bear FRN:* (2 × Six-Month LIBOR) − 9.10%

The treasurer for DEF knows that each of these floaters could be converted into a synthetic fixed-rate issue with the appropriate position in an interest rate swap. Accordingly, he contacts a swap dealer who provides the following actual/365 swap fixed-rate quotes for dollar-denominated, seven-year, plain vanilla agreements against six-month LIBOR:

- *Dealer's Bid Rate:* T + 85 basis points
- *Dealer's Offer Rate:* T + 95 basis points

At the time these quotes were obtained, the seven-year Treasury yield was 8.25 percent, leaving a bid–offer swap fixed-rate quote range of 9.10 percent to 9.20 percent.

As a first step in establishing whether any of these FRNs has the potential to generate a superior funding cost to the direct-issue alternative of 9.50 percent, the treasurer charts the nature of the swap agreement that would be required to convert each into synthetic fixed-rate debt. These diagrams are presented in Figure 3.5. The next step is to compute the net synthetic fixed-rate cost of funds implied by all three of the structures.

For the traditional FRN, this calculation is as follows:

$$(\text{LIBOR} + 0.25\%) \times \left(\frac{365}{360}\right) + \left[(9.20\%) - \text{LIBOR} \times \left(\frac{365}{360}\right)\right] = 9.453\%.$$

As in an earlier example, the coupon cash flows of the $50 million traditional floater are transformed with a $50 million pay-fixed swap, resulting in a net funding cost of 9.453 percent, slightly below the target of 9.50 percent. Recall, however, that this comparison cannot be made directly until the cost of a potential default by the swap counterparty is included in the synthetic rate. Also, although impossible to quantify in the present case, the treasurer would also need to consider the myriad "back office" costs associated with the swap-based alternative (e.g., accounting, documentation, and settlement calculations). Thus, although the "traditional floater/pay-fixed swap" combination cannot be dismissed as a possibility, it is unlikely to provide a compelling structure from DEF's point of view once all of the ancillary costs are included.

Figure 3.5 Charting the Structured Finance Alternatives

Converting a Traditional FRN

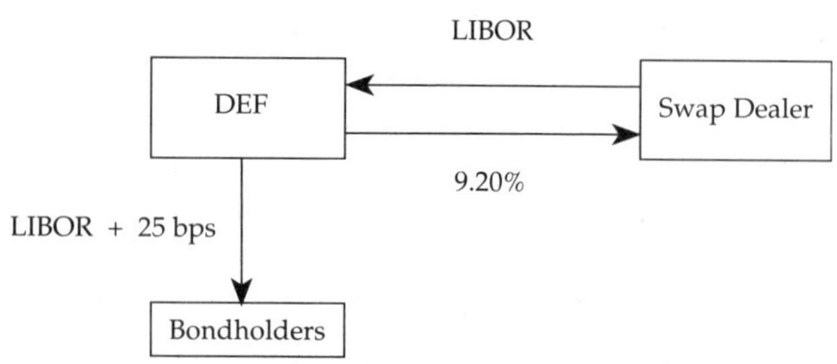

Converting a Reverse FRN

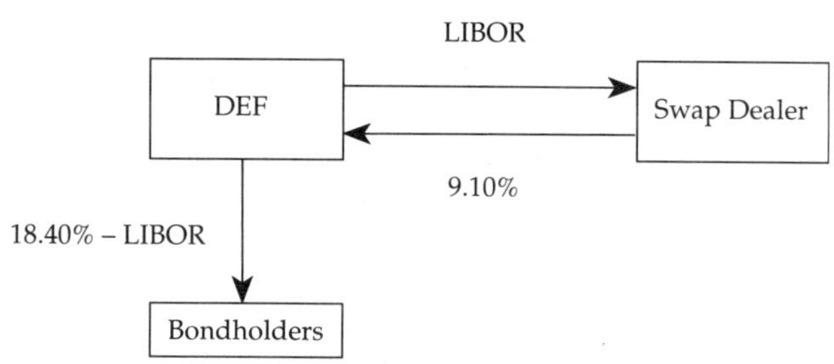

Converting a Bear FRN

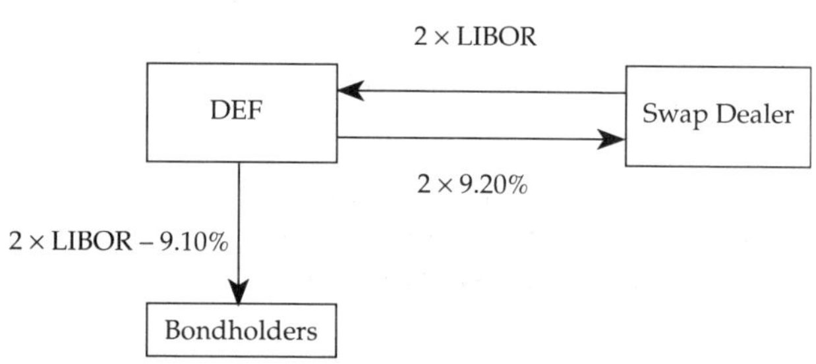

The restructuring of the reverse FRN, illustrated in the center panel of Figure 3.5, is by its nature a more involved process. First of all, notice that, from DEF's perspective, a \$50 million, receive-fixed swap will now be required. The best way to see why the firm would want to pay the floating rate on a swap in order to convert this type of floating-rate debt issue is to interpret the reverse FRN coupon (18.40 percent − LIBOR) as being equivalent to (1) a payment of 18.40 percent and (2) the receipt of LIBOR. The net effect is that the coupon payment will decline as LIBOR increases, thereby exacerbating the price decline that fixed-income securities typically suffer in rising rate environments. Thus, because the LIBOR exposure built into the reverse floater is opposite that of the traditional FRN, the opposite swap is required. As shown in the calculation below, the synthetic fixed rate associated with this structure is 9.556 percent:

$$(18.40\% - \text{LIBOR}) \times \left(\frac{365}{360}\right) + \left[\text{LIBOR} \times \left(\frac{365}{360}\right) - 9.10\%\right] = 9.556\%.$$

This percentage is in excess of the 9.50 percent direct-issue benchmark even before swap default risk concerns are taken into account.

Although the treasurer would not agree to this "reverse FRN/receive-fixed swap" deal anyway, the actual synthetic funding cost of the structure is even worse than it appears to be. Notice that the funding cost on this combination is only fixed if LIBOR is less than or equal to 18.40 percent, because the coupon on the floater would be zero on any settlement date when LIBOR exceeds 18.40 percent (i.e., DEF can never expect an interest payment *from* its bondholders). Thus, given that the reverse floater has effectively capped the benefits to the issuer at the point where LIBOR equals 18.40 percent, the treasurer will have to purchase an offsetting seven-year, semiannual settlement cap agreement (with a strike rate set at 18.40 percent) to protect against having to make too large a swap payment in a period of extremely high market rates. Although such a cap would not be particularly expensive under the presumed conditions, it would not be free, and its amortized cost would raise the overall synthetic fixed-rate funding expense even more.

Finally, the bear FRN (so called because the note appreciates in value as LIBOR rises, thereby creating a negative-duration asset) illustrated in the bottom panel of Figure 3.5 also has a few unique nuances embedded in it that make its conversion to a synthetic fixed-rate issue somewhat problematic. Like the reverse floater, this instrument's coupon can be decomposed into two parts: (1) a payment of twice the prevailing LIBOR and (2) a fixed-rate receipt of 9.10 percent. Consequently, to neutralize the floating-rate portion of the coupon payment, *two* pay-fixed, \$50 million swaps (or one with a notional principal of $100 million) are needed. Further, like both of the other swap-related structures, this deal involves the additional default exposure to the swap dealer, but now this exposure is twice as great because of a doubling of the notional principal. Lastly, notice that the funding cost on the "bear FRN/pay-fixed swap" combination is only fixed for LIBOR above 4.55 percent (i.e., 9.10/2). For LIBOR beneath this floor level, the coupon on the floater once again remains zero, and so Corporation DEF would need to supplement this structure with an interest rate floor agreement having a notional principal of $100 million and a strike rate of 4.55 percent.

The bear floater/swap package generates an attractive synthetic fixed rate of 9.174 percent, as shown in the following calculation:

$$(2 \times \text{LIBOR} - 9.10\%) \times \left(\frac{365}{360}\right)$$
$$+ \left\{2 \times \left[9.20\% - \text{LIBOR} \times \left(\frac{365}{360}\right)\right]\right\} = 9.174\%.$$

This rate is more than 30 basis points beneath the direct-issue target rate to absorb the amortized cost of the floor and the default and various other risks on the swap transaction. If after amortizing these costs and risks into the synthetic fixed rate, DEF finds it can fund for less than 9.50 percent, it should do so. All parties to the transaction would be satisfied: Corporation DEF would obtain superior synthetic fixed-rate funding, the investors would be able to acquire debt issued by DEF in a desired coupon package, and the swap dealer would make his or her spread on the agreement with DEF (and, possibly, fees for placing the underlying debt). Of course, the crucial elements in making this transaction work are having motivated end users and an intermediary with the ability to transform the cash flows cheaply and effectively with swap and option contracts.[4]

Asymmetric Information and Firm Credit Quality

The preceding applications have stressed how swap contracting is useful in managing undesirable economic exposures and repackaging cash flows to exploit windows of funding or investment opportunity. In a final general application, the swap product can also be adapted to help a manager make a choice of funding structures to take advantage of his or her superior knowledge of the firm's true financial condition. In particular, if a corporate treasurer faced with the decision of funding in either the short- or long-term debt markets has private (asymmetric) information as to the improving or deteriorating credit quality of the company, the swap can be an effective way to repackage the debt obligations accordingly.

To see how this process unfolds, consider the following scenario.[5] Suppose that the chief financial officer at Company IMP holds two beliefs as she considers the details of the firm's proposed debt financing program. First, she is quite concerned about the possibility that short-term interest rates will increase steadily and is therefore naturally reluctant to commit to a variable-rate structure. Second, based on her knowledge of changes planned for the internal operating structure of the organization, the credit quality of the company will *improve* substantially in the near future. Given that the capital market has not yet recognized these improvements, she is also concerned about locking in long-term, fixed-rate funding with a direct placement, even though this strategy would help to mitigate her perceived economic exposure.

To simplify the analysis, assume that the CFO has two financing choices: (1) borrow in a series of short-term commitments at market interest rates prevailing in the money market on each rollover date; or (2) lock in long-term

[4] An interesting addendum to this example is that Corporation DEF could also obtain $50 million of synthetic fixed-rate funding without accessing the swap market at all by issuing traditional and reverse floaters in two $25 million tranches. The resulting synthetic funding cost on such a structure would be (1/2) [(LIBOR + 0.25 percent) × (365/360)] + (1/2) [(18.40 percent − LIBOR) × (365/360)] = (1/2)[0.25 percent × (365/360)] + (1/2)[18.40 percent × (365/360)] = 9.4545 percent. Notice that although this scheme would avoid the additional credit risk associated with any of the swap-based solutions, it would still require the purchase of a cap agreement (with a notional principal of $25 million) to protect against LIBOR rising too high on the reverse FRN. Of course, the purchase of the cap would entail credit risk.

[5] This example was adapted from Titman (1992).

financing at the known fixed bond rate available now. Recognizing that any funding cost can be expressed as the relevant Treasury yield plus a credit adjustment, these rates can be written:

- Long-term funding rate = $T_L + BS$
- Short-term funding rate = $\tilde{T}_S + \tilde{MS}$

The tilde (˜) denotes a variable rate component, and $\tilde{MS}$ and BS represent the credit adjustments in the short-term money and long-term bond markets, respectively.

The important point to recognize from this design is that the long-term funding strategy locks in both the pure rate and credit spread components whereas the short-term format lets both components adjust to changing market circumstances. Unfortunately, neither of these direct-issue structures meets the needs of the CFO, who would like to lock in the Treasury rate while letting the firm-specific risk premium decline as the company's balance sheet strengthens. At this point, the swap agreement becomes useful. Recalling the earlier conventions in quoting plain vanilla interest rate swaps, we have

- Swap fixed rate = $T_L + SS$
- Swap floating rate = LIBOR = $\tilde{T}_S + \tilde{LS}$

SS is the swap spread and LIBOR has been broken down into the short-term Treasury yield plus an appropriate floating-rate spread (the so-called "TED" spread).

The top panel of Figure 3.6 illustrates what will happen if Company IMP adopts the short-term rollover borrowing strategy and then swaps into a fixed rate. Notice that the net cost of this combination is $T_L + SS - (\tilde{LS} - \tilde{MS})$. This conversion has accomplished two things. First, the CFO has no general yield curve exposure because a fixed, long-term base rate of ($T_L + SS$) has been established. Second, although she is exposed to an increased level of general risk aversion in the short-term credit markets (an increase in $\tilde{LS}$), she is now in a position to benefit from any improvement in firm credit quality that results in a lower level of $\tilde{MS}$. Thus, by repackaging the short-term funding alternative with a pay-fixed swap, she has been able to achieve both of her goals.

Conversely, suppose the treasurer of Company DCL has private information strongly suggesting that his firm's credit quality will *decline* at the same time he expects interest rates to fall. Once again, neither of the two direct-issue funding schemes produces a simultaneous attainment of the implied objectives. A swap-based strategy can, however. Assuming that DCL has the same market-determined credit rating as IMP at the present time, the lower panel of Figure 3.6 shows that both of the treasurer's goals can be satisfied by issuing a long-term bond and converting the fixed-rate liability into floating-rate payments. The net funding cost, $\tilde{T}_S + \tilde{LS} - (SS - BS)$, ensures that the treasurer

Figure 3.6 Exploiting Asymmetric Information about Company Credit Quality

Improving Credit Quality

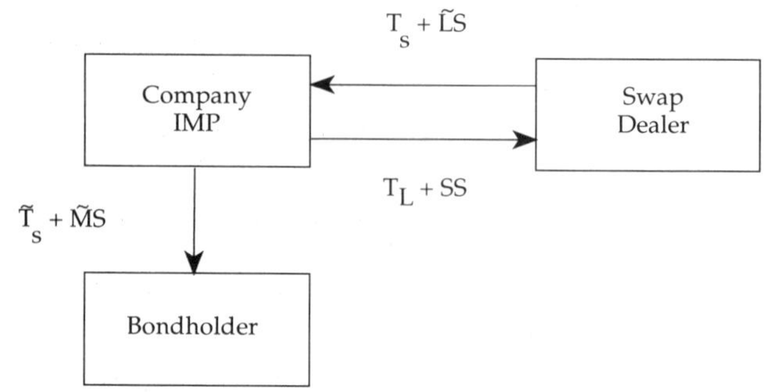

$$\text{Net Cost of Funds} = (\tilde{T}_S + \tilde{MS}) - [T_L + SS - (\tilde{T}_S + \tilde{LS})]$$
$$= T_L + SS - (\tilde{LS} - \tilde{MS})$$

Declining Credit Quality

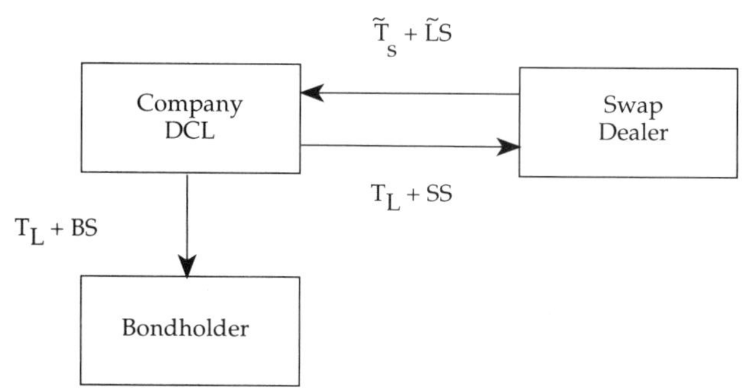

$$\text{Net Cost of Funds} = (T_L + BS) + [\tilde{T}_S + \tilde{LS} - (T_L + SS)]$$
$$= \tilde{T}_S + \tilde{LS} - (SS - BS)$$

will be able to take advantage of falling market rates while having locked in his credit spread at what he feels to be an overly generous assessment by the capital market.

Summary of Swap Applications

As the market for interest rate and currency swaps has matured, industry participants have become increasingly comfortable with how these derivative products function. One by-product of this rising level of comfort has been a more substantial appreciation for how swap contracts can be used to help a firm better achieve its financial objectives. In this chapter, we presented three broad reasons why the swap market has grown to its current stature. A common theme running through each set of examples is that these agreements provide a cost-effective way of repackaging an existing or proposed sequence of cash flows so as to align otherwise-conflicting goals among market participants. That is, rather than serve as investment or funding vehicles in themselves, interest rate and currency swaps add value through their ability to transform other securities into a more desirable format. This ability was true whether the ultimate goal was managing unwanted economic exposure, attempting to exploit an apparent pricing inefficiency across the various product markets, or taking advantage of private information. In evaluating the benefits from any swap-based strategy, however, two aspects must always be considered. First, the swap will have its own market-driven price, which can at times diverge from a level consistent with other market prices. Second, swaps inevitably entail some type of default risk, which makes credit assessment of the agreement itself a critical concern.

Exercises

Exercise 3.1: Table E-3.1 presents the asset and liability structure for a hypothetical financial corporation. Assume that all asset and liability positions are valued at par. (Thus, the yields on the nonamortizing loan portfolio and fixed-rate debt issue are 10 percent and 8 percent, respectively.)

Table E-3.1 A Hypothetical Balance Sheet

Item	Market Value	Duration
Assets		
Cash	$ 200	0.00
10-year, 10% business loan	800	4.17
Total	$1,000	
Liabilities		
6-year FRN (annual coupon reset at LIBOR)	$ 500	1.00
6-year, 8% coupon bond	350	5.00
Total	$ 850	

(a) After first obtaining the average duration of the asset and liability portfolios, calculate the duration gap for this bank and use this concept to describe the nature of the bank's interest rate exposure.

(b) Suppose that the firm attempted to eliminate this risk by formally restructuring some of the balance sheet accounts. In order to achieve a "zero-gap" position by altering the asset base, how much (in dollars) of the loan portfolio will have to be sold off and held in cash? Describe the practical and economic limitations of solving the rate exposure problem in this manner.

(c) Suppose that instead of formally restructuring the balance sheet, the bank considers lengthening the duration of its liabilities synthetically by converting a portion of its FRN position with a six-year, pay-fixed interest rate swap. If the fixed rate on this swap is 8 percent, how much of the floater position would have to be swapped?

Solution: (a) The asset and liability durations are as follows:

$$D_{\text{asset}} = \left(\frac{200}{1{,}000}\right) \times (0.00) + \left(\frac{800}{1{,}000}\right) \times (4.17) = 3.34 \text{ years}$$

and

$$D_{\text{liability}} = \left(\frac{500}{850}\right) \times (1.00) + \left(\frac{350}{850}\right) \times (5.00) = 2.65 \text{ years.}$$

These durations, in turn, produce the following duration gap statistic:

$$D_{\text{gap}} = (3.34) - \left(\frac{850}{1{,}000}\right) \times (2.65) = 1.09 \text{ years.}$$

As noted earlier, a positive duration gap value suggests that this financial corporation is exposed to rising interest rates; it is short funded, meaning that its average liability will have to be refinanced before its average asset can be reinvested.

(b) Assuming that the level and structure of the liability side of the balance sheet do not change, the percentage of assets that must be invested in cash (w_{cash}) to close the duration gap is given by:

$$D_{gap} = [(w_{cash})(0.00) + (1 - w_{cash})(4.17)] - \left(\frac{850}{1{,}000}\right) \times 2.65 = 0.00 \text{ years},$$

or $w_{cash} = 46$ percent. That is, the cash account must be increased by \$260, from \$200 to \$460. Beyond the obvious expense and logistical difficulties of liquidating a portion of what is likely to be a privately placed portfolio, this sort of physical transformation has a more fundamental economic flaw. Specifically, notice that before the restructuring, the firm was generating positive net interest income from its operations. For instance, assuming that LIBOR = 5.5 percent and that the cash account generates no income, revenues net of debt service were (800) × (0.10) − [(500) × (0.055) + (350) × (0.08)] = \$24.50. After the shift, however, this same figure would be (540) × (0.10) − [(500) × (0.055) + (350) × (0.08)] = −\$1.50. Even if the cash-equivalent account is assumed to earn some nominal return, the fact remains that formally restructuring the balance sheet to solve an interest rate risk-management problem takes this firm away from its main business (i.e., making and servicing loans) and, consequently, is an inferior solution.

(c) If the six-year floater is combined with a six-year, pay 8 percent fixed swap, the result will be a synthetic six-year, 8 percent fixed bond, which would have the same five-year duration as the actual fixed-rate issue already on the balance sheet. With the original asset accounts intact, the principal value of the floater position that would have to be converted to lengthen liability duration by a sufficient amount is determined as the solution to

$$D_{gap} = (3.34) - \left(\frac{850}{1{,}000}\right) \times \left[\left(\frac{500 - p_{swp}}{850}\right)(1.0) + \left(\frac{350 + p_{swp}}{850}\right)(5.0)\right] = 0.00 \text{ years}.$$

In this instance, $p_{swp} = \$273$, which becomes the notional principal on the swap.

Exercise 3.2: The chief financial officer of a large British retail store chain is considering issuing a five-year "geared reverse floater." The geared reverse floater would have a coupon-reset formula of 30 percent minus 2.5 times six-month (GBP) LIBOR, subject to a minimum coupon rate of 0 percent if LIBOR were to exceed 12 percent. The five-year, semiannual payment GBP 100 million floating-rate note can be issued at par value. The CFO intends to use derivative instruments to convert the geared reverse floater into synthetic fixed-rate funding. The following quotes for five-year, semiannual settlement interest rate swaps and caps on six-month GBP LIBOR are obtained from a market maker in derivative products:

- *Interest Rate Swaps:* The firm can pay a fixed rate of 8.16 percent and receive LIBOR, or the firm can receive a fixed rate of 8.10 percent and pay LIBOR.
- *Interest Rate Caps:* With a strike rate of 12 percent, the firm buys the cap at 150 basis points and writes the cap at 130 basis points. The premium on the cap is quoted as a percentage of the notional principal.

Indicate the specific combination of transactions that provides a synthetic fixed-rate liability. Calculate the all-in cost of funds. Assume that GBP LIBOR, the coupon rate on the geared reverse floater, the swap fixed rate, and the strike rate on the caps are all stated on a semiannual bond basis.

Solution: The British retailing firm would issue the geared reverse floater, enter two and one-half swaps (each for GBP 100 million or, more likely, one swap for notional amount of GBP 250 million) to receive the fixed rate of 8.10 percent, and buy two and one-half caps at a strike rate of 12 percent (or, just one for GBP 250 million). The caps on LIBOR assure a fixed rate if LIBOR were to rise above 12 percent. If LIBOR $\leq$ 12 percent, the interest expense on the FRN and the swaps will be (30 percent $-$ 2.5 $\times$ LIBOR) + (2.5 $\times$ LIBOR $-$ 2.5 $\times$ 8.10 percent) = 9.75 percent. But if LIBOR > 12 percent, the expense without the caps would be (2.5 $\times$ LIBOR $-$ 2.5 $\times$ 8.10 percent) > 9.75 percent. The cost of the caps, 375 basis points (2.5 $\times$ 150 bps each) raises the fixed rate cost of funds above 9.75 percent. Paying this premium at the time of origination would lower the net sale proceeds from the geared reverse floater to 96.25 percent of par.

The semiannual, all-in fixed cost of funds is 10.74 percent, calculated as the solution to

$$96.25 = \sum_{t=1}^{10} \frac{4.875}{(1 + y/2)^t} + \frac{100}{(1 + y/2)^{10}}.$$

Note that 9.75 percent is the synthetic fixed coupon rate; the all-in cost exceeds that in the same manner that the yield on a discount bond always exceeds its coupon rate.

Exercise 3.3: A Spanish pension fund is considering buying a five-year, floating-rate note named "El Oso Grande." El Oso Grande would have a coupon-reset formula of three times six-month (Spanish peseta) LIBOR minus 24 percent, subject to a minimum coupon rate of 0 percent if peseta LIBOR were to fall below 8 percent. Currently, six-month peseta LIBOR is 11.20 percent, so the initial coupon would be based on a rate of 9.60 percent. The five-year, semiannual payment, 100 million peseta floating-rate note can be bought at par value. The pension fund intends to use derivative instruments to convert El Oso Grande into a synthetic fixed-rate asset. Quotes for five-year, semiannual settlement interest rate swaps, caps, and floors on six-month Spanish peseta LIBOR, shown below, are obtained from a Madrid commercial bank specializing in derivative products.

- *Interest Rate Swaps:* The pension fund can pay a fixed rate of 13.50 percent and receive six-month peseta LIBOR, or the fund can receive a fixed rate of 13.35 percent and pay six-month peseta LIBOR.
- *Interest Rate Caps:* With a strike rate of 24 percent, the fund buys the cap at 125 basis points and writes the cap at 90 basis points.
- *Interest Rate Floors:* With a strike rate of 8 percent, the fund buys the floor at 175 basis points and writes the floor at 140 basis points.

(Recall that the premiums on the caps and floors are quoted as a percentage of the notional principal.) Indicate the specific combination of transactions that provides a synthetic fixed-rate asset to the pension fund. Calculate the all-in fixed rate of return. Assume that Spanish peseta LIBOR, the coupon rate on El Oso Grande, the swap fixed rate, and the strike rate on the caps and floors are all stated on a semiannual bond basis.

Solution: The Spanish pension fund would buy El Oso Grande, enter three swaps (each for a notional principal equal to the par value of the FRN or, equivalently, one swap with three times the notional value) to receive the fixed rate of 13.35 percent and write three floors at a strike rate of 8 percent (or, again, one with three times the notional amount).

The role of the floors is to create a fixed-rate asset even when LIBOR is less than 8 percent. Neglecting the floors, if LIBOR $\geq$ 8 percent, the return will be (3 $\times$ LIBOR $-$ 24 percent) + (3 $\times$ 13.35 percent $-$ 3 $\times$ LIBOR). The LIBOR flows net out by design, and the return is 16.05 percent. If LIBOR $<$ 8 percent, the return will be (3 $\times$ 13.35 percent $-$ 3 $\times$ LIBOR) $>$ 16.05 percent. Writing the floors in effect sells off the potential for a higher return if LIBOR is low. The receipt of 420 basis points (3 $\times$ 140 basis points for each floor) raises the fixed rate of return above 16.05 percent.

The net cost of the position is only 95.8 percent of par, the cost of the FRN less the premium received on writing the floors. So the all-in, semiannual fixed rate of return is 17.34 percent, calculated as

$$95.80 = \sum_{t=1}^{10} \frac{8.025}{(1 + y/2)^t} + \frac{100}{(1 + y/2)^{10}}.$$

Exercise 3.4: The corporate treasurer of BCD Corporation is considering a financially engineered, synthetic, fixed-rate funding package based on an innovative "collared floater," for which investors seem to have great demand in the marketplace. The collared note would have a coupon-reset formula of six-month LIBOR + 0.50 percent, subject to a minimum coupon rate of 7.50 percent and a maximum coupon rate of 12.50 percent. The five-year, semiannual payment $50 million floating-rate note can be issued at par value.

BCD obtains the following quotes for five-year, semiannual settlement interest rate swaps, caps, and floors on six-month LIBOR from its commercial bank:

- *Interest Rate Swaps:* BCD Corporation can pay a semiannual fixed rate of 8.75 percent and receive LIBOR. It can receive a semiannual fixed rate of 8.65 percent and pay LIBOR.
- *Interest Rate Cap Premiums* (as a percentage of the notional principal):

Strike Rate	*BCD Buys the Cap*	*BCD Writes the Cap*
12.0%	75 bps	65 bps
12.5	60	50
13.0	45	35

Interest Rate Floor Premiums (as a percentage of the notional principal):

Strike Rate	*BCD Buys the Floor*	*BCD Writes the Floor*
7.0%	90 bps	80 bps
7.5	105	95
8.0	120	110

Indicate the specific combination of transactions that provides a synthetic fixed-rate cost of funds. Calculate the all-in cost of funds. Note that the coupon rate on the collared floater and the strike rates on the caps and floors are on a money-market (360-day) basis. Describe the credit risk that BCD would bear in the synthetic fixed-rate package. Be exact in identifying the circumstances when credit risk is a concern.

Solution: BCD could engineer a synthetic fixed rate cost of funds by

- issuing the "collared" floater at a coupon of LIBOR + 0.50 percent, subject to a maximum rate of 12.50 percent and a minimum of 7.50 percent, at par value,
- "buying" a par-value swap to pay a fixed rate of 8.75 percent and to receive LIBOR,
- writing a cap on LIBOR at a strike rate of 12 percent for a premium of 65 basis points, and
- buying a floor on LIBOR at a strike rate of 7 percent for a premium of 90 basis points.

The funding cost of the collared floater alone is shown in Figure E-3.1, and the payoff diagrams for the three separate derivative transactions are illustrated in Figure E-3.2. The semiannual, synthetic fixed coupon rate resulting from these maneuvers is 9.26 percent [8.75 percent + 0.50 percent × (365/360)]. To find the all-in synthetic funding cost, recognize that the notional principals on the swap, cap, and floor equal the par amount of the collared floater. Thus, the cap–floor combination, effectively writing a 7 percent to 12 percent collar, requires a net payment of 25 basis points, so the net proceeds of the security at origination would be 99.75 percent of par. The yield is then the solution to the following equation:

$$99.75 = \sum_{t=1}^{10} \frac{4.63}{(1 + y/2)^t} + \frac{100}{(1 + y/2)^{10}},$$

or 9.32 percent on a semiannual bond basis.

This structure has two sources of credit risk for BCD: (1) on the swap when the counterparty is in financial distress and replacement swap fixed rates are higher than 8.75 percent; and (2) on the floor when the counterparty is in financial distress and LIBOR is less than 7 percent, or in fact, when the market premium on a replacement 7 percent floor exceeds the unamortized portion of the original 90-basis-point purchase price.

Figure E-3.1 Funding Cost of Collared Floater

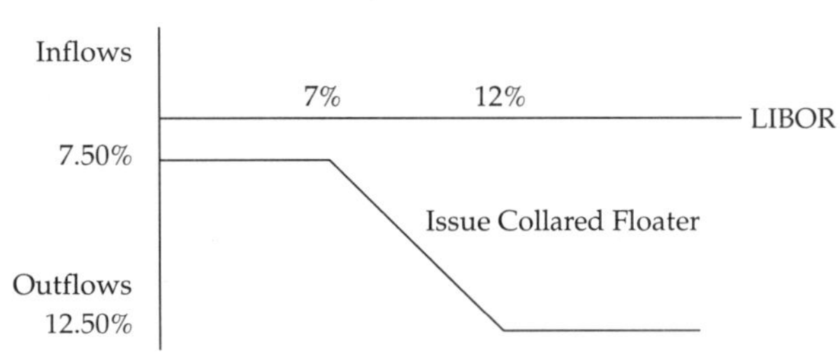

Figure E-3.2 Payoff Diagrams for Three Derivative Transactions

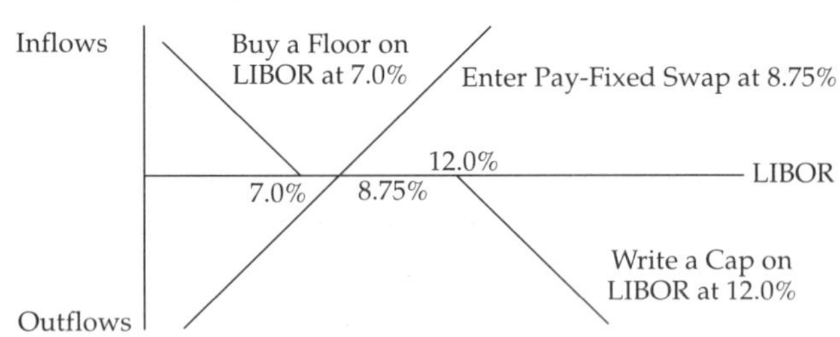

Chapter 4. Pricing Interest Rate and Currency Swaps

As we have seen, a swap's price is its fixed rate. The convention on U.S.-dollar-denominated plain vanilla transactions of quoting this fixed rate as a premium over the Treasury yield merely shifts the pricing problem to one of determining the appropriate swap spread. For instance, a swap fixed rate of, say, 6.45 percent on a three-year agreement, or equivalently, a swap spread of 45 basis points when the three-year Treasury yields 6 percent, is readily observable in the market. The question is why 6.45 percent (or 45 basis points) is the proper price in the first place.

Perhaps the simplest yet most revealing statement about interest rate swap pricing is that although the swap fixed rate is *quoted* off the Treasury yield curve, it is *priced* off a forward curve. The forward curve in question would be the sequence of future yields corresponding to the floating reference rate on the swap. That is, a LIBOR-against-fixed swap would be priced off the LIBOR forward curve and a Treasury bill-against-fixed swap would be priced off the Treasury forward curve. Pricing in this context suggests an averaging process; the swap fixed rate will be a "present value" average of the forward rates. That is, the swap's price will be established so that the present value of the fixed cash flows on the agreement equals the present value of the cash flows implied by the forward rates. Currency swaps, in turn, will be priced off the forward interest rate curves in each denomination, or the forward exchange rate curve.

Swap pricing is not the same as swap valuation. Pricing is the process of setting the fixed rate, usually so that the market value of the swap is initially zero (i.e., an at-market swap). Thereafter, the value of the swap is found by comparing that fixed rate to the current fixed rate on a swap having the same terms and remaining time to maturity as the original, a process identified earlier as mark-to-market valuation. In this chapter, we demonstrate that pricing swaps, including nonplain vanilla structures having forward start dates and varying levels of notional principal, is a rather straightforward and mechanical process once the forward curve is available. As a practical matter, these forward rates can be obtained by direct observation, calculation, and estimation.

Direct Observation: There are active over-the-counter markets in forward rate agreements and in foreign exchange, as well as in exchange-traded futures contracts on various interest and FX rates. These forward curves produce the most exact swap prices because they indicate directly the levels of the floating reference rate that can be locked in by hedging transactions for the future settlement dates on the swap.

Calculation: An *implied forward* curve can be inferred from the cash market yield curve, the sequence of implicit short-term rates obtained by successively extending the maturity in the cash market by one period. For instance, if the one-year rate is 5 percent and the two-year rate is 6 percent, the implied forward rate between Year 1 and Year 2 must be about 7 percent. Arbitrage transactions will drive rates along the implied forward curve to be virtually identical to those observed when explicit forward contracts are traded; any difference is because of transaction costs and limitations on short selling in the cash market.

Estimation: Some swaps need to be priced for tenors for which no corresponding delivery dates exist in the futures or cash markets. For example, pricing a 12-year interest rate swap on LIBOR will be challenging because futures contracts on U.S. dollar LIBOR currently extend to 10 years and the Eurodollar time deposit market is mostly short term. Consequently, the forward curve for LIBOR, at least in this maturity range, must be estimated off the forward curve for Treasury securities. An estimated forward curve will naturally produce less-exact swap prices because the future levels of the floating reference rate cannot be secured by hedging. This inexactness will be impounded in the bid–offer spread for the swaps; other things being equal, a short-term swap priced off an observed forward curve would have a tighter bid–offer spread than a long-term swap priced off an estimated forward curve.

Regardless of its source, the average of the relevant segment of the forward curve represents the theoretical swap fixed rate, the midpoint of the bid–offer spread. The midpoint is derived first and then adjustments are made for other factors such as credit risk, capital reserve requirements, back-office operations costs, and necessary profit levels. All of these factors together determine the particular fixed rates that a dealer will be willing to pay or receive. This point is a key one because it separates market risk from default risk in the pricing process. The midpoint swap fixed rate for a particular transaction would be the same for all market participants because they all can observe or estimate the same forward curve. At the bid–offer spread level, however, participants diverge in the fixed rates they ultimately pay or receive.

Pricing Interest Rate Swaps Off the FRA Curve

In Chapter 2, we showed that FRAs are merely one-date swaps; alternatively, a plain vanilla interest rate swap can be divided into a series of off-market FRAs. This fact can be used to aid swap pricing. Suppose that the midpoints (the average of the bid and offer rates) for a sequence of FRAs are 5.75 percent for the 3 × 6 agreement, 6.00 percent for the 6 × 9, and 6.25 percent for the 9 × 12. The current level of three-month LIBOR is 5.50 percent. These rates are all quoted on an actual/360 basis, meaning that in figuring a cash flow, the annual rate is adjusted by the actual number of days in the quarter divided by 360. For example, the payoff on a 3 × 6 FRA transacted on June 15th would depend on the level of three-month LIBOR revealed on September 15th compared with the FRA fixed rate of 5.75 percent. If LIBOR on September 15th is 5.50 percent and there are 91 days between September 15th and December 15th, the buyer of the FRA (the payer of the fixed rate and receiver of the "commodity" LIBOR) owes the counterparty on December 15th the rate difference (5.75 percent − 5.50 percent) times 91/360 times the notional principal or the present value of that amount if settlement is to be accelerated to September. This directly observed forward curve based on spot LIBOR and the strip of FRAs is pictured in Figure 4.1.

Now consider a one-year, quarterly settlement in arrears interest rate swap on three-month LIBOR. The subsequent rates on the floating-rate leg of the swap that will determine the settlement payments are, of course, unknown at present. Nevertheless, the presence of the explicit FRA market means that those unknown rates could be locked in at 5.75 percent, 6.00 percent, and 6.25 percent, respectively. In effect, FRAs could be used to completely hedge the uncertainty on the floating-rate side of the swap. Therefore, because the swap could be effectively reconstructed with a strip of FRAs, the swap fixed rate must be tied to that series of

Figure 4.1 A Directly Observed Forward Curve Based on Spot LIBOR and the Sequence of FRAs

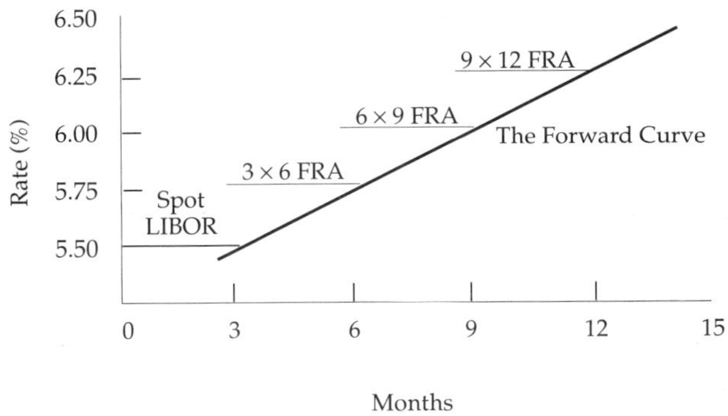

shorter term rates to eliminate the possibility of arbitrage.

Suppose that the trade date on this one-year swap is June 15th and that its day-count basis will be 30/360. Assume that there are 92 days between June 15th and September 15th, 91 days between September 15th and December 15th, 90 days between December 15th and March 15th, and 92 days between March 15th and June 15th. The swap fixed rate (SFR) will be the solution to the following equation:

$$\frac{5.50\% \times (92/360) \times \text{NP}}{1 + z_3} + \frac{5.75\% \times (91/360) \times \text{NP}}{1 + z_6} + \frac{6.00\% \times (90/360) \times \text{NP}}{1 + z_9} + \frac{6.25\% \times (92/360) \times \text{NP}}{1 + z_{12}}$$
$$= \frac{\text{SFR} \times (1/4) \times \text{NP}}{1 + z_3} + \frac{\text{SFR} \times (1/4) \times \text{NP}}{1 + z_6} + \frac{\text{SFR} \times (1/4) \times \text{NP}}{1 + z_9} + \frac{\text{SFR} \times (1/4) \times \text{NP}}{1 + z_{12}}.$$

The four terms to the left of the equal sign are the present value of the floating side of the swap, using the cash flows derived from the forward curve. This amount is calculated as the discounted value of the rate times the fraction of the year on an actual/360 basis times the notional principal. The sum of the last four terms is the present value of the fixed side of the swap, where the fraction of the year represented by each period is 90/360 (or 1/4).

Notice that the discount rates correspond to the timing of the cash flows. For instance, z_6 is the rate for discounting the cash flows on both the floating and fixed sides in 6 months and z_{12} is the rate for discounting the cash flows in 12 months. These discount rates, too, can be derived from the forward curve. The first discount rate, z_3, is based on current three-month LIBOR, 5.50 percent. The second discount rate, z_6, can be calculated from z_3 and the next point on the forward curve, the 3 × 6 fixed rate of 5.75 percent. The third discount rate, z_9, can be calculated from z_6 and the following point on the forward curve, the 6 × 9 fixed rate of 6.00 percent. This process is known as *bootstrapping*, whereby rates are obtained in sequence and at each point the previous calculations are used.

Taking account of the actual number of days in each period, the discount factors obtained from bootstrapping would be the following:

$$1 + z_3 = 1 + \left(\frac{92}{360} \times 0.0550\right) = 1.014056,$$

$$1 + z_6 = (1 + z_3) \times \left[1 + \left(\frac{91}{360} \times 0.0575\right)\right]$$
$$= 1.028795,$$

$$1 + z_9 = (1 + z_6) \times \left[1 + \left(\frac{90}{360} \times 0.0600\right)\right]$$
$$= 1.044226,$$

and

$$1 + z_{12} = (1 + z_9) \times \left[1 + \left(\frac{92}{360} \times 0.0625\right)\right]$$
$$= 1.060905.$$

Obtaining the discount rates in this manner is not substantively different from any other method for doing time value of money analysis. What we have done is calculate the sequence of zero-coupon rates that corresponds to the observed forward curve—the zero-coupon interest rates for 3, 6, 9, and 12 months that could be secured by the series of shorter term forward contracts.

The final step in the pricing process is to solve for SFR. On a plain vanilla swap, the notional principal is constant for all settlement dates, so the NP term conveniently drops out and the equation reduces to:

$$\frac{5.50\% \times (92/360)}{1.014056} + \frac{5.75\% \times (91/360)}{1.028795} + \frac{6.00\% \times (90/360)}{1.044226} + \frac{6.25\% \times (92/360)}{1.060905}$$
$$= \text{SFR} \times (1/4) \times \left[\frac{1}{1.014056} + \frac{1}{1.028795} + \frac{1}{1.044226} + \frac{1}{1.060905}\right].$$

Solving the equation reveals that SFR is 5.9516 percent, which when rounded to the nearest basis point becomes 5.95 percent. A market maker in this one-year swap would then set the bid–offer rates around this midpoint. For example, the market maker might be willing to pay a fixed rate of 5.93 percent and receive a fixed rate of 5.97 percent in exchange for LIBOR. Although a short-term swap such as this one is usually quoted using the fixed rate itself, the quoted price could be converted to a swap spread. If the one-year Treasury note yield, converted to conform to the quarterly basis of the swap rate, were 5.60 percent, the bid swap spread would be 33 basis points and the offered premium 37 basis points.

A significant aspect of this derivation is that it has avoided the word "expectations." Indeed, the midpoint fixed rate of 5.95 percent was calculated *without* assuming any particular path for future levels of LIBOR, let alone the path along the forward curve. To be precise, we do not necessarily assume that three-month LIBOR will be 5.75 percent in three months, 6 percent in six months, and 6.25 percent in nine months (or any other pattern, for that matter). Rather, this method of swap pricing is independent of any theory of the yield curve, in particular, the pure expectations hypothesis that contends that forward rates represent unbiased consensus forecasts of future cash market rates.

This averaging method of calculating the fixed rate on the swap rests only on the assumption of arbitrage-free markets. Neglecting all transaction costs (thereby reducing the bid–offer spreads to zero), an arbitrage opportunity would be present if the swap fixed rate were other than 5.95 percent. Suppose, for example, the swap rate is 6.05 percent. Then, the arbitrageur would "sell" the swap and "buy" spot LIBOR and the FRA strip. The former commits the trader to receive a fixed rate of 6.05 percent and pay out LIBOR on each settlement date; the latter commits him or her to receive LIBOR and pay out successively 5.50 percent, 5.75 percent, 6.00 percent, and 6.25 percent. The exposure to LIBOR is eliminated and the arbitrage gain is the difference in present value of cash flows based on a constant rate of 6.05 percent and the series of 5.50 percent, 5.75 percent, 6.00 percent, and 6.25 percent. This series, however, has the same present value as a constant rate of 5.95 percent. Consequently, the only assumption really needed in the swap pricing process is the presence of traders in the marketplace able to exploit mispricing across financial instruments.

This present value average is as precise a swap price as possible, given the available data. Worth noting, however, is that a more easily calculated approximation for that price typically is quite accurate. It comes from calculating the *internal rate of return* (IRR) on a par value, step-up coupon bond paying cash flows equal to the forward rates. In this example, the internal rate of return turns out to be 5.9517 percent, the solution to the following expression:

$$100 = \frac{(5.50 \times 92/360)}{1 + \text{IRR}} + \frac{(5.75 \times 91/360)}{(1 + \text{IRR})^2} + \frac{(6.00 \times 90/360)}{(1 + \text{IRR})^3} + \frac{[100 + (6.25 \times 92/360)]}{(1 + \text{IRR})^4}.$$

Although precise calculations obviously are needed when actually transacting in the swap market, a decent approximation can be quite useful when one merely wants to get a sense of the rates at which swaps are (or should be) trading. The IRR approximation can be easily obtained using a financial calculator; the present value average, in contrast, would typically require a computer spreadsheet, especially for longer maturity swaps.

Pricing Interest Rate Swaps Off the Eurodollar Futures Curve

Having just demonstrated that plain vanilla interest rate swap prices are easily determined given a sequence of rates on FRAs, we now consider how those FRA rates themselves are derived. Another way an FRA can be interpreted is as a customized, over-the-counter *Eurodollar futures* contract. Despite some logistical differences between the two, FRAs and Eurodollar futures are functionally equivalent in terms of managing interest rate risk, and so their rates must be very close. In fact, in practice, FRAs are priced off of Eurodollar futures rates.

The Eurodollar Futures Contract. Before pursuing the relationships between FRAs, futures, and interest rate swaps, some institutional aspects of the Eurodollar contract traded at the International Monetary Market (IMM) located at the Chicago Mercantile Exchange (CME) may be worth reviewing. This contract has become enormously successful since it was launched in the early 1980s. Delivery dates follow the March, June, September, December cycle (the "IMM dates") and now extend ten years into the future. The final trading and settlement date is the second London business day before the third Wednesday of the delivery month. The contract size is $1 million, and it allows for cash settlement only. The underlying interest rate is three-month (90-day) LIBOR, and it is quoted on a 360-day bank add-on basis. Like any futures contract, the Eurodollar rate contract requires participants to post a collateral account (i.e., margin), which is then marked to market on a daily basis.

Trading results for the Eurodollar contract for Monday, October 31, 1994, are displayed in Table 4.1. The total *open interest,* which is the number of outstanding contracts, is enormous. Those data are reported with a day lag, so on the previous Friday, total open interest for all 39 delivery dates out to September of 2004 exceeded 2.5 million contracts. Although the trading volume on the Treasury bond futures contract at the Chicago Board of Trade rivals the Eurodollar contract at the CME, its open interest is much less, averaging about one-half million contracts. In fact, the ratio of trading volume to open interest signals a key difference between the Treasury bond and Eurodollar futures contracts. The former has a high ratio, suggesting that it is a more speculative trading contract with participants turning over their positions frequently. The Eurodollar futures contract has a much lower ratio, suggesting that it is more a hedging contract whereby participants tend to be more inclined than T-bond futures investors to hold their positions until the delivery date nears. The Eurodollar contract is, in fact, commonly used by FRA and swaps market makers to hedge their books. The success of the contract, as measured by its open interest and number of delivery dates, parallels the growth of the over-the-counter swaps market.

To see how these instruments can be used as hedges, consider the March 1995 contract having a yield of 6.49 percent. This entry means that on October 31st, a borrower or lender was able to lock in a rate of about 6.49 percent for three-month LIBOR as of the following March. We must be cautious here because daily settlement cash flows into and out of the margin account will take place, generating either gains that can be invested or losses that need to be funded. Therefore, the performance of the hedge can vary depending on the particular path interest rates take up to the delivery date in March. This point—that the payoffs on a futures contract are *path dependent*—is best illustrated with a numerical example, summarized in Table 4.2.

Suppose a firm owes $10 million on a bank loan that has its interest rate tied to three-month LIBOR paid in arrears. That interest rate will be determined on the same date as the delivery date of the March futures contract. The first row in the table shows the June interest payment for four possible levels of LIBOR in March. The example is simplified by assuming a 90-day time period so the interest payments are just one-quarter of the rate times $10 million. If LIBOR is 8 percent in March, the interest payment in June would be $200,000. Concerned with the possibility of rising LIBOR, the firm elects to hedge that risk by selling ten March Eurodollar futures contracts. This short position will gain as futures rates rise and futures prices fall.

Notice that the futures prices quoted in Table 4.1 (i.e., the opening price for the day, the high, the low, and the closing price that is used

Table 4.1 Eurodollar Futures Trading Results for October 31, 1994

Month	Open	High	Low	Settle	Change	Yield Settle	Yield Change	Open Interest
December	94.06	94.06	94.03	94.05	− 0.01	5.95	+ 0.01	430,382
March 1995	93.62	93.62	93.59	93.51	− 0.01	6.49	+ 0.01	408,222
June	93.15	93.15	93.11	93.14	− 0.01	6.86	+ 0.01	296,969
September	92.80	92.80	92.77	92.80	− 0.01	7.20	+ 0.01	239,577
December	92.48	92.48	92.44	92.47	− 0.01	7.53	+ 0.01	181,070
March 1996	92.37	92.37	92.34	92.37	− 0.01	7.63	+ 0.01	155,906
June	92.23	92.23	92.20	92.23	− 0.01	7.77	+ 0.01	129,711
September	92.12	92.12	92.09	92.12	− 0.01	7.88	+ 0.01	120,677
December	91.98	91.99	91.96	91.99	− 0.01	8.01	+ 0.01	99,430
March 1997	91.99	91.99	91.96	91.99	− 0.01	8.01	+ 0.01	86,472
June	91.92	91.92	91.89	91.93	–	8.07	–	72,351
September	91.86	91.87	91.83	91.87	–	8.13	–	56,755
December	91.75	91.76	91.73	91.76	–	8.24	–	52,543
March 1998	91.77	91.78	91.75	91.78	–	8.22	–	43,214
June	91.71	91.74	91.70	91.72	–	8.28	–	37,080
September	91.66	91.69	91.65	91.67	–	8.33	–	26,570
December	91.55	91.57	91.54	91.56	–	8.44	–	24,346
March 1999	91.57	91.59	91.56	91.58	–	8.42	–	22,166
June	91.50	91.54	91.50	91.52	–	8.48	–	16,774
September	91.46	91.49	91.45	91.47	–	8.53	–	11,046
December	91.36	91.36	91.34	91.36	–	8.64	–	7,669
March 2000	91.40	91.41	91.38	91.40	–	8.60	–	7,651
June	91.34	91.36	91.34	91.35	+ 0.01	8.65	− 0.01	5,070
September	91.29	91.31	91.27	91.30	+ 0.01	8.70	− 0.01	7,943
December	–	–	–	91.20	+ 0.01	8.80	− 0.01	6,940
March 2001	–	–	–	91.25	+ 0.01	8.75	− 0.01	6,792
June	–	–	–	91.21	+ 0.01	8.89	− 0.01	5,536
September	91.17	91.17	91.16	91.18	+ 0.01	8.82	− 0.01	5,083
December	–	–	–	91.09	+ 0.01	8.91	− 0.01	3,943
March 2002	–	–	–	91.14	+ 0.01	8.86	− 0.01	2,838
June	–	–	–	91.11	+ 0.01	8.89	− 0.01	2,673
September	–	–	–	91.09	+ 0.01	8.91	− 0.01	2,021
December	–	–	–	91.01	+ 0.01	8.99	− 0.01	1,359
March 2003	–	–	–	91.05	+ 0.01	8.95	− 0.01	1,673
June	–	–	–	91.02	+ 0.01	8.98	− 0.01	1,488
September	–	–	–	91.00	+ 0.01	9.00	− 0.01	1,344
December	–	–	–	90.90	+ 0.01	9.10	− 0.01	1,225
March 2004	–	–	–	90.94	+ 0.01	9.06	− 0.01	1,515
June	–	–	–	90.91	+ 0.01	9.09	− 0.01	155
September	90.85	90.88	90.85	90.88	+ 0.01	9.12	− 0.01	70

Note: Estimated volume, 240,341; volume Friday, 656,910; open interest, 2,584,249, +39,653.
Source: Wall Street Journal, November 1, 1994.

Table 4.2 Hedging a Bank Loan with Eurodollar Futures

	Hypothetical Levels for LIBOR in March			
	5%	6%	7%	8%
Interest on a $10 million bank loan at LIBOR, set in March, paid in June (shown as a negative flow)	−$125,000	−$150,000	−$175,000	−$200,000
Cumulative payoff on ten short Eurodollar futures contracts sold at 93.51 ($25/bps per contract)	−$ 37,250	−$ 12,250	$ 12,750	$ 37,750
All-in cost of funds	$162,250	$162,250	$162,250	$162,250

for daily settlement) are merely 100 minus the yield. This *price index* has no meaningful interpretation in terms of money; its purpose is simply to preserve the dictum in financial markets that the long position gains when prices rise and the short gains when prices fall. Even though the contract is cash settled, it is as if the buyer commits to purchase (and the seller commits to deliver) a three-month, $1 million Eurodollar time deposit having a coupon rate equal to the futures rate. The buyer, therefore, gains if rates fall, because the contract represents an agreement to lend at an above-market rate. The seller gains if rates rise, because then the contract provides for borrowing at what is a below-market cost of funds.

Daily settlement adjustments in the Eurodollar futures market are figured as $25 per basis point per contract, where $25 is the basis point value of one contract (calculated as ($1,000,000 × (90/360) × 0.01 percent). The exact number of contracts needed to hedge a particular risk exposure is determined by dividing the basis point value for the entire position by $25. Returning to the example in Table 4.2, we can now calculate the cumulative gain or loss over the hedging interval. These results are shown in the second row of the table. If LIBOR is 8 percent, the futures price index would be 92.00. Because the firm went short at 93.51 (e.g., 100 − 6.49), the cumulative gain is 151 basis points. So, 151 basis points times $25 per basis point times ten contracts generates a cumulative gain of $37,750. For each assumed level of LIBOR in March, the net interest cost, combining the proceeds on the futures contracts with the loan payment, is $162,250. That amount corresponds to an annualized interest rate of 6.49 percent ($162,250 divided by $10 million times the four 90-day periods in the 360-day year).

The firm's all-in cost of funds will probably not turn out to be exactly 6.49 percent for two reasons. First, the cumulative gain or loss on the futures in the table neglects the time value of money. Suppose that the daily settlement payments or receipts can be funded or invested at, say, 6.25 percent. If LIBOR ended up at 8 percent, the 151 cumulative basis points credited would correspond to total gains in excess of $37,750, especially because those gains can remain invested until June when the bank loan payment is made. At the end of the period, the all-in cost of funds would be less than 6.49 percent. If LIBOR ended up at 5 percent, funding the 149 cumulative basis points lost would correspond to total losses in excess of $37,250. The result is an all-in cost of funds that exceeds 6.49 percent. Notice that the firm is *overhedged* whether rates rise or fall. Both gains and losses are too high to attain a cost of funds of 6.49 percent. This overhedging problem can be remedied by an adjustment known as *tailing the hedge*, which is described in the next chapter.

The Relationship Between Futures, FRA, and Swap Prices. With this background, the connection between FRAs and Eurodollar futures is immediate. The FRA offer rate will be a markup over, and the FRA bid rate a markdown from, the futures rate corresponding to the contracts used to hedge the position. This relationship is easy to see for FRAs that coincide with the IMM delivery dates. For example, suppose the March 1995 futures rate is still 6.49 percent on December 13, 1994, which is three months prior to the delivery date. If a 4-basis-point spread is needed to cover the market maker's costs, 3 × 6 FRAs would likely be priced at 6.51 percent offered and 6.47 percent bid. If the market maker sold the FRA at its offered rate, it would hedge its position by going short March futures. The exact number of contracts would depend on the basis point value of the FRA and would be "tailed" to avoid overhedging. If the market maker bought the FRA at its bid rate, it would hedge its position by going long March futures. These hedging decisions might at first seem to be reversed, given that ordinarily one thinks of selling futures to hedge a long cash position and vice versa. Any confusion is semantic, however; payoffs in futures are expressed by prices, but they are expressed in rates for FRAs (and swaps), and those metrics are inversely related.

Pricing FRAs on non-IMM dates requires some further calculation. Suppose we need to price a 3 × 6 FRA on October 31st. The payoff on that FRA would depend on three-month LIBOR on the valuation date, January 31, 1995. The problem is that the available futures allow for delivery either in December, at 5.95 percent, or in March, at 6.49 percent. In such a case, market makers will take a weighted average of those two futures rates using the extent of overlap with the FRA time frame as the weights. This situation is illustrated in Figure 4.2. The averaged futures rates will be 6.24 percent; that is,

$$\left(\frac{41}{89} \times 5.95\%\right) + \left(\frac{48}{89} \times 6.49\%\right) = 6.24\%.$$

So, the 3 × 6 offered FRA rate might be 6.26 percent while the bid rate is 6.22 percent. These weights also indicate the distribution of the hedge for the FRA across the Eurodollar futures contracts. Notice this hedge is riskier than one based on the IMM date because it implicitly assumes parallel shifts in the forward curve. The market maker would like to price the FRA at a wider spread to compensate for the risk, but in practice, the FRA market is quite competitive and the sizes of the bid–offer spreads tend not to change as IMM dates near.

Another practical problem is to price FRAs based on six-month LIBOR off the Eurodollar futures strip. With no futures contract on six-month LIBOR, a 6 × 12 FRA would be derived from rates on the 6 × 9 and 9 × 12 agreements. Those two would be obtained as above, typically interpolating along the futures rates for three-month LIBOR. Suppose that the midpoints for the 6 × 9 and 9 × 12 FRAs are 6.86 percent and 7.20 percent, respectively. Also, those quarterly periods span 90 and 91 days, respectively, for a total of 181 days. The six-month rate for the 6 × 12 FRA would then be the solution for $FRA_{6\times12}$ in the following equation:

$$\left[1 + \left(\frac{90 \times 0.0686}{360}\right)\right] \times \left[1 + \left(\frac{91 \times 0.0720}{360}\right)\right] = \left[1 + \left(\frac{181 \times FRA_{6\times12}}{360}\right)\right].$$

Here $FRA_{6\times12}$ equals 7.09 percent, so the offered rate on the 6 × 12 agreement might be 7.11 percent with a bid rate of 7.07 percent.

Figure 4.2 Pricing a 3 x 6 FRA on a Non-IMM Date

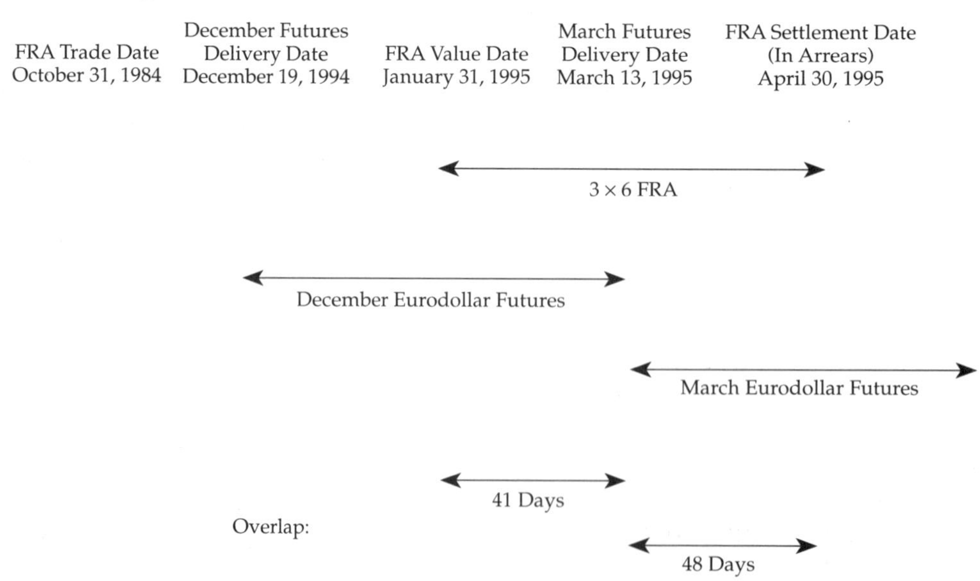

As the discussion in both this and the preceding section illustrates, FRAs can be viewed as an intermediate stage between rates on exchange-traded futures and fixed rates on interest rate swaps. Even in pricing swaps directly off the futures curve for LIBOR, the process is the same; that is, the futures rates can be strung together to derive a sequence of zero-coupon discount factors, which are used to solve for the present value average of the relevant segment of the Eurodollar futures curve. This, in turn, permits calculation of a midpoint swap fixed rate off the observed futures curve as easily as we can derive it from the observed forward curve in the FRA market. In short, swap prices are linked to forward rates, and whether this curve is found in exchange-traded or over-the-counter markets does not affect the calculation of the proper theoretical level.

Pricing Interest Rate Swaps Off the Implied Forward Curve

Suppose that we need to price an interest rate swap in a market having no directly observed futures or forward curve but ample trading in the underlying cash market for coupon-bearing securities of various maturities. The methods described above for pricing a swap contract can still be used after deriving an *implied forward curve*. Essentially, such a curve represents where explicit forward (or futures) rates would have to be if such markets did exist. In this process, we first must calculate an *implied zero curve* based on an assumption that bond market arbitrage activities are not profitable. The implied zero curve is then used to generate the forward curve that also will be consistent with the absence of arbitrage.

A straightforward numerical example illustrates these techniques. (In practice, these methods must address more complex institutional detail but still follow the same pattern and are easily adapted to computer-based solutions.) Suppose that the task is to price a three-year swap with annual settlements in arrears based on the one-year Treasury rate. One-, two-, and three-year cash market Treasuries yield 8 percent, 10 percent, and 12 percent, respectively. Each trades at par value so the coupon rates equal the yields and, to avoid complications from accrued interest, are presumed to be on a coupon payment date. The implied zero curve is the series of zero-coupon Treasury rates consistent with the observed yield curve on coupon-bearing securities in the sense of permitting no arbitrage opportunities. Mathematically, the implied zero curve is the solutions for z_1, z_2, and z_3 (the subscript here indicates years, above it was months) in the following equations:

$$100 = \frac{108}{(1 + z_1)^1}, \text{ or } z_1 = 8.00\%;$$

$$100 = \frac{10}{(1 + 0.08)^1} + \frac{110}{(1 + z_2)^2}, \text{ or } z_2 = 10.1020\%;$$

and

$$100 = \frac{12}{(1 + 0.08)^1} + \frac{12}{(1 + 0.10102)^2}$$

$$+ \frac{112}{(1 + z_3)^3}, \text{ or } z_3 = 12.3437\%.$$

Although the *par curve* is 8 percent, 10 percent, and 12 percent, the implied zero curve (sometimes called the *term structure* of interest rates or the *spot yield curve*) lies above the par curve at 8 percent, 10.1020 percent, and 12.3437 percent. The solution method is another example of bootstrapping. The first point on the implied zero curve, z_1, is obtained from the first equation. That term is plugged into the second equation to get z_2; z_1 and z_2 are plugged into the third equation to get z_3; and so forth out the yield curve.

With these values, we can now calculate the implied forward curve, which is the sequence of short-term rates indicating the marginal return for extending the maturity for an additional period. Note that calculating the implied zero curve is a necessary step in the procedure. No general formula exists for calculating implied forwards directly from yields on coupon-bearing bonds.[1] The implied forward rate between Year

[1] General formulas to calculate implied forward rates depend on how the spot rates are quoted. If they are on a bond basis, meaning the rates are all annualized assuming the same number of periods in the year (e.g., U.S. Treasuries are commonly quoted on a semiannual bond basis so that the quoted yield will be the yield per six-month period

1 and Year 2 (denoted $IFR_{1\times2}$) will be the solution to the expression

$$1.08 \times (1 + IFR_{1\times2}) = (1.101020)^2.$$

So, $IFR_{1\times2}$ equals 12.245 percent. Similarly, the implied forward rate between Year 2 and Year 3 (denoted $IFR_{2\times3}$) can be established by solving

$$(1.101020)^2 \times (1 + IFR_{2\times3}) = (1.123437)^3,$$

or $IFR_{2\times3}$ equals 16.965 percent. The implied forward curve will consist of the current one-year rate, 8 percent (for the 0×1 period); the one-year rate, one year forward of 12.245 percent (for the 1×2 period); and the one-year rate, two years forward of 16.965 percent (for the 2×3 period). Both the implied zero and forward curves are plotted in Figure 4.3. Notice that the time reference on the horizontal axis differs for the curves: The implied zeros are yields to maturity with each point representing a different time to maturity; the implied forwards are all one-year yields.

Assuming that these implied forwards indicate the rates at which explicit forward contracts would be trading if they existed, this curve can now be used to price the three-year interest rate swap. We have the forward curve and the zero-coupon discount rates; we need only calculate the present value average to set the mid-point of the swap dealer's bid–offer spread. Solving for SFR, the swap fixed rate, in the following formulation:

Figure 4.3 Implied Zero Curve and Implied Forward Curve

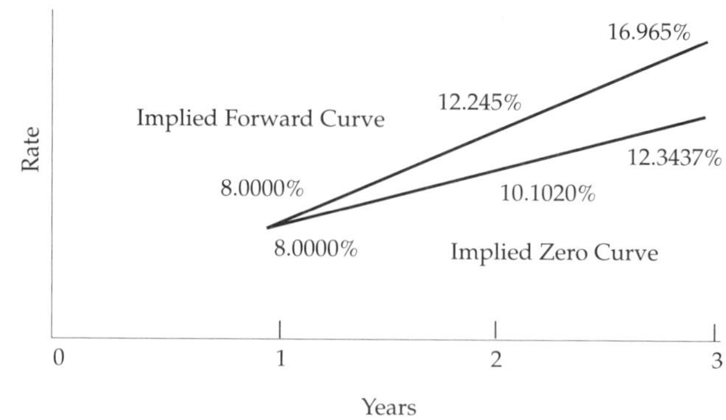

$$NP \times \left[\frac{8}{(1.08)^1} + \frac{12.245\%}{(1.10102)^2} + \frac{16.965\%}{(1.123437)^3}\right]$$

$$= NP \times \left[\frac{SFR}{(1.08)^1} + \frac{SFR}{(1.10102)^2} + \frac{SFR}{(1.123437)^3}\right]$$

yields a value of 12 percent. Notice that, as before, the notional principal, NP, is the same for each date and will therefore cancel out from each side of the equation. Thus, the three-year swap in this example would have its bid–offer spread based on a midpoint of 12 percent. A different way of visualizing this averaging process is shown in Figure 4.4. The swap fixed rate should be selected so that the present value of the settlement payments that the pay-fixed and receive-fixed counterparties will make to one another will be equal, if future LIBOR was locked in by hedging transactions. Swap pricing does not require that the counterparties actually hedge the floating side of the agreement, only that they could and would do so if it captured an arbitrage opportunity. These discounted settlement payments are represented by the shaded squares in the figure.

Recognize that the same midpoint swap fixed rate would be obtained whether the forward curve comes from observed futures rates or is implied by the underlying spot yield curve. The size of the bid–offer spreads would differ, however. A futures rate can be secured more precisely and easily than locking in an implied forward rate, which requires offsetting short and long positions in the cash market. Of course,

---

times two periods in the year), the following formula can be used:

$$\left(1 + \frac{Z_{0\times A}}{n}\right)^{n\times A} \times \left(1 + \frac{IFZ_{A\times B}}{n}\right)^{n\times(B-A)} = \left(1 + \frac{Z_{0\times B}}{n}\right)^{n\times B},$$

where $Z_{0\times A}$ is the spot yield for A years to maturity, $Z_{0\times B}$ the spot yield for B years, and $IFZ_{A\times B}$ the implied forward rate between years A and B. Each yield is annualized for "n" periods a year. If the rates are quoted on a money market basis (e.g., LIBOR), the formula above is not applicable because rates with different maturities are annualized for a different number of periods in the year. No n corresponds to all rates. In this case, the following formula can be used:

$$\left[1 + \left(\frac{A}{360} \times R_{0\times A}\right)\right] \times \left[1 + \left(\frac{B-A}{360} \times IFR_{A\times B}\right)\right]$$

$$= \left[1 + \left(\frac{B}{360} \times R_{0\times B}\right)\right],$$

where $R_{0\times A}$ is the money market rate for A days to maturity, $R_{0\times B}$ the rate for B days, and $IFR_{A\times B}$ the implied forward rate between days A and B.

Figure 4.4 Pricing a Plain Vanilla Interest Rate Swap

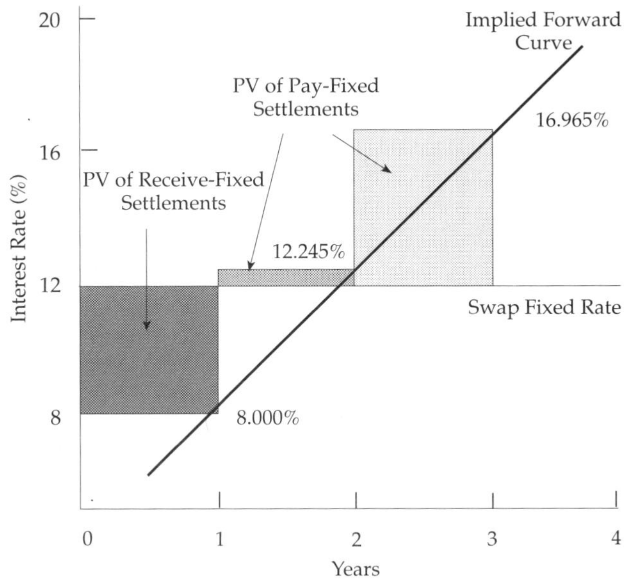

these additional transactions represent a more expensive endeavor, and that higher cost would be built into the bid–offer spread.

Pricing Nonplain Vanilla Interest Rate Swaps

So far, we have only priced interest rate swaps having a constant notional principal over the lifetime of the agreement and an immediate start date. Varying the notional principal and postponing the start date create innovative, non-plain vanilla structures. In any case, these can be priced using the same present-value-average methodology just used for plain vanilla swaps. To extend the earlier example, suppose the spot yield curve for zero-coupon transactions and the forward curve are the same as displayed in Figure 4.3. The yields on one-, two-, and three-year zero-coupon securities are 8 percent, 10.1020 percent, and 12.3437 percent, and the forward rates are 8 percent, 12.245 percent, and 16.965 percent.

Assume now that we need to price a three-year *amortizing swap* for which the notional principal will be \$30 million for the first year, \$20 million for the second year, and \$10 million for the third. To solve for the swap fixed rate in this case, we need only adjust the relative weights for each settlement date in the basic pricing formula,

$$\frac{30 \times 8\%}{(1.08)^1} + \frac{20 \times 12.245\%}{(1.10102)^2} + \frac{10 \times 16.965\%}{(1.123437)^3}$$

$$= \frac{30 \times \text{SFR}}{(1.08)^1} + \frac{20 \times \text{SFR}}{(1.10102)^2} + \frac{10 \times \text{SFR}}{(1.123437)^3},$$

which generates a value for SFR equal to 10.60 percent. The fixed rate on the amortizing swap is lower than the plain vanilla structure (i.e., 12 percent) because more weight is placed on the early part of the forward curve. Given that the forward curve is upward sloping, the weighted average is reduced compared with the plain vanilla swap, which places equal weight on each cash flow. The same process applies to other types of varying notional principal swaps such as *accreting swaps*, on which the notional amounts increase over time, and *roller-coaster swaps*, which have notional amounts that rise and fall over the swap's lifetime so as to follow the estimated outstanding amount of principal on a revolving-credit agreement.

A *forward swap*, which was introduced in Chapter 3, is also easily priced once we have the forward curve and the set of discount rates. Suppose that we need to price a 1 × 3 forward swap, meaning a two-year swap that is deferred for one year. The fixed rate and all other terms to the agreement (e.g., the settlement dates, the reference rate, the governing law) are set in advance, but the transaction does not begin at once. The fixed rate on the forward swap will merely be the present value average of the relevant segment of the forward curve, as portrayed in Figure 4.5. The bid–offer spread will surround the midpoint SFR value of 14.42 percent, calculated as the solution to

$$\frac{12.245\%}{(1.10102)^2} + \frac{16.965\%}{(1.123437)^3}$$

$$= \frac{\text{SFR}}{(1.10102)^2} + \frac{\text{SFR}}{(1.123437)^3}.$$

As noted earlier, when the forward curve is upward sloping, deferred-start swaps will have higher fixed rates than plain vanilla structures, which would commence immediately. Recognize that the same methodology can be used to price combinations of varying notional principals and forward start dates. As we have stressed, the forward curve is the key to pricing interest

Figure 4.5 Pricing a Forward Interest Rate Swap

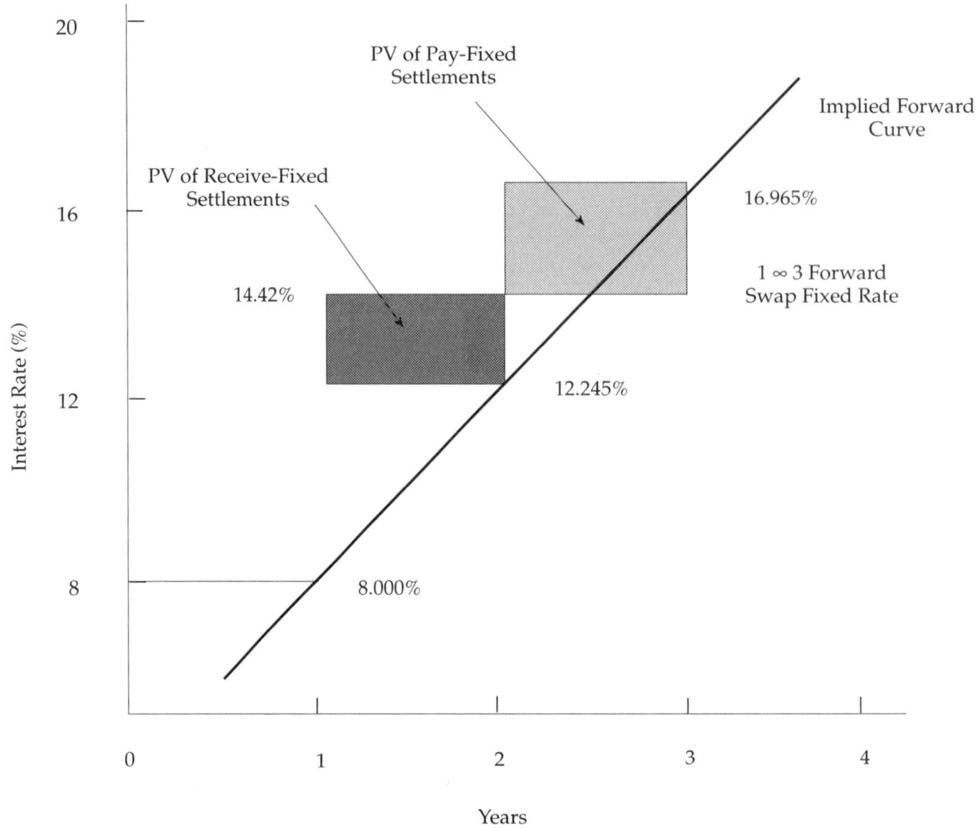

rate swaps, even on such a complex structure as a roller-coaster swap with a delayed starting date.

Pricing Interest Rate Swaps Off the Treasury Curve

Many financial markets have no interest rate futures contract from which to observe the forward curve directly. Moreover, many markets have no underlying yield curve from which to calculate the implied forward rates. This deficiency has been as much a problem in the U.S. dollar market in the past as it is in emerging markets in the present. Only in the past few years has the Eurodollar futures contract extended out beyond three years of delivery dates. Furthermore, no ready series of LIBOR-equivalent, long-term, coupon-bearing cash market securities is available for computing the implied zero and forward curves, even in U.S. dollars. The Treasury market is the best source of data for yield curve analysis because of its size, depth, and liquidity.

The LIBOR forward curve can be estimated from the Treasury forward curve, which itself can be derived using any of the techniques described above. The difference between a forward rate on LIBOR and a Treasury bill is known as the *TED spread.* (Formally, the TED spread is the difference between the price index on the Treasury bill futures contract and the price index on the Eurodollar contract deliverable on the same date.) Once the Treasury forward curve has been established, the LIBOR forward curve is obtained by estimating and adding the average TED spread for the future time periods. To be precise, the present values of the cash flows based on the T-bill forward rates plus the TED spread would equal the present value of the cash flows based on the LIBOR forward curve. This process is illustrated in Figure 4.6.

Figure 4.7 summarizes the pricing of interest rate swaps off the forward curve for the floating reference rate, assumed here to be LIBOR. Two pricing "zones" are shown: one in which the forward curve is directly observed in the futures

Figure 4.6 Estimating the LIBOR Forward Curve Off of the Treasury Curve

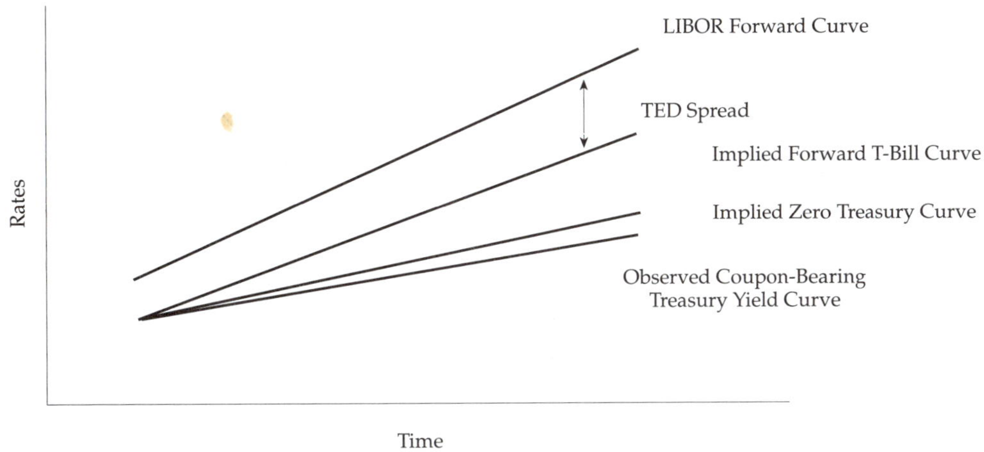

market and one in which it must be estimated from yields on government debt. The direct observation method produces more exact swap prices and narrower bid–offer spreads than does Treasury-based estimation of the LIBOR forward curve. In the U.S. dollar market, the segmentation line has moved to the right over the years, meaning that more swaps with longer tenors are being priced off of the Eurodollar futures strip. A market for long-dated swaps will still exist, however, for which the forward curve must be estimated, typically by forecasting future levels of the TED spread. Those forecasts largely determine the swap spread over the Treasury yield curve. Whatever its source, though, the forward curve determines the midpoint of the bid–offer spread. Other factors such as the precision of the forward curve and default risk determine the width of the spread.

Figure 4.7 Directly Observed Versus Estimated Forward Curves

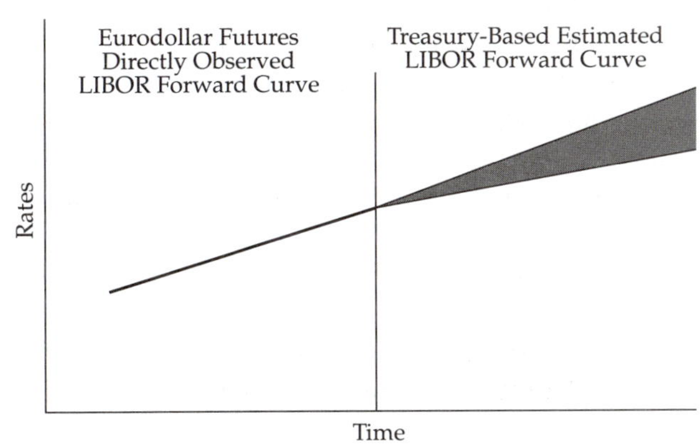

Pricing Currency Swaps

The salient difference between an interest rate swap and a currency swap, besides the obvious fact that the latter involves an exchange across currencies, is that principal as well as coupon interest is exchanged in a typical currency swap. Ironically, this principal exchange will make it easier to price a plain vanilla currency swap than a *currency annuity swap*, for which no such exchange takes place at maturity. The intuition behind this observation is that the plain vanilla currency swap with its re-exchange of principal at maturity looks very much like a package of bonds, as suggested in Chapter 2 by the capital market interpretation of the swap. The annuity, or coupon-only, swap has no comparable capital market analog, making its pricing more difficult.

Plain Vanilla Currency Swap Pricing. Assume that two firms, Companies ABC and XYZ, are equal in credit rating and access to international capital markets. Suppose further that these firms can both issue three-year, floating-rate notes at one-year deutschemark LIBOR flat or at one-year dollar LIBOR flat for principal amounts of DEM 150 million or USD 100 million. The spot market FX rate is assumed to be DEM 1.50/USD. Currently, one-year deutschemark LIBOR and dollar LIBOR are assumed to be 9 percent and 4 percent, respectively. ABC and XYZ can also issue par-value, annual-payment, fixed-rate debt at the following yields (and coupon rates), stated on a 365-day basis:

Maturity	*Yield in DEM*	*Yield in USD*
One year	9%	4%
Two years	8	5
Three years	7	6

So, the deutschemark yield curve on coupon-bearing securities is downward sloping and the dollar curve is upward sloping.

The implied zero-yield curves, calculated by the process described earlier, are as follows:

Maturity	*Yield in DEM*	*Yield in USD*
One year	9.0000%	4.0000%
Two years	7.9604	5.0252
Three years	6.9069	6.0829

The implied forward curves in each currency can then be calculated using these implied zero-coupon rates:

In DEM:

$$(1.09) \times (1 + \text{IFR}_{1\times2}) = (1.079604)^2, \text{ or } \text{IFR}_{1\times2} = 6.9307\%$$

$$(1.079604)^2 \times (1 + \text{IFR}_{2\times3}) = (1.069069)^3, \text{ or } \text{IFR}_{2\times3} = 4.8306\%,$$

and in USD:

$$(1.04) \times (1 + \text{IFR}_{1\times2}) = (1.050252)^2, \text{ or } \text{IFR}_{1\times2} = 6.0605\%$$

$$(1.050252)^2 \times (1 + \text{IFR}_{2\times3}) = (1.060829)^3, \text{ or } \text{IFR}_{2\times3} = 8.2304\%.$$

Because we have the forward curve and the zero-coupon discount rates, the theoretical interest rate swap fixed rates are easy to calculate. For three-year plain vanilla swaps, the fixed rates are derived from the following equations:

In DEM:

$$\left[\frac{9\%}{(1.09)^1} + \frac{6.9307\%}{(1.07904)^2} + \frac{4.8306\%}{(1.069069)^3}\right] = \left[\frac{\text{SFR}}{(1.09)^1} + \frac{\text{SFR}}{(1.07904)^2} + \frac{\text{SFR}}{(1.069069)^3}\right],$$

and in USD:

$$\left[\frac{4\%}{(1.04)^1} + \frac{6.0605\%}{(1.050252)^2} + \frac{8.2304\%}{(1.060829)^3}\right] = \left[\frac{\text{SFR}}{(1.04)^1} + \frac{\text{SFR}}{(1.050252)^2} + \frac{\text{SFR}}{(1.060829)^3}\right].$$

From these equations, the three-year swap fixed rate in deutschemarks would be 7 percent (versus DEM LIBOR flat), and the dollar swap fixed rate would be 6 percent in exchange for dollar LIBOR flat. These results are not at all surprising given the assumption that Companies ABC and XYZ could issue three-year debt at LIBOR flat in either currency or at 7 percent fixed in deutschemarks or 6 percent fixed in dollars. These swap calculations merely demonstrate that we can enter the pricing cycle at various points: the coupon curve, the zero curve, or the forward curve. From any starting point, we can derive the others using the assumption that these markets are free from arbitrage.

Chapter 1 listed four plain vanilla currency swap structures: floating/floating, floating/fixed, fixed/floating, and fixed/fixed. For these DEM/USD currency swaps, the no-arbitrage swap prices for three-year transactions between counterparties ABC and XYZ would have to be DEM LIBOR/USD LIBOR, DEM LIBOR/6 percent USD, 7 percent DEM/USD LIBOR, and 7 percent DEM/6 percent USD. The standard for quotation is most likely to be the third of these, the nondollar fixed rate versus dollar LIBOR. The others all can be obtained from plain vanilla interest rate swap quotes in each currency. Notice again that we are focusing on the mid-point of the bid–offer spread; other considerations such as default risk enter when determining the spread around this value.

Currency Annuity Swap Pricing. The plain vanilla currency swap just considered assumes an exchange of principal at origination and re-exchange at maturity. Will the swap prices change if the re-exchange is dropped? The answer is yes, as long as the yield curves in the two currencies differ in level or shape. The reason is that the principal exchanges at origination and maturity are typically based on the same FX rate: the original spot rate. When the yield curves differ, however, this rate will very likely be an off-market forward rate at the time of maturity. To see this, first calculate the FX forward rates that would be consistent with interest rate parity.

One-year FX Forward:

$$\text{DEM } 1.5/\text{USD} \times \left(\frac{1.09}{1.04}\right)^{1} = \text{DEM } 1.5721/\text{USD}$$

Two-year FX Forward:

$$\text{DEM } 1.5/\text{USD} \times \left(\frac{1.079604}{1.050252}\right)^{2}$$

$$= \text{DEM } 1.5850/\text{USD}$$

Three-year FX Forward:

$$\text{DEM } 1.5/\text{USD} \times \left(\frac{1.069069}{1.060829}\right)^{3}$$

$$= \text{DEM } 1.5352/\text{USD}.$$

In this example, the dollar is at a forward premium to the deutschemark because the dollar interest rates are lower than in deutschemarks.

Suppose Companies ABC and XYZ enter a cross-currency basis swap, trading deutschemark LIBOR for dollar LIBOR for three years. This transaction is shown in Figure 4.8, which casts ABC as the payer of dollar LIBOR and XYZ as the payer of deutschemark LIBOR. In the plain vanilla structure, USD 100 million would be exchanged for DEM 150 million on the Date 3 settlement in addition to the final coupon exchange. That implicit off-market forward FX rate of DEM 1.5/USD matches the current spot market but not the interest rate parity result of DEM 1.5352/USD for a forward FX transaction. Clearly, the plain vanilla structure benefits XYZ as the payer of deutschemarks and the receiver of dollars on the re-exchange of principal. Company ABC, the counterparty who is paying dollars, should be getting the parity rate of DEM 153.52 million for the payment of USD 100 million, but it gets only DEM 150 million. ABC benefits on the first two coupon exchanges in an amount just sufficient to offset the loss on the final settlement. That is the nature of swap pricing—the present values of the positions should be equivalent.

Figure 4.8 A Plain Vanilla Cross-Currency Floating/Floating Swap

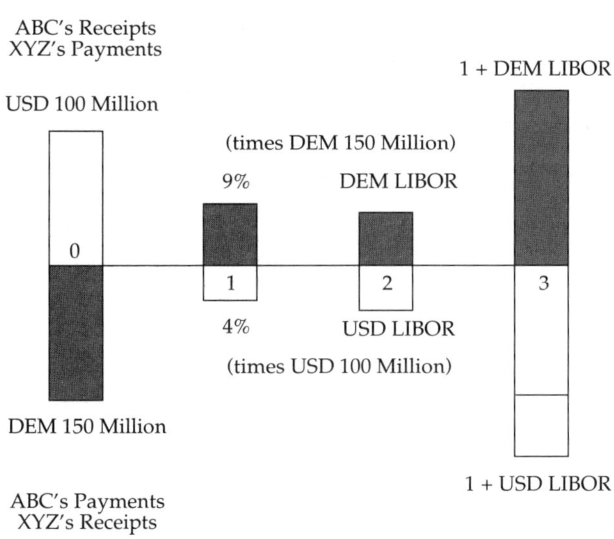

Now, suppose that the cross-currency deutschemark-for-dollar LIBOR swap is structured on an annuity basis without the principal trade at maturity. Company ABC will now have to compensate XYZ for the absence of the favorable Date 3 transaction. To determine the amount of the payment, assume that the receipt of DEM 150 million by ABC at maturity on the plain vanilla cross-currency basis swap can be sold forward at the three-year rate of DEM 1.5352/USD. That transaction translates to a Date 3 receipt of USD 97.707139 million (DEM 150 million ÷ DEM 1.5352/USD). The net dollar outflow for the re-exchange of principal on Date 3, therefore, is a payment of USD 2.292861 million from ABC to XYZ. The present value of that amount is USD 1.920621 million, using the implied three-year dollar zero-coupon rate of 6.0829 percent as the discount factor.

Figure 4.9 summarizes the resultant cash flows on the cross-currency annuity swap. ABC

Figure 4.9 A Cross-Currency Annuity Swap

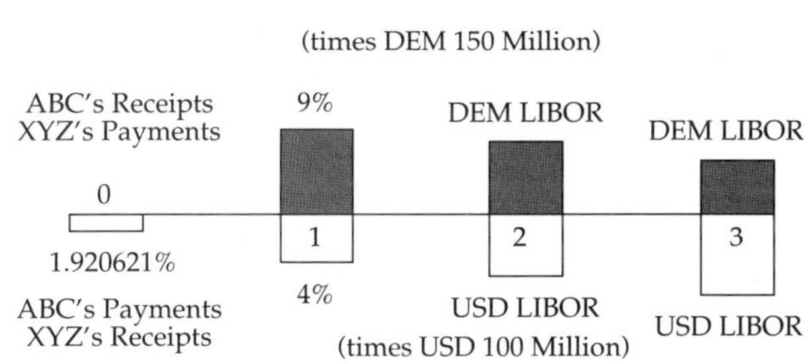

would have to pay XYZ 1.920621 percent of the USD notional principal up front. Instead, if spread out over the three years and paid as a margin over dollar LIBOR on the swap, the amortized amount would be 71 basis points. This amount can be obtained as the margin that when discounted by the dollar zero-coupon interest rates, equals the up-front payment; that is,

$$1.920621 = \frac{\text{Margin}}{1.04} + \frac{\text{Margin}}{(1.050252)^2} + \frac{\text{Margin}}{(1.060829)^3}, \text{ or Margin} = 0.70982\%.$$

In conclusion, the plain vanilla basis swap would be an exchange of deutschemark LIBOR for dollar LIBOR, which follows directly from the capital market interpretation of the swap. Barring default, the cash flows on a combination of buying one FRN and issuing the other will be the same as the currency basis swap. This result is particularly evident in the exchange of principals that the capital market transactions, as well as the plain vanilla currency swap, would entail. The annuity swap, however, would require a margin over dollar LIBOR in exchange for deutschemark LIBOR. The same result would hold for the other varieties of currency swaps. For instance, the plain vanilla three-year, fixed/fixed swap would be priced at 7 percent DEM versus 6 percent USD. The fixed/fixed annuity swap would be an exchange of 7 percent DEM against 6.71 percent USD.

Summary of Interest Rate and Currency Swap Pricing

This chapter emphasized two central themes. First, swap pricing can be separated into two parts: the theoretical value that is based on arbitrage-free pricing and the bid–offer spread around that midpoint that contains the other relevant pricing variables (e.g., default risk, liquidity risk, hedging costs, operations costs, and profit). The assumption that prices will move to eliminate arbitrage opportunities is central to modern financial analysis. This assumption, however, does not mean that arbitrage opportunities will never exist. Quite to the contrary, those opportunities will sometimes exist but will be exploited until the risk–return trade-off is back to normal. We used arbitrage-free pricing in several key analytic techniques, including the implied zero curve, implied forward rates, implied FX forward rates, and in establishing the link between the FRA and Eurodollar futures markets. The power of no-arbitrage pricing results is that little need be assumed about the behavior and information of market participants.

The second theme that was stressed is the importance of the forward curve in swap pricing. Plain vanilla swaps, as well as some basic modifications such as those having varying notional principal or a deferred start date, can be priced by calculating the present value average of the relevant segment of the forward curve. The problem ultimately is to establish the forward curve in the first place, a task made easier when an actively traded futures contract exists in the swap's reference rate, such as the Eurodollar futures contract in the U.S. dollar market. When a directly observed forward curve is not available, the curve must be estimated, which is where logistical difficulties often arise, even with a well-established forward curve in government securities. Finally, currency swaps present a different sort of problem, mainly because of the exchange (or nonexchange) of principal at maturity.

Exercises

Exercise 4.1: It is mid-June of 1994, and as the short-term swap trader for a "boutique" derivatives house, you are routinely asked to quote a two-way market for plain vanilla deals with maturities ranging out as far as five years. The most recent request has come from the treasurer of a middle-market consumer services company that is trying to convert the last year of an outstanding debt issue from a floating rate to a fixed rate. This debt issue has a face value of $30 million and requires four more LIBOR-based quarterly payments, the next of which is scheduled in September of 1994 based on today's three-month rate.

You base the pricing for short-term swaps such as this one on the exchange-traded Eurodollar futures contract at the CME. To be specific, you set your bid and offer fixed rates off the midpoint of the "average" of the futures rates. Because competition is strong in this maturity range, you will only be able to add (subtract) 2 basis points when quoting your offer (bid) rate on the swap. In the Eurodollar futures markets, the current settlement prices are 95.02 for delivery in September 1994, 94.78 for delivery in December 1994, and 94.43 for delivery in March 1995. At this time, the level of three-month LIBOR is 4.70 percent.

(a) Based on this information, what swap fixed rate would you quote the treasurer for this deal? You may assume that each quarter has exactly 91.25 days, that LIBOR is on a 365-day basis, and that all quoted rates can be converted to a quarterly rate simply by dividing by four. For example, if LIBOR is 4.70 percent, the periodic coupon payment on the outstanding debt would be exactly $352,500. Also, the swap fixed rates are quoted on a quarterly bond basis (the quarterly rate times four). With these simplifying assumptions, no day-count conversions need be made.

(b) What positions in Eurodollar futures contracts would you enter to hedge your market risk if the company elects to enter the swap with you? Indicate the specific futures position (i.e., long or short), the delivery dates, and the specific number of contracts.

Solution: In general, you will set the swap fixed rate according to the present value average of the futures strip—the rate such that when you discount the cash flows that can be locked in for the future levels of LIBOR, you get the same present value as the discounted cash flows for the swap rate. That fixed rate will turn out to be 5.11 percent, giving a bid rate of 5.09 percent and an offer of 5.13 percent. The company will want to pay the fixed rate on the swap to hedge its cost of funds, thereby paying your offer rate of 5.13 percent. Upon "selling" the one-year swap, you become exposed to higher market rates. Your hedge must be to sell Eurodollar futures contracts so that you gain when futures rates rise and prices fall. The exact number of contracts will be based on "tailing" the hedge. The basic hedge ratio is 30 contracts in each delivery month, the September, the December, and the March. The tailed-hedge ratio will be the present value of 30 in 6, 9, and 12 months.

(a) The spot rate for LIBOR is 4.70 percent. The futures rates are 4.98 percent in September, 5.22 percent in December, and 5.57 percent in March. Recall that the futures rate is merely 100 minus the price index. Those points are the first four on the Eurodollar futures strip. Now find the break-even SFR that solves the following equation:

$$\$30\text{ million} \times \frac{1}{4} \times \left[\frac{\text{SFR}}{1+z_3} + \frac{\text{SFR}}{1+z_6} + \frac{\text{SFR}}{1+z_9} + \frac{\text{SFR}}{1+z_{12}}\right]$$

$$= \$30\text{ million} \times \frac{1}{4} \times \left[\frac{4.70\%}{1+z_3} + \frac{4.98\%}{1+z_6} + \frac{5.22\%}{1+z_9} + \frac{5.57\%}{1+z_{12}}\right],$$

where the zero-coupon discount factors derived by "repackaging" the futures data are

$$1 + z_3 = 1 + (0.0470/4) = 1.01175$$

$$1 + z_6 = (1 + z_3) \times [1 + (0.0498/4)] = 1.02435$$

$$1 + z_9 = (1 + z_6) \times [1 + (0.0522/4)] = 1.03771$$

$$1 + z_{12} = (1 + z_9) \times [1 + (0.0557/4)] = 1.05216.$$

The solution, which becomes the midpoint of the bid–ask spread, is SFR = (19.83121 percent/3.87870) = 5.11285 percent. Adding 2 basis points onto this value and then rounding gives an offer rate of 5.13 percent. Similarly, your bid-side quote to clients wishing to receive the swap fixed rate would be 5.11 percent less 2 basis points, or 5.09 percent.

(b) You will need to hedge your own market risk on the swap by selling the September, December, and March futures contracts. Notice that the first settlement of the swap is set at today's LIBOR and need not (in fact, cannot) be hedged. For each delivery date, you will need 30 contracts prior to tailing the hedges. The basis point value of the exposure on the \$30 million swap is \$750. To see this, calculate the floating-rate payment if LIBOR is 5 percent. It would be \$375,000, the notional principal of \$30 million times the day-count factor of 1/4 times 5 percent. Then, recalculate the payment if LIBOR is 5.01 percent—a 1-basis-point change. It would be \$375,750, a difference of \$750. The basis point value of each futures contract is \$25. The 30 contract requirement is the ratio of the difference in payment to the basis point value of the contract, or \$750 divided by \$25.

Thirty contracts for each delivery date, however, would lead to overhedging as gains and losses on the futures are realized daily. Theoretically, the optimal number of September contracts to enter at once would be 30 divided by $1 + z_6$, or 29.3 contracts. Notice that the six-month discount rate is used even though the futures are for delivery in three months. The idea is that the gains or losses on the futures hedge would be invested or funded until the in-arrears settlement in December. Similarly, the other tailed-hedge ratios would be 28.9 December contracts and 28.5 March contracts.

Exercise 4.2: Suppose that the spot and implied forward rates shown in Table E-4.1 prevail in the market for zero-coupon time deposits. The rates are quoted on a semiannual bond basis, so a 5.0-year time deposit in the amount of \$1 million at a stated rate of 8.68 percent would pay \$1 million $\times$ $[1 + (0.0868/2)]^{10}$ = \$1,529,355 at maturity. Likewise, a 4.5-year time deposit at a rate of 8.27 percent would pay \$1 million $\times$ $[1 + (0.0827/2)]^9$ = \$1,440,027 at maturity. The implied forwards represent break-even reinvestment rates and are calculated from the zero-coupon rates. For example, the forward rate implied by the 4.5-year and 5.0-year spot market zero-coupon rates is 12.41 percent, which is the solution to the following expression:

$$\left(1 + \frac{0.0827}{2}\right)^9 \times \left(1 + \frac{\text{IFR}}{2}\right) = \left(1 + \frac{0.0868}{2}\right)^{10}.$$

Calculate the midpoint fixed rate on a five-year, \$25 million, plain vanilla interest rate swap.

Solution: The swap fixed rate will be the present value average of the implied forward curve. Note that the current six-month rate of 6.14 percent will be the first point on the forward curve. The remaining points will be the implied forward rates (i.e., the 0.5 $\times$ 1.0, the 1.0 $\times$ 1.5, and so forth). The swap fixed rate will be the solution for SFR in the following expression:

Table E-4.1 Hypothetical Spot and Implied Forward Rates in Market for Zero-Coupon Time Deposits

Maturity (years)	Zero-Coupon Rates	Forward Rates
0.5	6.14%	
		6.70%
1.0	6.42	
		6.96
1.5	6.60	
		7.56
2.0	6.84	
		7.74
2.5	7.02	
		8.46
3.0	7.26	
		9.23
3.5	7.54	
		10.84
4.0	7.95	
		10.85
4.5	8.27	
		12.41
5.0	8.68	

$$\$25 \text{ million} \times \frac{1}{2} \times \left[\frac{6.14\%}{(1 + 0.0614/2)^1} + \frac{6.70\%}{(1 + 0.0642/2)^2} + \frac{6.96\%}{(1 + 0.0660/2)^3} + \frac{7.56\%}{(1 + 0.0684/2)^4}\right.$$

$$+ \frac{7.74\%}{(1 + 0.0702/2)^5} + \frac{8.46\%}{(1 + 0.0726/2)^6} + \frac{9.23\%}{(1 + 0.0754/2)^7}$$

$$\left.+ \frac{10.84\%}{(1 + 0.0795/2)^8} + \frac{10.85\%}{(1 + 0.0827/2)^9} + \frac{12.41\%}{(1 + 0.0868/2)^{10}}\right]$$

$$= \$25 \text{ million} \times \frac{1}{2} \times \left[\frac{SFR}{(1 + 0.0614/2)^1} + \frac{SFR}{(1 + 0.0642/2)^2} + \frac{SFR}{(1 + 0.0660/2)^3}\right.$$

$$+ \frac{SFR}{(1 + 0.0684/2)^4} + \frac{SFR}{(1 + 0.0702/2)^5} + \frac{SFR}{(1 + 0.0726/2)^6} + \frac{SFR}{(1 + 0.0754/2^7)}$$

$$\left.+ \frac{SFR}{(1 + 0.0795/2)^8} + \frac{SFR}{(1 + 0.0827/2)^9} + \frac{SFR}{(1 + 0.0868/2)^{10}}\right].$$

SFR is 8.4504 percent, and the five-year bid and offer fixed rates will be based on this midpoint value.

Exercise 4.3: Based on the same spot market and implied forward curves as in Exercise 4.2, calculate the fixed rates on the following nonplain vanilla swaps:

(a) A three-year accreting swap that starts with a notional principal of \$25 million and then adds \$5 million every six months until it reaches \$50 million for the last settlement period.

(b) A \$25 million, 2×5 forward swap; that is, a three-year swap that has its start time deferred for two years.

Solution: These swaps will be priced off the forward curve. On the accreting swap, the notional principal cannot be factored out of the present value expressions. On the forward swap, the averaging process takes place on the 2×5 segment of the curve. Otherwise, the pricing methodology is the same as on plain vanilla swaps.

(a)

$$\frac{1}{2}\times\left[\frac{25\times 6.14\%}{(1+0.0614/2)^1}+\frac{30\times 6.70\%}{(1+0.0642/2)^2}+\frac{35\times 6.96\%}{(1+0.0660/2)^3}+\frac{40\times 7.56\%}{(1+0.0684/2)^4}\right.$$

$$\left.+\frac{45\times 7.74\%}{(1+0.0702/2)^5}+\frac{50\times 8.46\%}{(1+0.0726/2)^6}\right]=\frac{1}{2}\times\left[\frac{25\times SFR}{(1+0.0614/2)^1}+\frac{30\times SFR}{(1+0.0642/2)^2}\right.$$

$$\left.+\frac{35\times SFR}{(1+0.0660/2)^3}+\frac{40\times SFR}{(1+0.0684/2)^4}+\frac{45\times SFR}{(1+0.0702/2)^5}+\frac{50\times SFR}{(1+0.0726/2)^6}\right].$$

Solving for SFR produces 7.3849 percent.

(b)

$$\$25\text{ million}\times\frac{1}{2}\times\left[\frac{7.74\%}{(1+0.0702/2)^5}+\frac{8.46\%}{(1+0.0726/2)^6}+\frac{9.23\%}{(1+0.0754/2)^7}\right.$$

$$\left.+\frac{10.84\%}{(1+0.0795/2)^8}+\frac{10.85\%}{(1+0.0827/2)^9}+\frac{12.41\%}{(1+0.0868/2)^{10}}\right]$$

$$=\$25\text{ million}\times\frac{1}{2}\times\left[\frac{SFR}{(1+0.0702/2)^5}+\frac{SFR}{(1+0.0726/2)^6}+\frac{SFR}{(1+0.0754/2)^7}\right.$$

$$\left.+\frac{SFR}{(1+0.0795/2)^8}+\frac{SFR}{(1+0.0827/2)^9}+\frac{SFR}{(1+0.0868/2)^{10}}\right].$$

On the 2×5 forward swap, SFR equals 9.7872 percent.

Exercise 4.4: Your new job is on the currency derivatives trading desk of a New York bank subsidiary in Toronto. You have primary responsibility for pricing, trading, and hedging the bank's book of Canadian dollar (CAD)/U.S. dollar currency swaps. One day you are asked by a steady customer to price a three-year, annual settlement, fixed/fixed CAD/USD annuity swap. You immediately check the yield curves in each currency and find, to your surprise and delight, that each curve is exactly flat—in CAD at 10 percent, in USD at 8 percent, both rates on an annual payment basis. This situation is indeed quite rare, but because of it, the implied zero and implied forward curves will also be flat in CAD and USD at 10 percent and 8 percent, respectively. In the spot FX market, the exchange rate is CAD 1.3333/USD.

What is your theoretical pricing (before setting the bid–offer spread) for the annuity swap? Assume that the customer wants the fixed rate in CAD to be 10 percent on a notional principal of CAD 53,332,000, or USD 40,000,000 at the current spot rate.

Solution: Start with the plain vanilla, 10 percent in CAD versus 8 percent in USD currency swap. The annual coupon exchanges will be CAD 5,333,200 for USD 3,200,000. These amounts are just the annual interest rates times the principal amounts. Note that they imply a very favorable FX rate of CAD 1.6666/USD to the U.S.

payer. The principal exchange at maturity in Year 3 will be at the current spot rate of CAD 1.3333/USD, or CAD 53,332,000 for USD 40,000,000.

The innovation with a currency annuity swap is the absence of the principal exchange. In that case, the U.S. dollar payer will have to pay a higher fixed rate because CAD 1.6666/USD is higher than available in the current spot market. In fact, the fixed/fixed annuity swap should end up at the average FX rate of the one-, two-, and three-year points on the FX forward curve. To identify where in theory that curve should be, calculate the FX forwards that would be consistent with interest rate parity and flat yield curves at 10 percent in Canadian dollars and 8 percent in U.S. dollars.

One-year FX Forward:

$$\text{CAD } 1.3333/\text{USD} \times \left(\frac{1.10}{1.08}\right)^{1} = \text{CAD } 1.357991/\text{USD}$$

Two-year FX Forward:

$$\text{CAD } 1.3333/\text{USD} \times \left(\frac{1.10}{1.08}\right)^{2} = \text{CAD } 1.383139/\text{USD}$$

Three-year FX Forward:

$$\text{CAD } 1.3333/\text{USD} \times \left(\frac{1.10}{1.08}\right)^{3} = \text{CAD } 1.408752/\text{USD}.$$

Assume now that you can sell the Year 3 principal flow of CAD 53,332,000 at the implied FX forward rate of CAD 1.408752/USD. That amount corresponds to USD 37,857,622. The U.S. dollar payer on the plain vanilla currency swap, therefore, loses USD 2,142,378 on the principal exchange. That loss can be amortized at 8 percent a year over the three years at USD 659,924, an annual loss of 1.649811 percent of the notional principal of USD 40,000,000. The annuity swap fixed rates will be 10 percent in Canadian dollars and 9.649811 percent in U.S. dollars. Now convert that to annual cash flows: CAD 5,333,200 in exchange for USD 3,859,924, the latter found as the product of 9.649811 percent and USD 40,000,000.

The accuracy of this pricing can be established by finding the present value of each side in the annuity swap. The present value of a three-year annuity of CAD 5,333,200 a year discounted at 10 percent is CAD 13,262,879. The present value of the three-year annuity of USD 3,859,924 at 8 percent is USD 9,947,399. At the spot exchange rate of CAD 1.3333/USD, that amount corresponds to CAD 13,262,867, which differs from the present value of the Canadian dollar leg of the swap only because of rounding errors.

Notice also that the implicit FX rate is CAD 1.3817/USD, found as CAD 5,333,200 divided by USD 3,859,924, which is the average of the implied FX forward rates. A currency annuity swap is comparable to a plain vanilla interest rate swap. The fixed rate on the latter is an average of the forward interest rates. The implicit fixed FX rate on the former is an average of the FX forward curve. The plain vanilla currency swap took its standard form to include the exchange of principal at origination and maturity at a time when most transactions were based on newly issued bonds. As more swaps are motivated by financial restructuring and risk management, the number of annuity swaps is likely to increase because they represent cleanly a package of FX forwards.

Chapter 5. The Risks in Swap Contracting

In financial analysis, risk is usually defined in the context of the return volatility and the stochastic processes that drive price variables. This chapter addresses risk in its more colloquial sense: Swap risk is all the things that can go wrong after a counterparty enters an interest rate or currency swap. For example, if a company is using a receive-fixed/pay-floating swap transaction to speculate that LIBOR will decline, two types of risk will predominate. One is that the speculator will be incorrect and LIBOR will move to a much higher level than expected. This type of risk is *market risk*: the risk that the mark-to-market value of the swap moves against the firm and the transaction becomes a significant liability. If the speculation is right, however, and rates do indeed fall as expected, the swap becomes a significant asset. The threat now is one of *credit risk*, the risk that the counterparty will fail to perform its side of the contract and the firm will suffer a loss when replacing the swap under disadvantageous conditions.

These two aspects of swap risk are not additive; total swap risk is not the sum of market risk and credit risk. If the firm using a swap to speculate on lower short-term rates gets worried about market risk because it is losing money, it is not likely to be concerned with the credit risk of the counterparty. If the swap is a liability to one party, it must be an asset to the other. Therefore, market risk and credit risk, as mirror images of the same process, are inversely related. Also, swap risk can depend on the motivation for the swap. A firm that is truly hedging is not concerned with market risk, only default risk. If the MTM value of the swap moves against the firm, the firm will gain elsewhere on the balance sheet or income statement; that is the essential nature of a hedge.

This chapter outlines the myriad risks that anyone contracting in the swap market is likely to face. Consistent with the attention swap credit risk attracts from participants and regulators, the discussion begins with an analysis of this dimension, including the current methods for measuring it, as well as how it is handled in practice. We next adopt the perspective of a corporation using swaps to hedge an interest rate or currency exposure and examine the additional sources of uncertainty, including the significant *enterprise, accounting,* and *tax* risks that must be analyzed when structuring a swap transaction. Even after these elements are accounted for, however, there is usually some *basis* risk that cannot be hedged away. We conclude with a discussion of the special risks swap dealers face, including those associated with hedging their swap books and the vagaries of the legal system.

Swap Credit Risk

Default risk on swap transactions has two dimensions. *Potential* credit risk, which involves an assessment of future interest and FX rates and the likelihood that the counterparty will default in those environments, is inherently *bilateral.* That is, depending on future market conditions, either participant to an agreement could be hurt by the default of the counterparty. This possibility is of practical concern for banks that make markets in swaps, because they cannot require the same set of restrictive covenants as they might on a loan document. Negotiations over swap documentation are more on a "level playing field" than a typical debt agreement is. In the extreme, a strong corporation might refuse to enter a swap with a lower rated commercial bank that lends it money.

Actual credit risk is the loss, in present value terms, that a participant would suffer if its counterparty defaulted now. In this regard, an event of default is not limited to the nonpayment of an owed amount. For example, a common inclusion in a swap document is a *cross-default clause,* which brings the contract to early termination if a third party files bankruptcy proceedings against the distressed firm. Actual credit risk, which is simply the MTM value of the swap, is based on the current fixed rate for a replacement swap having the same remaining tenor, settlement dates, and reference rate. At origination, actual credit risk is zero on an at-market swap because no initial payment is made. After origination, however, the MTM amount will become positive or negative as market-fixed rates change over time. Therefore, actual credit risk is always *unilateral* in that a swap is a "zero-sum" game. One side's loss is the other side's gain, so the swap can have positive MTM value to only one counterparty at a time.

Measuring Actual Credit Risk. Suppose that one year ago a corporation agreed to pay the fixed offer rate of 7.05 percent (against three-month LIBOR) to a swap dealer on a three-year, quarterly settlement contract with a notional principal of \$50 million. Now, with exactly two years remaining on the agreement, the firm defaults on its remaining obligations. To measure its loss, the dealer will use the average quoted market rates from a number of other dealers. These quoted rates represent the fixed rates the other dealers would be willing to pay to receive LIBOR. The idea is that if the dealer truly had to replace the defaulted swap, it would have to transact at the prevailing market rate. Assume that the average of the other dealers' quoted bid rates is 6.13 percent quoted on a 30/360 day-count basis to match the original transaction. The default loss to the dealer will be the present value of an eight-period annuity of \$115,000 a period, calculated as

$$(7.05\% - 6.13\%) \times \left(\frac{90}{360}\right) \times \$50{,}000{,}000 = \$115{,}000.$$

By having to receive a lower fixed rate on the new swap than on the original contract, the dealer will be losing the equivalent of \$115,000 each quarter, no matter what LIBOR happens to be. In fact, notice that the difference in these two swap fixed rates is what matters, not current LIBOR. Current LIBOR, as the anchor to the forward curve, is merely part of the 6.13 percent replacement swap fixed rate.

Calculating the present value of that annuity requires the selection of a discount factor. In presenting the default loss to the bankruptcy court, the dealer would like as large a dollar amount as can be justified and so would argue for low discount rates, perhaps the dealer's own cost of borrowed funds or perhaps using different zero-coupon rates for each settlement date. Using the new swap fixed rate of 6.13 percent, the present value of the loss is found to be \$859,664, or

$$\sum_{t=1}^{8} \frac{\$115{,}000}{(1 + 0.0613/4)^t} = \$859{,}664.$$

Notice that this loss is a small fraction, just 1.72 percent, of the \$50 million transaction amount, which highlights the point that the notional principal is a very misleading summary statistic for default risk.

Clearly, the dealer (i.e., the receive-fixed party) will suffer a loss if the corporation defaults when the replacement swap rate is below 7.05 percent. Suppose, however, the default occurs when the two-year swap fixed rate is above 7.05 percent, say at 8.13 percent. The MTM value of the swap to the dealer at that time would be a *negative* \$987,556. The present value of the loss per period is

$$(7.05\% - 8.13\%) \times \left(\frac{90}{360}\right) \times \$50{,}000{,}000 = \$135{,}000,$$

so that

$$\sum_{t=1}^{8} \frac{-\$135{,}000}{(1 + 0.0813/4)^t} = -\$987{,}556.$$

The swap in this environment is an asset to the corporation and a liability to the dealer, meaning that the dealer's actual credit exposure to the firm is effectively zero. What happens if the corporation goes into default, whether or not it has missed a payment to the dealer? Will the dealer have to pay the corporation the MTM value? The answers to these questions depend on the termination clause specified in the swap documentation. The two standard alternatives in the ISDA document are (1) *limited* two-way settlements, which would not allow the defaulting party to receive a net settlement payment upon termination if the value of the swap is determined to be in its favor, or (2) *full* two-way settlements, which require the nondefaulting party to make a termination payment if the value of the swap favors the defaulting party.

Until recently, limited two-way settlement has been the norm for the swap market. Under this system, the dealer would not have to pay the corporation anything if the event of default occurred when the swap fixed rate had risen to 8.13 percent. With full two-way settlement, the dealer would pay the corporation $987,556, the MTM value of the swap. In current practice, the industry recommends full two-way settlement in the context of a single master agreement for all derivative transactions. In July 1993, the Group of Thirty, a financial services industry committee chaired by Paul Volcker, published a set of recommendations for dealers and end users of derivatives, including Recommendation 13:

> Dealers and end-users are encouraged to use one master agreement as widely as possible with each counterparty to document existing and future derivatives transactions, including foreign exchange forwards and options. Master agreements should provide for payments netting and close-out netting, using a full two-way payments approach.

Putting all transactions under one agreement is intended to eliminate "cherry-picking," which is the deliberate selection of transactions to default on (i.e., those with negative values) and not to default on (i.e., those with positive values). *Close-out netting* means that the mark-to-market value of all positions held by the defaulting party are calculated using market quotations. Those are added up, including all positive and negative amounts, with any accrued interest or settlement payments due added in as well. Under full two-way settlement, this net amount, if positive to the defaulting party, is paid by the nondefaulter; if negative, it is paid by the defaulter. If the defaulting firm is insolvent, the owed party becomes a general unsecured claimant, unless the swap agreement was initially collateralized. The reason for recommending full two-way settlement is to make the value of the ultimate net position under the single master agreement more certain and to avoid costly litigation. Limited two-way settlement tends to discourage (and postpone) default, creating uncertainty about the ultimate resolution of the problem. Note that eliminating limited two-way settlements might also have the effects of excluding lower rated firms from accessing the swap market and of promoting the use of collateral.

Measuring Potential Credit Risk. Swap market makers must calculate their potential credit risk to be sure they are holding sufficient loss reserves. Unlike actual credit risk, which can be accurately measured given current market conditions, potential default risk is simply an estimate of the MTM exposure that *might* occur in the future if the counterparty defaults at some later date. Therefore, potential, or *fractional*, exposure depends on both the financial distress of the counterparty and an adverse movement in interest rates since origination. The potential credit risk calculation is often done using *Monte Carlo simulation,* an empirical technique of running thousands of randomly selected rate scenarios, calculating the MTM value associated with each one, and then compiling the outcomes. For any given settlement date in the future, potential exposure can then be measured as either the average or the "worst case" (e.g., the 95th percentile) of the random MTM outcomes. The potential credit risk for the entire swap is simply the largest of the settlement-date-specific exposures.

Figure 5.1 illustrates potential credit risk on five-year and ten-year swaps for typical assumptions about interest rate movements. Notice that the point of maximum loss occurs on a settlement date in the middle of the swap's life. This pattern results from two offsetting factors: the number of remaining settlements, which obviously goes down as time passes, and the possibility that the current swap fixed rate might go up or down as time passes, thus diverging from the original level. At origination, potential credit risk is zero, assuming an at-market swap. Just before maturity, potential credit risk is limited to the largest likely change in LIBOR times the notional principal. At intermediate dates, the potential loss is higher because multiple remaining settlements would be affected by a movement in market rates. In general, the amount of maximum exposure depends on the credit quality of the counterparty, the tenor of the swap, and the parameters chosen for the stochastic process for future rates.

As an example of the simulation process, consider the potential credit risk borne by the fixed-rate payer on a new 8 percent, five-year swap with semiannual settlement and a notional principal of $25 million at a time when the yield curve is upward sloping. Table 5.1 reports the mean and 95th percentile of the distribution of potential MTM exposures based on 2,000 randomly generated interest rate paths for each of the ten future settlement dates.[1] Two facts from this table support the previous analysis. First, even under the worst-case scenario, the potential estimated default loss on the swap is a small fraction of the $25 million notional principal. Second, this fractional exposure reaches its maximum of 2.20 percent on the fourth settlement date (i.e., two years into the life of the agreement).

Figure 5.1 The Potential Credit Risk Profile of an Interest Rate Swap

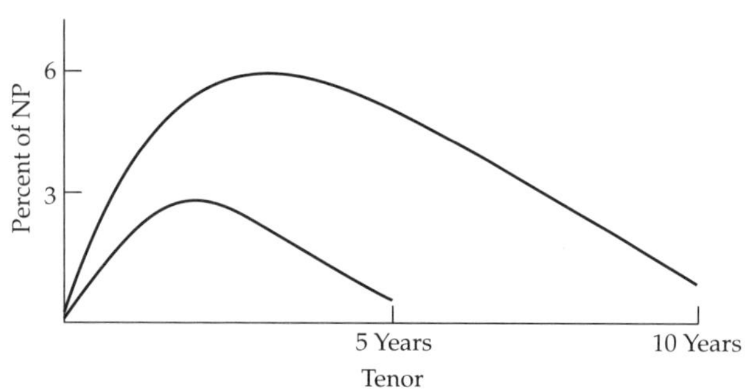

[1] Specifically, this simulation assumed that changes in the original swap fixed rate would follow a mean-reverting stochastic process of the form $dr = a(b - r)dt + \sigma[r]^{1/2}dz$, with the parameters a = 0.2, b = 8.50 percent (i.e., the long-term trend rate), σ = 0.01, t = the number of settlement periods into the future, and dz generated as a standard normal random variable. For each of the 2,000 projected rates corresponding to a particular settlement date, the MTM value of the swap was calculated and set equal to zero if negative (i.e., if the swap was a liability to the pay-fixed position).

Table 5.1 Estimating Potential Credit Risk: Monte Carlo Simulation Results

	Average		95th Percentile	
Settlement Date	Exposure	Percent of NP[a]	Exposure	Percent of NP[a]
0.5 years	$102,233	0.41%	$344,142	1.38%
1.0	145,840	0.58	485,947	1.94
1.5	156,974	0.63	520,676	2.08
2.0	181,753	0.73	549,996	2.20
2.5	182,737	0.73	548,107	2.19
3.0	176,666	0.71	505,915	2.02
3.5	146,560	0.59	419,028	1.68
4.0	110,726	0.44	309,742	1.24
4.5	63,470	0.25	172,304	0.69
5.0	0	0.00	0	0.00

[a]NP = Notional principal.

A key reason for the diminution of potential credit risk on an interest rate swap as maturity nears is the absence of any exchange of principal. In contrast, the presence of such an exchange on plain vanilla cross-currency swap contracts dramatically alters the time profile of credit risk in that it peaks at the maturity date and at a much greater percentage of the principal amount. Another, more technical factor concerns the assumed stochastic process that drives the volatility. Many processes for interest rates, such as the one governing the preceding example, assume *mean reversion*, implying a tendency for rates to move toward some long-term average. Thus, if market forces keep interest rates from moving too much, the potential exposure on the swap is muted. In a currency swap, however, mean reversion in nominal FX rates is not an obvious assumption. Consequently, extensive changes in FX rates over the lifetime of the currency swap can lead to a large amount of credit risk on the maturity date when the principal re-exchange is to be made.

This discussion underscores yet another risk to swap management: *model risk*. Theoretical models are used in a number of ways in derivatives operations, from pricing the swaps to figuring out how to hedge them to calculating default loss. The risk is that the model is wrong, that the assumptions implicit in the model turn out not to hold. For example, theoretical valuation models often assume continuous trading without any large or discrete jumps in prices from day to day. These models can break down in times of illiquidity and market disruption. As another example, recognize that mean reversion in interest rates is really a political assumption. That is, it presumes that the government and central bank have the ability and, more importantly, the will to do what is necessary to keep inflation under control (e.g., by allowing a recession to drive unemployment rates up). Although economic conditions alone might suggest mean reversion in real rates, mean reversion in nominal rates has a political context. The risk to the swap dealer, therefore, is that the reserves held for default loss turn out to be inadequate.

Adjusting Swap Pricing for Credit Risk. Broadly speaking, swap dealers manage credit risk either by pricing it into the bid–offer spread or with credit enhancements. Other things being equal, the dealer would pay a lower, or receive a higher, fixed rate on an unsecured swap the greater the credit risk of the counterparty. Alternatively, instead of adjusting the bid–offer spread, the dealer could require that the counterparty either have a certain credit rating or provide equivalent assurance through a letter of credit or by posting collateral. Some swap contracts limit the amount of MTM value, and hence credit risk, that can build up over time. When that threshold is reached, a termination clause is triggered and the swap is closed out at the MTM value.

The credit adjustment to the bid–offer spread will depend on several factors, including the credit quality of the dealer, the credit quality of the counterparty, and the shape of the yield curve. When the dealer is the stronger party, the bid–offer spread will widen. Because potential credit risk is bilateral, the bid–offer spread would have to narrow for a weaker dealer to transact with a stronger counterparty. In practice, the supranationals and the strongest corporations tend to limit their swap activity to include only the strongest dealers. To gain access to that market, a number of investment banks have set up special-purpose swap subsidiaries that are sufficiently capitalized and possess sufficient "firewalls" to warrant a AAA rating.

To see why the shape of the yield curve matters in the credit-adjustment process, consider again a pay-fixed swap in an upwardly sloped yield curve environment. The swap fixed rate will be an average of the forward curve. During the first half of the swap's life, this side of the deal would have negative MTM values because the fixed-payer is paying a higher rate than on the comparable FRAs or futures (hence a "negative carry"). The second half would then have positive values, which implies credit risk. So, under these conditions, potential credit risk on a pay-fixed swap is "back-loaded," or concentrated in the last half of the tenor. The opposite result holds for receive-fixed swaps; concern over credit risk is focused in the first half. Given that the ability to assess financial distress in the counterparty is more difficult the more distant the horizon, potential credit risk would be greater when paying the fixed rate than when receiving it when the forward curve slopes up.

The opposite conclusion can be drawn, of course, when the curve is downward sloping.

The risk adjustment around the theoretical value extracted from the forward curve need not be symmetric. In a steep yield curve setting, the market maker would want a larger adjustment on the bid side than the offer side. Suppose the present value average of the forward curve is 7.55 percent. The bid–offer spread in a rising yield curve market might be 7.51 percent bid and 7.57 percent offered. In an inverted yield curve market generating the same theoretical midpoint, however, the pricing might be 7.53 percent bid and 7.59 percent offered. Notice that we have once again made this argument without regard to expectations about future rates. We have based it on the arbitrage-free method of pricing and the idea that credit risk is an increasing function of the time to maturity. Thus, the result should hold whether or not LIBOR is expected to rise in line with prices on a corresponding strip of Eurodollar futures contracts.

Figure 5.2 illustrates the credit risk adjustment from the perspective of an A-rated swap dealer paying the fixed rate to BBB-rated, A-rated, and AA-rated counterparties in rising, flat, and inverted yield curve environments. With a flat yield curve, a swap with the equally creditworthy counterparty would not be adjusted. When the counterparty is better than A-rated, the dealer would pay a higher fixed rate (about 5 basis points in the diagram). When the curve is upward sloping, the dealer, as payer of the fixed rate, views its credit risk as greater than that of its counterparty, so it reduces its bid fixed rate. If the yield curve is inverted, the dealer is willing to pay a higher rate because the credit risk problem is not back-loaded as it is when the curve is rising.

End-User Swap Risk

In addition to market and credit risks, which all swap participants confront to varying degrees, end users face additional risks that must be analyzed when evaluating the quality of any particular swap-related transaction. The most important of these are measurement risk, basis risk, and accounting risk.

Measurement Risk. Consider a nonfinancial corporation that has the stylized balance sheet portrayed in Figure 5.3. Its assets consist of cash, inventory, and plant and equipment, which are funded by short-term and floating-rate debt; long-term, fixed-rate debt; and equity. Given our risk-management focus, the liabilities have been grouped by duration, rather than maturity. In that regard, recall that long-term, floating-rate notes have low implied-duration statistics and, therefore, have more in common with short-term debt than with long-term, fixed-rate bonds. (See the appendix for further discussion of duration.)

Is this corporation exposed to rising or falling interest rates? Looking only at the liabilities, an easy conclusion would be that rising interest rates will lead to a higher cost of funds. If the corporate treasury is operated as a cost center, management would certainly conclude that the exposure is to higher rates. That perspective can be limiting, however. From an *enterprise* point of

Figure 5.2 Credit Adjustments to the Bid–Offer Spread

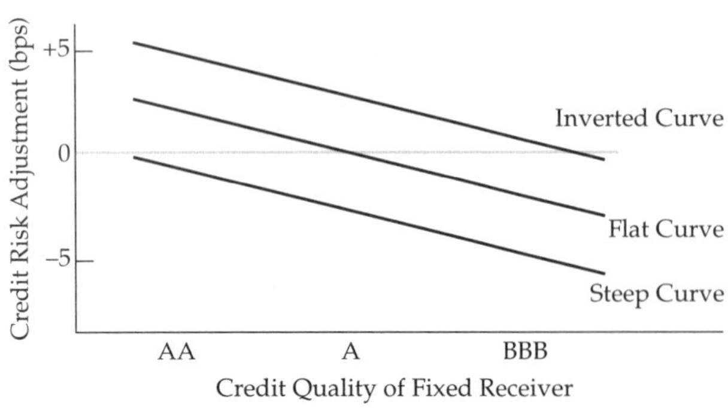

Source: Sorensen and Bollier (1994)

Figure 5.3 A Stylized Balance Sheet for a Nonfinancial Corporation

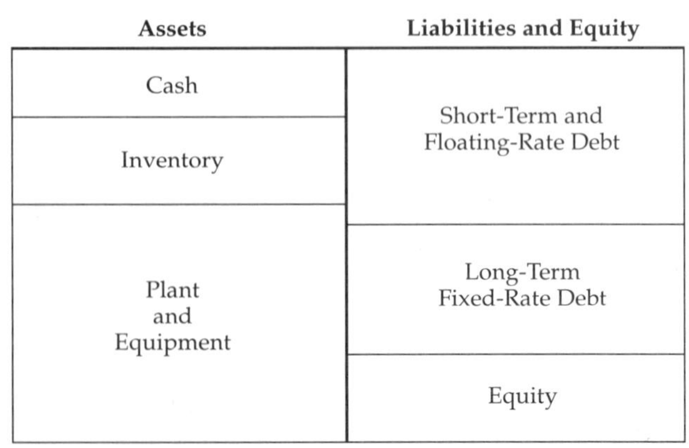

view, the interest sensitivity of the revenues must be considered along with the expenses. Suppose that the corporation's net revenues are positively correlated to interest rates because each is driven by inflation. Then, higher commodity prices that raise operating revenues might fully compensate the firm for higher interest rates that raise the cost of short-term and floating-rate debt. In that case, the corporation already is *internally hedged* against interest rate risk.

A common problem in corporate risk management is measuring the extent of the exposure itself. Suppose the corporate treasurer, given the myopic perspective of debt management alone, were to enter a pay-fixed swap to hedge the firm's apparent exposure to higher rates. By ignoring the revenue side of its operations, the firm could end up overhedged, effectively speculating on higher rates. Although evaluating risk on an enterprise basis might be the proper thing to do, it is quite difficult to implement in practice. The interest sensitivity of revenues to interest rates might not be stable over time. Rather, it might depend on the pricing strategies of competitors and the reason *why* interest rates have changed. Revenues might rise if rates increase because of inflation but fall with higher real (i.e., inflation-adjusted) rates.

The measurement problem also arises with foreign exchange and commodity prices, especially when considering what is known as *strategic* risk management. Suppose this corporation's operations are entirely based in U.S. dollars and its major competitor is a foreign firm entirely based in Canadian dollars. From a strategic point of view, the corporation can be exposed to the CAD/USD exchange rate even though it never has a transaction in Canadian dollars. The reason is that a favorable swing in the FX rate to the competitor can worsen the corporation's market share and profits. The same could hold for commodity price exposure if, say, the competitor's technology makes it very dependent on hydroelectric energy prices and the corporation's technology does not. Again, the corporation's share price could be correlated to a variable in which it does not itself transact.

These examples illustrate one thing that can go wrong with the use of any derivative contract: It could be the right solution to the wrong problem. Unless risk has been correctly measured, the correct hedging program is quite difficult to put together. Some risks are themselves correlated to other risks; for instance, commodity prices, FX rates, and interest rates are all connected by inflation. This correlation suggests that overall financial risk should be measured by the *covariances,* as well as the variances, of prices and rates. Although viewing risk from a full balance sheet perspective, including its strategic dimension, might be elegant in theory, accounting and tax considerations often force a manager to treat risk on a transaction-by-transaction basis. Thus, what is hedging and what is speculation often turns out to be a gray area, yet that designation can matter a great deal in how industry analysts, regulators, and even the corporation's shareholders view the outcome of the swap.

Basis Risk. Returning to the balance sheet in Figure 5.3, suppose the corporation's operating revenues are not correlated at all with market interest rates so that the firm is unambiguously exposed to an upward shift in the yield curve. Assume further that its short-term debt is largely commercial paper (CP). The CP is issued regularly with maturities of 30 to 90 days depending on market conditions and the corporate treasurer's view on future rates. Concerned with higher rates brought on by tightening monetary policy, the treasurer has already lengthened maturities as much as the CP market will allow. To lengthen the average maturity of debt even more, the treasurer decides to pay the fixed rate on a three-year interest rate swap. The nature of the problem and the swap solution can be laid out in a matrix, as below, to highlight the fact that the payoffs on the hedge product must be negatively correlated with the underlying exposure.

Event	*Exposure (Issue CP)*	*Hedge (Pay-Fixed Swap)*
Rates Rise	Lose	Gain
Rates Fall	Gain	Lose

Assume that a swap dealer offers the corporation the two alternatives for the swap shown in Figure 5.4. In the LIBOR-based hedge, the corporation would pay 7.05 percent fixed for three years and receive LIBOR flat. (This plain vanilla transaction is the same as that used in the actual credit risk example above.) Alternatively, the corporation could pay 6.75 percent fixed and receive a cash flow tied to a CP index based on a set of A1/P1-rated issuers. The treasurer expects the spread between LIBOR and the CP index to average 30 basis points during the next three years; if not, a clear preference would exist between the swap structures. Notice that in neither case would the cost of funds be constant over the three years. In the first deal, the all-in rate each period will vary with the difference between LIBOR and the corporation's CP rate. In the second, the all-in rate depends on the difference between the industrywide CP index and the firm-specific CP rate.

Figure 5.4 Pay-Fixed Swap Alternatives

A LIBOR-Based Hedge

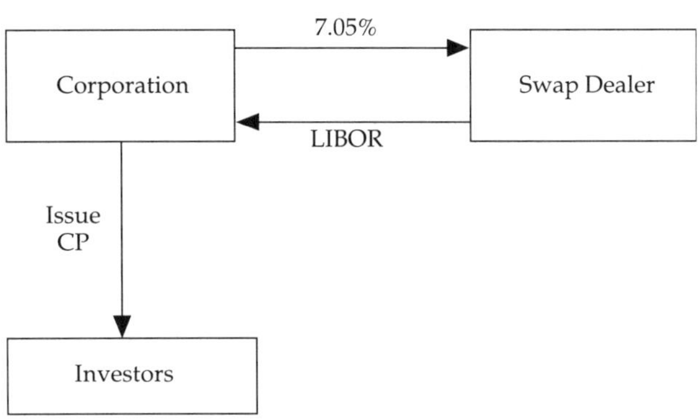

Cost of Funds: 7.05% – (LIBOR – CP Rate)

A CP-Based Hedge

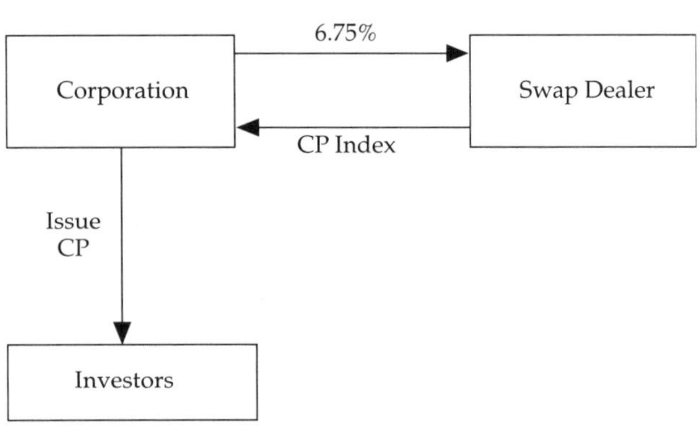

Cost of Funds: 6.75% – (CP Index – CP Rate)

The treasurer's choice between the two alternatives will likely turn on the perceived trade-off between the better liquidity of the LIBOR swap versus the lesser basis risk of the CP index swap. In this context, basis risk arises from the extent to which the firm's own CP rate does not track perfectly the floating reference rate on the swap. Because LIBOR picks up bank risk and the CP index picks up nonbank corporate risk, the plain vanilla swap presumably would have the greater degree of basis risk. If, however, the treasurer foresees the possibility of unwinding the swap prior to maturity, perhaps because his or her view on market conditions might change, the LIBOR swap might be preferred because the market in this structure is the deeper of the two. Assuming that the treasurer chooses the LIBOR-based transaction, another element that could go wrong with the swap is that the corporation's own CP rate might increase much more than LIBOR. This eventuality would raise the cost of funds more than expected and render the swap a less effective hedge.

Accounting Risk. Table 5.2 presents a numerical example of how the preceding hedge is supposed to work for the corporation. The example assumes that the CP rate, LIBOR, and the swap fixed rate are all converted to the same conventions and that the LIBOR–CP spread is 30 basis points. Regardless of the actual level of market rates, the all-in cost of funds is shown to be 6.75 percent, the sum of the interest expense on the CP and the net settlement on the swap. This formulation ignores the accounting treatment of the payments, however.

The implicit assumption in the numerical example is the application of *hedge accounting*. If hedge accounting applies, the two transac-

Table 5.2 A Numerical Example of the Hedge

CP Rate	LIBOR	Net Payment on Swap[a]	All-in Cost of Funds[b]
4.70%	5.00%	2.05%	6.75%
5.70	6.00	1.05	6.75
6.70	7.00	0.05	6.75
7.70	8.00	−0.95	6.75
8.70	9.00	−1.95	6.75

[a]Net payment of swap = 7.05 percent − LIBOR.
[b]All-in cost of funds = CP rate + net payment of swap.

tions—the interest payments on the CP and the net settlements on the swap—are effectively combined. The reported interest expense for the period would be 6.75 percent times the principal. The benefit of this arrangement is that the swap would not be marked to market on the current year's financial statement because the underlying CP liability is carried at book value. Therefore, gains or losses represented by the MTM value are deferred until any subsequent transaction is actually made.

If hedge accounting does not apply, the MTM value of the swap would have to be recognized even though such gains or losses are unrealized in the current period. That recognition could lead to more volatility in the firm's financial statements than the economics of the transaction warrant. So, when the swap is used for hedging, the appropriate accounting treatment is hedge accounting. If the swap is speculative, the appropriate treatment would be to mark the position to its market value. Consequently, the distinction between hedging and speculation matters, even if they are often difficult to distinguish. The current criteria for hedge accounting generally include:

- Designation of the swap as a hedge to a particular transaction at the time of initiation. This practice prevents a firm from sorting through its positions at the end of a year to manipulate reported income by identifying some swaps as hedges and others as not hedges.
- Commitment to a future transaction that must represent a bona fide risk. This commitment is to prevent the deferral of swap losses on what are no more than vague intentions to transact in the future.
- Correlation between the exposed position and the hedge product. Typically the correlation must be on the order of 80 percent.

Now reconsider the LIBOR-based, pay-fixed swap to hedge the corporation's exposure to higher future CP rates. Will it qualify for hedge accounting? Most likely it will, but with a couple of potential problems. First, is the firm a regular issuer of CP or new to the market? This distinction would not be a problem if the swap were attached to an FRN that pays coupons tied to a CP Index. It could be a problem, though, if this transaction were a forward swap structured around a view of current low rates but higher future rates. Second, what is the degree of correlation? Clearly, this question is an empirical one that can depend on the time frame of the data series and whether it is *ex post* or *ex ante* correlation that matters. Suppose a firm hedges FX risk exposure to one currency with another to which it is pegged for political reasons (e.g., the British pound and the deutschemark prior to September 1992). Should hedge accounting still apply if for some reason the currencies become delinked, as when Britain exited the Exchange Rate Mechanism?

Accounting risk arises from uncertainty over the treatment that the swap will get from its outside auditors or from the regulators. A historical problem has been that some instruments have guidelines (mostly dealing with FX risk) and others do not. Some rules, such as the fact that the deferral of gains and losses is intended for legitimate hedges and not speculative positions, have been clear, but the rules for hedge accounting are tremendously ambiguous, with different standards and treatments for FX and interest rate risk, as well as for hedging with futures, swaps, and options. Further complicating these matters is a growing movement within the accounting profession to eliminate hedge accounting treatment altogether. Such a change in practice would force firms to mark all positions to market regardless of their intended use.

Tax Risk. A risk-management strategy must work on both a pretax and after-tax basis. In practice, this condition requires a *timing* match, a *character* match, and a *sourcing* match for the cash flows (or MTM values) on the underlying exposure and the hedge product. In this setting, timing is a matter of whether the cash flows correspond to the current tax period or are deferred to a future period, character is whether the income or expense (or change in MTM value) is treated as an ordinary or capital gain or loss, and sourcing refers to whether the income or expense is treated as domestic or foreign.

In recent years, there has been a great deal of uncertainty about possible character mismatches that could seriously undermine the efficiency of many risk-management strategies. This uncertainty arose from the Internal Revenue Service's application of the Supreme Court's ruling in the 1988 Arkansas Best case (*Arkansas Best Corporation* v. *Commissioner of Internal Revenue*) and in several well-publicized audits and tax court cases, notably against the Federal National Mortgage Association. The Supreme Court ruled that Section 1221 of the IRS Code clearly states that all property used in the course of doing business is to be regarded as capital, with five specific exceptions (including accounts receivable and inventory) that give rise to ordinary income and expense.

Based on that ruling, the IRS argued that the net cash flows on most positions in derivatives should be treated as capital gains and losses. Even if the firm was hedging what is an ordinary expense, the swap or futures contract would be a capital asset because it did not fall among the five exceptions. Under this interpretation, a classic liability hedge—using a pay-fixed interest rate swap to transform floating-rate debt—would have a character mismatch in that the settlement payments on the swap would be capital and the interest expense on the floating-rate debt ordinary. Returning to the numerical example in Table 5.2, the problem is that the CP rate is ordinary interest expense but the net payment on the swap is a capital loss when LIBOR is less than 7.05 percent and a capital gain when LIBOR is above 7.05 percent. Only ordinary losses are deductible against ordinary income. Capital losses are deductible only to the extent that capital gains exist and the timing of carry-forwards and carry-backs is limited.

This tax risk was immense in the early 1990s. The risk hanging over many corporations that had actively used derivatives in risk management was that the IRS would retroactively characterize reported losses during an audit of an open tax year. Fortunately for corporate end users of derivative products, the tax court ruled unanimously (16-0) against the IRS in the Fannie Mae case. In October 1993, the Service announced it was revising its litigating position with respect to Arkansas Best and in 1994 issued new rules clarifying the character treatment of derivatives. Many tax issues remain unresolved, however, so tax treatment has not completely gone away as a source of risk on a swap transaction.

Dealer Swap Risk

Although the market maker can be viewed as just another corporate participant in the swap market and therefore subject to all of the exposures listed above, some additional risks come with managing a swap book.

Managing Swap Market Risk With Futures. In an earlier example, the dealer agreed to receive the fixed rate of 7.05 percent on a three-year swap from a corporate counterparty. Immediately upon selling this swap, the dealer would be exposed to increases in swap fixed rates, which determine the MTM value of its newly acquired position. The dealer could, of course, do nothing and simply speculate that swap rates will fall, but the more likely event is that the open position will be covered. In practice, large swap market makers use a portfolio approach to book management, meaning that individual swaps are not separately hedged. Rather, each new contract merely contributes to the portfolio's overall duration and convexity characteristics. Depending on the degree of aggregation (i.e., if products such as FRAs, swaps, caps, and floors are all combined), the residual risk of the swap book then will be hedged as its own entity. To draw attention to additional sources of risk, though, we assume that the dealer hedges this particular three-year, receive-fixed swap using Eurodollar futures contracts.

As noted, the dealer's market risk is that the swap fixed rates will rise, rendering 7.05 percent a below-market, fixed-rate receipt for payment of LIBOR. Notice that we avoid saying that the risk involved in this transaction is that current LIBOR goes up. The market risk is exposure to movement in the entire forward curve, not just to its end point. To hedge this exposure, the dealer sells Eurodollar futures contracts, because higher futures rates will equate to lower futures prices. (Recall from the discussion of these instruments in Chapter 4 that the futures price index is 100 minus the futures rate and that the seller gains $25 a contract per basis point increase.) Figure 5.5 illustrates the dealer's hedge position.

Figure 5.5 Dealer's Hedge Using Eurodollar Futures

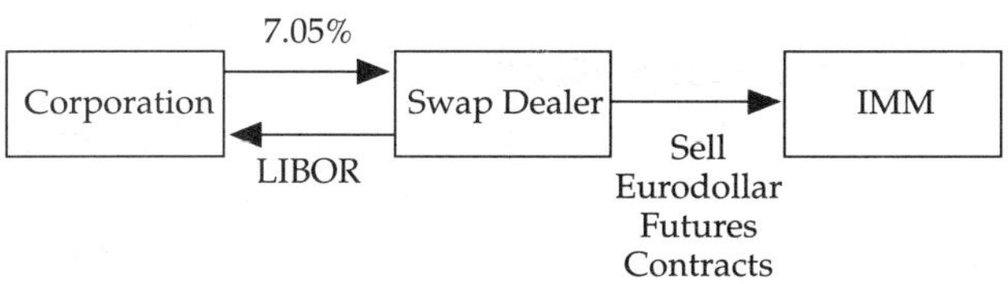

The dealer has to make a number of decisions beyond deciding to go short, such as which contract month and how many. A major decision is whether to use a *strip hedge* or a *stack hedge*. With the former, the dealer would sell the requisite number of contracts for all the delivery dates corresponding to the settlement dates of the swap. With the latter, the dealer "stacks up" all the contracts on the nearest few delivery dates. This decision would be based on the trade-off of greater liquidity (as measured by open interest) in the nearer-to-delivery contracts against greater basis risk. The basis risk of a stack hedge derives from the chance of a nonparallel shift of the yield curve.

The effectiveness of the strip versus stack hedge is illustrated in Figure 5.6. The original swap fixed rate is the present value average of the original forward curve (plus the dealer's offer spread). Additionally, the figure shows two new forward curves, one representing a parallel shift and the other a steepened curve. Notice that the new swap fixed rate—and the amount of loss in MTM value—is the same for either shift. If the parallel shift prevails, both hedges would work equally well because all futures rates rise by the same amount. If the forward curve steepens, the strip hedge would still work because of gains on the distant delivery dates but the stack hedge would fail because it is located entirely at the near end of the curve, which did not move much. Not shown is an inversion in the forward curve whereby the near-term rates rise dramatically; in this case, the stack hedge would overperform and more than cover the loss on the swap. Essentially, the decision to use a stack hedge becomes a bet on the likelihood of a nonparallel shift in the forward curve. Sometimes, this exposure is unavoidable because, for example, in most non-USD currencies, futures contracts do not offer delivery dates much beyond one year.

Figure 5.6 Hedging the Swap with a Futures Strip or Futures Stack

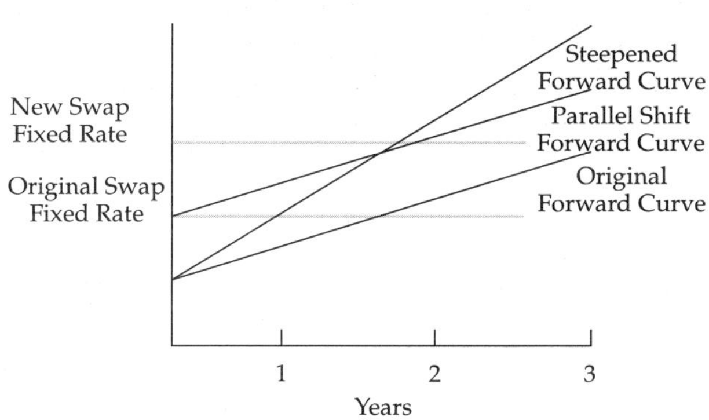

Assuming the dealer chooses the strip hedge, the issue of determining the number of contracts for each delivery date remains. Suppose the swap is for quarterly settlement and a notional principal of \$50 million. Selling 50 futures contracts for each delivery date, each for \$1 million, would lead to overhedging, because the gains and losses on the hedge would be realized each day while the gains and losses on the swap would remain unrealized until the settlement date. This overhedging can be remedied by tailing the hedge ratio. In effect, tailing the ratio is accomplished by selling the present value of the "untailed" number of contracts. If the three-year interest rate is 7.25 percent, the dealer would sell only 40 or 41 contracts for delivery in three years ($50/1.0725^3 = 40.5$). The idea is that gains on the hedge as rates rise can be invested while losses as rates fall need to be funded. The amount to be invested or borrowed should be the present value of the amount eventually needed. Tailing the hedge corrects for the time value of money.

Another source of risk in swap book management using futures contracts concerns the actual investment or funding rate compared with the assumed rate that is used to calculate the tailed hedge. Notice that the seller of the futures contracts is in a propitious position. The assumed rate is 7.25 percent, but if market rates rise, the short position benefits from daily settlement, given that the chances are good that the receipts can be invested at a rate above 7.25 percent. Moreover, if market rates fall, the short might be able to fund the losses at a rate below 7.25 percent. Thus, if rates move in either direction, the short hedge stands to benefit. Because futures are a zero-sum game, a systematic bias in favor of the short position must imply a systematic bias against the long position. Indeed, the buyer of the Eurodollar futures contract gains if prices rise (and rates fall) and loses if prices fall (and rates rise). The buyer, therefore, gets to invest gains into the low-rate environment but must fund losses when rates have gone up. This phenomenon is called the *convexity of the tail.*

The convexity-of-the-tail problem becomes an issue in pricing swaps, as well as in hedging them. Recall that a swap can be viewed as a series of FRAs; in fact, one source of the forward curve in pricing swaps is the observed fixed rates on FRAs. In Chapter 4, we saw that FRAs are priced around the futures rates that are used to hedge the positions. On some *long-dated* FRAs, however, the systematic bias toward the short hedge and against the long hedge becomes a factor in pricing. This bias is illustrated in Figure 5.7. The bid–offer spread is shown to widen at more distant delivery dates for several reasons, including the greater difficulty in assessing credit risk, the operational costs of managing the hedges for longer time periods, and the inherent risks of managing long-term positions (e.g., adverse regulatory, legal, or accounting rulings). The midpoint of the bid–offer spread also diverges from the futures rate for more distant FRAs. The bid rate would come down because the required hedge would be the adversely affected long positions. Recognizing that fact, the dealer is willing to pay only a lower fixed rate than otherwise. The offer rate would come down because of competition, because the dealer in a competitive market might be forced to share with the counterparty some of the favorable circumstance of hedging the position by selling Eurodollar futures. In practice, this convexity-of-the-tail effect appears to be small, with the midpoint of the FRAs maturing beyond three years tending to be anywhere from 5 to 15 basis points below the corresponding futures rate. Nevertheless, neglecting to deal with tailing and the convexity issue would lead to swap mispricing, which itself would be a source of business risk.

Figure 5.7 Implication of the Convexity of the Tail on the Pricing of Long-Dated FRAs Off of Eurodollar Futures

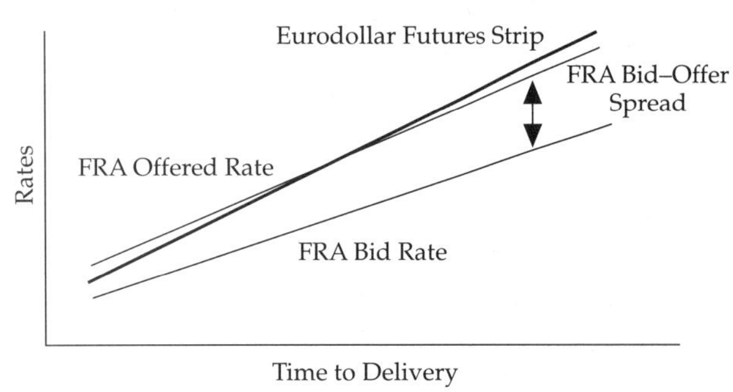

Managing Swap Market Risk in the Cash Market. Suppose the swap dealer chooses to hedge the market risk following the sale of the three-year swap by using the cash market in Treasury notes, a situation that might arise if no Eurodollar futures market exists in which to lay off the risk of an upward move in market rates. The alternative hedge would be to sell three-year Treasury notes to a government securities dealer. The proceeds from this short sale would likely be invested in the overnight repo (i.e., sale–repurchase agreement) market. This hedge position is illustrated in Figure 5.8.

The idea of this hedge is that changes in the MTM value of the swap will track market movements at the three-year point of the Treasury yield curve. The short sale will produce a gain if rates rise, because the dealer would be able to buy the T-note in the cash market at a lower price to close out the position. That gain offsets the loss on the value of the swap, as shown in Figure 5.9. The original swap fixed rate is an average of the forward curve and is quoted as a spread over the three-year Treasury. Thus, when the agreement is hedged in the cash market, the swap spread becomes a source of basis risk. To the extent that any change in the swap fixed rate fully corresponds to a change in the Treasury rate, the swap spread must remain

Figure 5.8 Dealer's Hedge Using Cash Market Treasury Notes

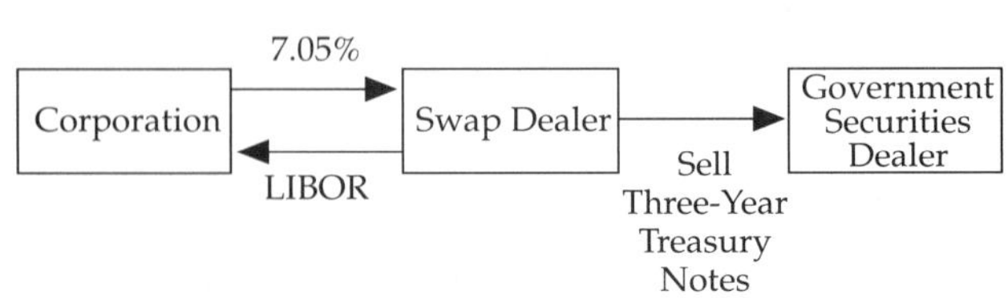

constant. The hedge fails if the source of the higher swap rate is an increase entirely in the swap spread without a commensurate move in the Treasury note. Similarly, the hedge overperforms if the swap spread falls from its original level.

Figure 5.9 Hedging the Swap in the Cash Market

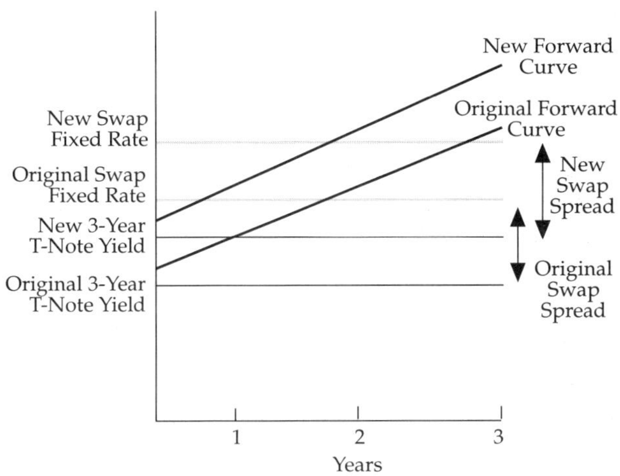

The swap spread can be broken down into two components: the average TED spread, which is the difference between LIBOR and the T-bill rate for each future settlement date; and the *coupon bias*, which is the difference between the yield on a coupon-bearing Treasury note and a zero-coupon Treasury having an equivalent maturity.[2] Forecasting the swap spread then dissolves into forecasting those variables. The coupon bias can be directly measured from the Treasury yield curve and the implied zero curve. It is larger when the Treasury yield curve is higher or steeper and the time to maturity is longer. Increases in these factors, other things being equal, should correlate with increases in observed swap spreads in the market.

Used by analysts as a barometer of market conditions, the TED spread is difficult to forecast because it is essentially picking up the credit risk differential between a money-center bank and the Treasury. The TED spread widens during "flights to quality," because investors flock to Treasuries, driving their prices up and yields down. The dealer could attempt to hedge the exposure to the swap spread itself by taking positions in the TED spread to the extent that LIBOR and T-bill futures contracts are available. If the reason for hedging in Treasuries in the first place is the absence of those contracts, however, the swap spread will remain a source of risk to the dealer in managing its book.

Legal Risk. After the events of 1994, swap risk will be impossible to discuss without addressing its legal dimension. Recent litigation involving swap transactions, most notably the *Procter & Gamble* v. *Bankers Trust* case, makes the existence of legal risk undeniable. The critical issues that all market makers must consider are the *suitability* of the transactions for their clients and *disclosure* of each deal's various risks. These can be challenging matters, even on what appear to be straightforward, plain vanilla agreements. If a corporation has difficulty in measuring its own interest rate and FX risk and, therefore, in knowing whether a particular swap moves it to a more speculative or hedged position, how can the swap dealer hope to assess suitability? How can all the risks be disclosed, particularly the tax and accounting risks, when authoritative rulings are not available?

Concern about the legal status of derivatives was heightened by the 1991 British High Court *ultra vires* ruling regarding a number of swap and options contracts transacted between banks and local authorities (notably the London borough of Hammersmith and Fulham). The local governments, although originally intending to hedge, ended up with large speculative positions. The court essentially ruled that they were not authorized to enter such contracts, thereby voiding their losses of about £500 million, even though the Bank of England had approved the original hedging strategies.

Another aspect of swap legal risk comes from a lesser known case, a 1992 Indiana State Court

[2] The swap spread is the difference between the swap fixed rate and the yield on the comparable-maturity coupon Treasury note. The swap fixed rate is the average of the LIBOR path, and the zero-coupon Treasury yield is the average of the T-bill path. The coupon bias is the difference between the yield on the coupon-bearing note and the zero-coupon note for the same maturities. After some substitution and rearrangement of terms, one gets that the swap spread can be expressed as the difference between the average LIBOR path and the T-bill path, which is simply the average TED spread plus the coupon bias.

ruling in *Brane* v. *Roth*. This case involved the management of a grain co-operative. Co-op shareholders successfully sued the manager and directors for *not* using derivatives to hedge losses following from an unexpected decline in grain prices. The court ruled that management was negligent in not adequately using grain futures to hedge the risk exposure. The co-operative's accountant had advised the directors to authorize management to use futures contracts. The directors did so, but management covered only a very small fraction of the exposure. The court also ruled that the directors had an obligation to understand hedging techniques.

Summary of Swap Risk

The risk in swap transactions is partly unavoidable and partly a reflection of their history, as short a time period as that might be. Accounting and tax risks are largely attributable to the newness of the swap market. The accounting profession moves slowly in formulating new doctrine. This deliberation is, perhaps, a matter of bureaucracy, but it also reflects the rapid pace of financial innovation in recent years. Only if an innovation persists, as interest rate and currency swaps have, will it reach the agenda of the Emerging Issues Task Force of the Financial Accounting Standards Board. As the financial and tax accounting for derivatives is clarified, some of their risk will diminish.

Market risk, however, is quite unlikely to go away. Fortunately, as different financial risks dominate at different times, swap contracts can be designed to hedge the movements of any variable price, a point emphasized in the next chapter. Conversely, credit risk is the mirror image to market risk. In this respect, the history of swaps, and in particular the practice of setting a single fixed rate to all settlement periods, impacts risk. For example, although the plain vanilla design was needed in early arbitrage transactions, it does generate more risk than would a series of fixed rates that follow the forward curve. The risk of default can be effectively managed, though, by pricing the risk into the swap fixed rate, by holding capital reserves for potential credit risk, by netting provisions under master agreements, by holding collateral, or by limiting the buildup of value before early termination is triggered.

Swap market makers face other business risks. As intermediaries in these markets, they must hedge their open positions in some manner. Whether they use futures markets or cash markets in Treasuries, some degree of basis risk will always remain. Legal risk is the latest concern to the derivatives industry. As litigation is resolved, however, both in and out of court, the swap market will emerge with a better understanding of the legal rights and responsibilities of end users and market makers.

Exercises

Exercise 5.1: A midsized regional commercial bank funds its acquisition of commercial and real estate loans mostly in the retail deposit and brokered CD (certificates of deposit) markets. Brokered CDs are large, negotiable time deposits typically purchased in the national market by institutional investors via specialized CD brokers. The bank's president is concerned with rising market rates and the higher cost of borrowed funds, particularly on its brokered CDs, which very quickly reflect changes in money market conditions. The banker decides to enter a \$50 million, three-year, 7.75 percent pay-fixed interest rate swap with a New York money-center bank as the counterparty. The reference rate is chosen to be three-month LIBOR, even though the regional bank has very few deposits tied to LIBOR. The reason for choosing this swap structure is its liquidity—should management's view on the market change, the hedge using a plain vanilla instrument can be more readily unwound than a swap tied to bank CD rates. If you were a risk-management consultant asked to make a presentation to the bank's board of directors, what specific risks to the transaction would you discuss?

Solution: You would always discuss *default risk* because swaps are credit instruments with a potential unrealized buildup of value and, therefore, credit risk. To be specific, the credit risk is that the money-center bank will default at a time when the fixed rate on a replacement swap is higher than 7.75 percent. If market swap rates are above that level, the existing transaction is an asset to the regional bank because it would be paying a below-market fixed rate for receipt of LIBOR. If the counterparty were to default, the regional bank would have to replace the swap at the higher market rate.

The *basis risk* on the swap arises from hedging an exposure to CD rates with a plain vanilla swap tied to LIBOR. The synthetic fixed rate created by attaching the swap to CDs is 7.75 percent plus the CD rate minus LIBOR. For example, if LIBOR is 6 percent and the CD rate is 5.90 percent, the all-in cost of funds would be 7.65 percent. As the difference between the rates varies, the all-in cost will vary. The risk to the bank is that its CD rate rises relative to LIBOR. Note that the CD rate is specific to this regional bank, whereas LIBOR in the swap is an average of prime money-center banks. (The swap document will specify exactly how LIBOR is to be determined).

Your presentation should cover *accounting risk*. Unless the bank marks its liabilities to market, which it probably does not, it will want hedge accounting treatment on the swap, if permissible. In that case, its reported interest expense on the CDs over the three years will be fixed, at least to the extent that the spread between LIBOR and the CD rate does not vary. If hedge accounting does not apply, the bank will have to book the mark-to-market value of the swap. Of the three criteria for hedge accounting, designation should not be a problem if the bank has its bookkeeping operations in order. The correlation between the CD rates and LIBOR is an empirical matter that can be easily tested. Given that most money market rates track closely together, the correlation is likely to be sufficiently strong. Commitment could be problematical, however. If the bank has an ongoing relationship with the CD brokers and regularly uses that market as a source of funds, hedge accounting would seem to be justified. If the bank is new to the brokered CD market, then an auditor or regulator could conceivably argue that a swap that has a tenor beyond the current accounting period is speculative because the bank has no commitment to the underlying position. The risk is that an adverse ruling could force the bank to mark the swap to market when it has a significant negative value, thereby reducing its capital adequacy ratios.

Tax risk should be mentioned as well, even though the threat of an "Arkansas Best" ruling by the IRS that would recharacterize losses on hedge positions has abated. The efficiency of the swap should be examined on both a before-tax and after-tax basis.

Exercise 5.2: Suppose that on April 15, 1987, a French corporation entered into an annual-settlement, three-year currency swap to receive 12.72 percent in U.S. dollars and to pay 14.88 percent in French francs. Suppose that the spot market exchange rate was FRF 8.4435/USD at the time, or USD 0.118433/FRF. The principal on the swap was USD 100 million, which equals FRF 844.35 million. The scheduled cash flows on the swap from the perspective of the French corporation were the following:

Date		*Receive*		*Pay*
April 15, 1988	USD	12,720,000	FRF	125,639,280
April 15, 1989		12,720,000		125,639,280
April 15, 1990		112,720,000		969,989,280

On April 15, 1988, just after the initial coupon exchange, the counterparty to the swap filed for bankruptcy. On that date, plain vanilla, two-year, fixed/fixed currency swaps were quoted by a number of dealers at 10.20 percent in dollars versus 12.78 percent in francs. The spot market exchange rate was FRF 9.4829/USD, or USD 0.105453/FRF.

(a) Calculate the mark-to-market value of the currency swap. Did the French corporation experience a loss because of the default? Assume the swap document called for limited two-way settlement.

(b) If the French corporation chose to replace the swap on April 15, 1988, and wanted to continue receiving 12.72 percent in dollars for USD 100 million in principal, what franc interest rate would it have been willing to pay? What would have been the specific cash flows on this replacement swap?

Solution:

(a) The MTM value of the swap was the present value of the dollar inflows converted to francs at the spot rate, less the present value of the franc outflows. The reduction in the dollar interest rate from 12.72 percent to 10.20 percent raised the value of the swap (and the default loss), and the reduction in the franc rate from 14.88 percent to 12.78 percent lowered the value. Adding the appreciation in the dollar relative to the franc from FRF 8.4435/USD to FRF 9.4829/USD suggests that the net effect should have been a positive MTM value. This result is confirmed by the following calculations:

$$PV_{\text{USD}} = \frac{\text{USD } 12{,}720{,}000}{1.1020} + \frac{\text{USD } 112{,}720{,}000}{(1.1020)^2} = \text{USD } 104{,}361{,}843$$

$$PV_{\text{FRF}} = \frac{\text{FRF } 125{,}639{,}280}{1.1278} + \frac{\text{FRF } 969{,}989{,}280}{(1.1278)^2} = \text{FRF } 874{,}012{,}546$$

$$\text{Value} = \frac{\text{USD } 104{,}361{,}843}{\text{USD } 0.105453/\text{FRF}} - \text{FRF } 874{,}012{,}546 = \text{FRF } 115{,}640{,}124.$$

The default by the counterparty caused the French corporation to lose FRF 115,640,124, the market value of the swap that had become an asset.

(b) The at-market, plain vanilla currency swaps that were available in the market on April 15, 1988, were priced such that the French corporation could receive a fixed rate of 10.20 percent in dollars and pay a fixed rate of 12.78 percent in francs. If the corporation wanted an off-market swap to receive 12.72 percent (an additional 252 basis points in dollars), it would need to pay a higher rate in francs. First calculate the value, in francs, of 252 basis points in dollars:

$$\frac{252 \text{ bps}}{1.1020} + \frac{252 \text{ bps}}{(1.1020)^2} = \frac{x}{1.1278} + \frac{x}{(1.1278)^2}$$

or $x = 260.7375$ bps.

The off-market swap fixed rates would be 12.72 percent in dollars versus 15.387375 percent in francs (15.387375 percent = 12.78 percent + 2.607375 percent). The principal on the swap would be USD 100 million = FRF 948,290,000.

The scheduled cash flows on the two-year swap from the perspective of the French corporation would be:

Date	*Receive*	*Pay*
April 15, 1989	USD 12,720,000	FRF 145,916,938
April 15, 1990	112,720,000	1,094,206,938

The MTM value of the currency swap can also be measured as the present value of the lost (or gained) cash flows from entering into a replacement swap at current rates. Because the remaining scheduled and replacement cash receipts are the same, the value of the swap is the difference between the payments. Those differences are FRF 20,277,658 on April 15, 1989, and FRF 124,217,658 on April 15, 1990. Discounting those amounts by 12.78 percent provides the value of the swap.

$$\text{MTM Value} = \frac{\text{FRF } 20{,}277{,}658}{1.1278} + \frac{\text{FRF } 124{,}217{,}658}{(1.1278)^2} = \text{FRF } 115{,}640{,}383.$$

Note that the value of the swap obtained by the replacement swap method is virtually identical to the more direct mark-to-market method (differing only because of rounding).

Exercise 5.3: A leasing company is in serious financial distress and is teetering on the brink of bankruptcy. Although no event of default has yet taken place, senior management is seriously considering relief under Chapter 11. At issue is the timing of the filing; the company could keep going as is for several more months, perhaps for a year or so. Management decides to hinge its timing decision on the single largest transaction on its books, an interest rate swap on which it pays a fixed rate of 7.50 percent and receives six-month LIBOR semiannually for a notional principal of $82.5 million. The swap, which was entered two years before, has exactly three years remaining. Settlement payments are based on an actual/360 day count for LIBOR and 30/360 for the fixed rate, and they are paid in arrears. The swap document specifies limited two-way settlement in event of default.

Indicate the strategy you would recommend for the company in each of the following yield curve environments:

	Current Six-Month LIBOR	*Three-Year Swap Fixed Rate*
A	7.00%	7.00%
B	7.00	8.00
C	8.00	7.00
D	8.00	8.00

Assume that there are 181 days in the next six-month time period. These yield curve environments are pictured in Figure E-5.1.

Solution: The key point is that current LIBOR will determine the direction and amount of the next scheduled settlement payment, whereas the swap fixed rate determines the MTM value of the swap.

Figure E-5.1 Hypothetical Yield Curve Environments

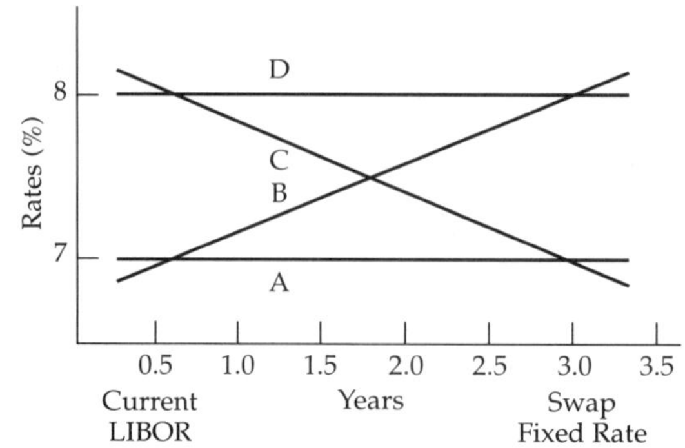

Scenario A: The MTM value of the swap will be negative \$1,099,014, calculated as a six-period annuity of \$206,250 per period using 7 percent as the discount rate.

$$(7.50\% - 7.00\%) \times \frac{1}{2} \times \$82{,}500{,}000 = \$206{,}250$$

$$\sum_{t=1}^{6} \frac{\$206{,}250}{[1 + (0.0700/2)]^t} = \$1{,}099{,}014.$$

The company is scheduled to make the next settlement payment to the counterparty in the amount of \$190,208:

$$\left[\left(7.50\% \times \frac{1}{2}\right) - \left(7.00\% \times \frac{181}{360}\right)\right] \times \$82{,}500{,}000 = \$190{,}208.$$

The swap is a liability to the corporation, and the next settlement payment is an outflow. The company appears to have no reason not to enter bankruptcy proceedings at this time, but it could defer default until the payment date in six months because market rates could possibly rise dramatically to reverse the sign on the value of the swap.

Scenario B: The company is still scheduled to make the next settlement payment in the amount of \$190,208, but the MTM value of the swap now will be positive \$1,081,191, calculated using 8 percent as the discount factor. That is,

$$(8.00\% - 7.50\%) \times \frac{1}{2} \times \$82{,}500{,}000 = \$206{,}250$$

$$\sum_{t=1}^{6} \frac{\$206{,}250}{[1 + (0.0800/2)]^t} = \$1{,}081{,}191.$$

The company should attempt to sell the swap to capture its market value as much as possible. Any event of default would definitely be postponed because of the limited two-way settlement clause.

Scenario C: The MTM value of the swap again will be negative \$1,099,014, but the company is scheduled to receive \$244,583 on the next settlement date.

$$\left[\left(8.00\% \times \frac{181}{360}\right) - \left(7.50\% \times \frac{1}{2}\right)\right] \times \$82{,}500{,}000 = \$224{,}583.$$

Here the case for deferring default is strong because the firm can collect the payment in six months and then default. The role of cross-default clauses is to protect the counterparty from this sort of "default-timing" option.

Scenario D: The MTM value of the swap will be positive $1,081,191, and the company is scheduled to receive $244,583 on the next settlement date. The swap should be sold if possible, and any event of default postponed.

Exercise 5.4: A Savings and Loan Association (S&L) has just been taken over by the Office of Thrift Supervision, an event of default that triggers early termination of the S&L's two swap contracts with a commercial bank. The swaps are under a master agreement that calls for close-out netting with full two-way settlement. The terms of the two swaps are as follows:

> *Swap #1.* The S&L pays 6.32 percent and receives three-month LIBOR (quarterly settlement in arrears) on a two-year, $37 million, plain vanilla interest rate swap.
>
> *Swap #2.* The S&L receives 5.89 percent and pays three-month LIBOR (quarterly settlement in arrears) on a three-year, $25 million, plain vanilla interest rate swap.

Who owes whom how much to close out these positions? To simplify the calculations, assume that the current date is a settlement date. A survey of market makers reveals the following average bid and offer fixed rates for two-year and three-year swaps against three-month LIBOR; these are the rates the surveyed dealers would be willing to pay to or receive from the bank soliciting the quotations:

Settlement Date	*Bid*	*Offer*
Two years	7.02%	7.06%
Three years	7.41	7.45

Solution: The two- and three-year swaps are compared in Figure E-5.2. For the two-year swap, the close-out value will be based on the surveyed market makers' bid rate of 7.02 percent. The idea is that if the bank were to replace the swap, it would enter a new transaction "selling" LIBOR and getting the dealer's bid rate. This swap is an asset to the S&L because it is paying a below-market fixed rate for receipt of LIBOR. The bank would owe the S&L $479,373 on this position:

Figure E-5.2 The Savings and Loan Swaps

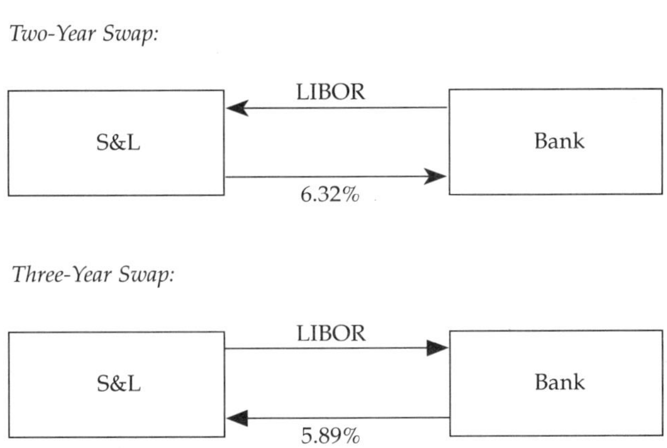

$$(7.02\% - 6.32\%) \times \frac{1}{4} \times \$37{,}000{,}000 = \$64{,}750$$

$$\sum_{t=1}^{8} \frac{\$64{,}750}{[1 + (0.0702/4)]^t} = \$479{,}373.$$

The close-out value for the three-year swap will be based on the market makers' offered rate of 7.45 percent. If the bank were to replace this swap, it would have to "buy" LIBOR and pay the dealer's offered rate. This swap is a liability to the S&L because it is receiving a below-market fixed rate for payment of LIBOR. The S&L would owe the bank $1,039,857 to close out this position.

$$(7.45\% - 5.89\%) \times \frac{1}{4} \times \$25{,}000{,}000 = \$97{,}500$$

$$\sum_{t=1}^{12} \frac{\$97{,}500}{[1 + (0.0745/4)]^t} = \$1{,}039{,}857.$$

Combining the two positions, the bank's claim to the Office of Thrift Supervision would be for $560,484.

Chapter 6. Swap Design Variations and Extensions

The preceding chapters demonstrated that interest rate and currency swaps are an extremely flexible form of financial contracting. In this chapter, we describe several ways in which these agreements have been adapted to make them even more appealing to their ultimate end users. In presenting these innovations, we have made a somewhat arbitrary distinction between those that are merely variations on the basic swap theme, such as the forward swap and varying notional principal swap contracts, and those that extend the concept to applications in new markets such as equity and commodity risk management.

Variations on the Basic Swap

Some of the more popular contract adjustments that have been introduced by financial intermediaries in recent years include basis swaps, constant-maturity swaps, "diff" swaps, arrears swaps, MTM swaps, indexed amortizing rate swaps, and corridor swaps.

"Floating/Floating" (or Basis) Swaps. The simplest departure from the plain vanilla format is to link each of the swap cash flows to different reference rates that are allowed to vary over time. For example, in lieu of making fixed-rate payments in exchange for LIBOR-based receipts, a corporate cash manager might choose to have the swap payments tied to a commercial paper index (plus or minus a spread). In this manner, the manager would be able to maintain the short duration of any outstanding debt payments linked to LIBOR but convert the effective rate basis to a preferable exposure. In general, any short-term rate can be built into this contract design, including the prime rate or the Treasury bill yield. In fact, a *TED spread swap*, in which the counterparties exchange cash flows based on LIBOR and a spread-adjusted T-bill rate, could be used to speculate on an increase or decrease in the market-driven risk premium built into LIBOR.

Constant-Maturity Swaps. An interesting form of the basis swap is the constant-maturity swap (CMS). Also known as yield curve swaps, these agreements call for the exchange of cash flows tied to the short end of the yield curve (e.g., three- or six-month LIBOR) for those based on movements farther out the curve. The contract draws its name from the fact that the maturity of the security underlying this latter movement—typically a Treasury note or a plain vanilla swap—remains fixed throughout the tenor of the agreement. A typical application for the CMS structure is illustrated in Figure 6.1. In this case, a bond manager who is invested in a LIBOR-linked FRN has used the swap to

Figure 6.1 A Constant-Maturity Basis Swap

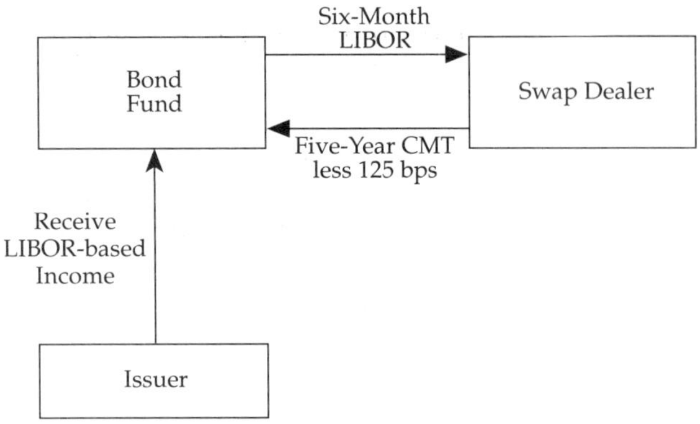

convert the basis for his receipts into the five-year constant-maturity Treasury bond (CMT) yield less 1.25 percent. That is, every settlement date for the life of the swap, the manager will receive a swap flow linked to the five-year T-bond yield prevailing at that time. (The data series for the CMT is maintained by the Federal Reserve Board.)

The innovative aspect of the constant-maturity swap is that it allows the counterparties to participate in changes in the *shape* of the curve over the life of the contract. In this example, the bond manager will benefit from a steepening yield curve—at least in the six-month to five-year segment—because his net settlement receipt (payment) will be successively larger (smaller). In contrast, an unanticipated flattening or inversion of the yield curve benefits the CMT payer.

Notice that the CMS payments can also be adapted to a more traditional fixed/floating format by replacing LIBOR with a fixed rate exchanged against CMT flat. Of course, this fixed rate would now be an average of the forward five-year CMT rates, rather than the forward six-month LIBOR, and will be appropriately higher in an upward-sloping yield curve environment.

Rate-Differential (or "Diff") Swaps. Another way basis swaps have been structured involves the exchange of cash flows based on short-term rates from two different countries but denominated in the same base currency. The primary advantage of this sort of arrangement is that it allows an investment fund to take views on the changes in the shape of a yield curve in another country (relative to its own) without having to hold foreign securities directly. To see how this swap might work, suppose that a British money manager is holding GBP 10 million worth of two-year securities paying quarterly coupons equal to sterling LIBOR. The manager's view is that British money rates will decrease significantly over the next few years at the same time short-term German rates rise. Further, assume that the present levels of sterling- and deutschemark-denominated LIBOR are 6.25 percent and 5.15 percent, respectively, and both rates are adjusted to reflect an actual/365 day count.

Figure 6.2 captures the essence of how a diff swap could be designed to assist this manager. The swap agreement would allow for the transformation of the sterling coupons into receipts based on deutschemark LIBOR plus a spread of 1.85 percent. Both of the swap cash flows would be denominated in sterling and the same GBP 10 million notional principal would apply to each. The 185-basis-point spread would have been determined by several factors, including the levels and shapes of the pound and deutschemark yield curves, the assumed correlation between yields in each currency, and the exchange rate between them.

An immediate implication of this structure is that during the first quarterly settlement period on the swap (assumed to be 91 days), the British manager will receive a net settlement payment from the swap dealer equal to:

Figure 6.2 A Rate-Differential Swap

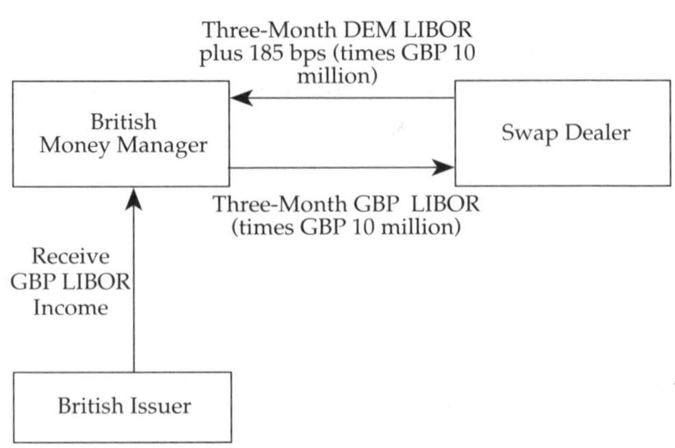

$$[(0.0515 + 0.0185) - 0.0625] \times \left(\frac{91}{365}\right) \times (\text{GBP } 10{,}000{,}000) = \text{GBP } 18{,}699,$$

which adds to the coupon interest of the GBP 155,822 (calculated as GBP 10,000,000 × (91/365) × 0.0625) received on the sterling floater. Of course, because the spread adjustment was set, in part, by the market's anticipation that sterling rates will increase far more rapidly than deutschemark LIBOR, the money manager is likely to be making the net settlement payments to the dealer later in the lifetime of the agreement.

Arrears Swaps. An arrears swap is equivalent to a plain vanilla agreement in which the floating rate is both set *and* paid at the end of a settlement period. In addition to modifying a traditional fixed/floating structure, the arrears concept can also be extended to become a basis swap by, say, exchanging LIBOR set in advance for LIBOR set in arrears. In either case, the main benefit of the arrears format is that it allows end users to lock in the dynamics of a yield curve that is more upwardly sloped than previously (e.g., the U.S. curve in the early 1990s). For instance, a floating-rate issuer seeking a pay-fixed swap and believing rates will rise more rapidly than the rates priced into the existing curve will prefer an agreement that sets the LIBOR receipt at the end of the settlement period. Conversely, a LIBOR-based investor can arrange to receive the fixed rate on an arrears swap if he or she thinks future rates will either decline or rise by less than the rates implied by the forward curve and hence priced into the fixed rate on the swap.

To see the difference between traditional and arrears swap pricing, consider the cash flows associated with two-year, semiannual-settlement versions of each agreement using the rate calculations summarized in Tables 6.1 and 6.2. Table 6.1 presents the current LIBOR yield curve (based on a hypothetical set of long-dated, zero-coupon Euro-time deposits adjusted to a semiannual bond basis) and the sequence of six-month implied forward rates, calculated as in Chapter 4. Table 6.2 indicates the floating rate applicable to each settlement date, given these implied forward rates. Notice that with an upward-sloping yield curve, the implied forward LIBOR rates also increase with successively distant investment dates. The importance of this pattern is that the anticipated floating-rate payments for the arrears swap will be larger on each settlement date than those for the traditional agreement. The result is a larger swap fixed rate on the arrears swap—4.74 percent versus 4.39 percent—which can be established by setting the "fixed rate" present value formula,

$$\frac{\text{SFR}}{(1 + 0.0400/2)^1} + \frac{\text{SFR}}{(1 + 0.0410/2)^2} + \frac{\text{SFR}}{(1 + 0.0420/2)^3} + \frac{\text{SFR}}{(1 + 0.0440/2)^4},$$

equal, in turn, to each of the following "arrears floating" and "traditional floating" discount equations:

$$\frac{4.20\%}{(1 + 0.0400/2)^1} + \frac{4.40\%}{(1 + 0.0410/2)^2} + \frac{5.00\%}{(1 + 0.0420/2)^3} + \frac{5.40\%}{(1 + 0.0440/2)^4},$$

and

Table 6.1 LIBOR Yield Curve and Associated Implied Forward Rates

Maturity (months)	Current LIBOR	Forward Date (months)	Forward Rates
6	4.00%	—	—
12	4.10	6	4.20%
18	4.20	12	4.40
24	4.40	18	5.00
30	4.60	24	5.40

Table 6.2 Floating-Rate Determination for Two-Year Traditional and Arrears Swaps

Settlement Period (months)	Traditional Swap LIBOR	Arrears Swap LIBOR	Difference
0–6	4.00%	4.20%	+0.20%
6–12	4.20	4.40	+0.20
12–18	4.40	5.00	+0.60
18–24	5.00	5.40	+0.40

$$\frac{4.00\%}{(1 + 0.0400/2)^1} + \frac{4.20\%}{(1 + 0.0410/2)^2} + \frac{4.40\%}{(1 + 0.0420/2)^3} + \frac{5.00\%}{(1 + 0.0440/2)^4},$$

and then solving for the separate SFR values. That is, pricing the arrears swap entails averaging a two-year segment of the forward curve shifted out by one period.

"Mark-to-Market" (MTM) Swaps. The mark-to-market swap was developed specifically to reduce the amount of actual credit risk either of the two counterparties to the transaction must carry during the life of the contract. To see how this can be accomplished, consider the time line illustrated in Figure 6.3, which assumes that a $(T + N)$-period swap was negotiated at date $-T$ relative to the current date, 0. In short, the MTM swap is designed to eliminate the actual exposure on the swap accumulated from the origination date (or, alternatively, the last "marking" date) to the present.

Figure 6.3 Time Line for Mark-to-Market Swap Example

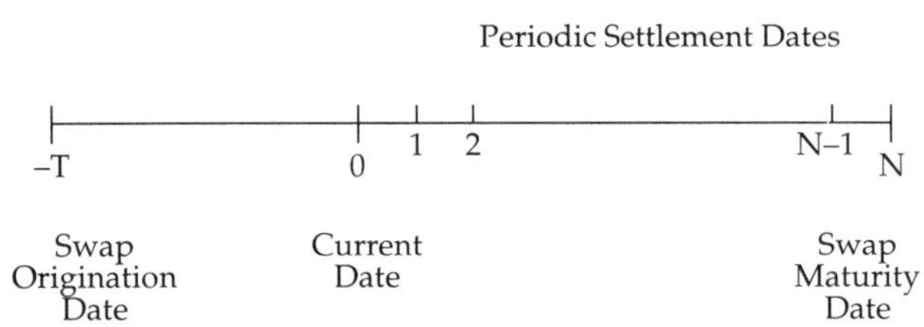

The basic premise of this agreement can be seen in the following example. Imagine that a swap dealer and a corporate counterparty had structured the following agreement at date $-T$:

- Enter into a plain vanilla interest rate swap for $T + N$ periods with the corporation paying and the dealer receiving the prevailing swap fixed rate.
- On the first settlement date, the counterparties make their respective fixed- and floating-rate payments on the existing swap and then liquidate the remaining portion of the existing swap using the new swap fixed rate for an agreement that continues through the original maturity as the discount factor for all future cash flows.
- Immediately upon unwinding the old swap, the participants enter into a new swap at the current fixed rate and with the same notional principal as the original but one fewer settlement periods to maturity.
- Repeat the previous two steps on each settlement date until the maturity date of the original swap.

As an example of how this procedure might work in practice, suppose that a corporate borrower arranges a two-year, nonamortizing loan from a commercial bank in the amount of \$100 million. The interest rate on the loan is set at six-month LIBOR plus 1 percent, with semiannual payments in arrears. The corporate treasurer, fearing higher market rates could cut into operating margins, seeks to transform the debt into a synthetic fixed-rate liability using a pay-fixed interest rate swap. The best terms offered the corporation are a pay-fixed rate of 6 percent for a mark-to-market swap. The top panel of Table 6.3 illustrates a hypothetical path for the future LIBOR and swap fixed rates that govern the settlement cash flows on the loan/swap package. To simplify the calculations, assume that LIBOR and the swap rates are on a semiannual bond basis for payment in arrears on a 30/360 day count. This means that cash flows will be the annualized rate times 0.5 times the principal. These settlement date flows are shown in the lower panel of the table.

The all-in, realized cost of funds (COF) for the loan/swap combination is found by solving

$$100{,}000{,}000 = \frac{3{,}854{,}428}{(1 + \text{COF}/2)^1} + \frac{2{,}897{,}498}{(1 + \text{COF}/2)^2} + \frac{4{,}234{,}756}{(1 + \text{COF}/2)^3} + \frac{103{,}000{,}000}{(1 + \text{COF}/2)^4}$$

for COF, which equals 7.00 percent. Notice that this outcome is exactly the same as would have resulted from combining the loan at LIBOR plus 1 percent with a plain vanilla pay-fixed swap at 6 percent. The difference is that in the latter scheme, the actual credit exposure would build up throughout the life of the agreement, whereas the MTM format calls for cash payments that eliminate this exposure on each

Table 6.3 Mark-to-Market Swap Mechanics

Assumed LIBOR and Future Swap Fixed-Rate Paths

Date 0	LIBOR = 4.00%	2.0-year swap fixed rate = 6.00%
Date 1	LIBOR = 4.25%	1.5-year swap fixed rate = 5.75%
Date 2	LIBOR = 4.75%	1.0-year swap fixed rate = 6.25%
Date 3	LIBOR = 5.00%	0.5-year swap fixed rate = 5.00%

Settlement-Date Cash Flows

Date 1
Swap settlement: (6% − 4%)(0.5)($100,000,000) = $1,000,000
Mark-to-market settlement:

$$\sum_{t=1}^{3} [(0.06 - 0.0575)(0.5)(100{,}000{,}000)] \div (1.02875)^t = \$354{,}428$$

Loan payment: (4.00% + 1.00%)(0.5)($100,000,000) = $2,500,000
Total payment: $3,854,428

Date 2
Swap settlement: (5.75% − 4.25%)(0.5)($100,000,000) = $750,000
Mark-to-market settlement:

$$\sum_{t=1}^{2} [(0.0575 - 0.0625)(0.5)(100{,}000{,}000)] \div (1.03125)^t = -\$477{,}502$$

Loan payment: (4.25% + 1.00%)(0.5)($100,000,000) = $2,625,000
Total payment: $2,897,498

Date 3
Swap settlement: (6.25% − 4.75%)(0.5)($100,000,000) = $750,000
Mark-to-market settlement:
[(0.0625 − 0.05)(0.5)(100,000,000) ÷ (1.025) = $609,756
Loan payment: (4.75% + 1.00%)(0.5)($100,000,000) = $2,875,000
Total payment: $4,234,756

Date 4
Swap settlement: (5% − 5%)(0.5)($100,000,000) = $0
Mark-to-market settlement: $0
Loan payment: (5.00% + 1.00%)(0.5)($100,000,000) = $3,000,000
Total payment: $3,000,000

settlement date. Importantly, although the practice of mark-to-market valuation and settlement changes the timing of the cash flows, the internal rate of return is the same (barring default) as it would have been with a regular swap. A corollary to this result is that the ultimate cost of funds does not depend on any "errors" in the fixed rates used to mark the swap to market; this independence will hold as long as the same fixed rate is used to calculate the required MTM payment and to set the new fixed rate on the replacement swap. This condition is important because an active market in swaps might not exist on the reset date as a result of a general decline in swap transactions or inactivity in that particular tenor.

Indexed Amortizing Rate (IAR) Swaps. An IAR swap is a traditional fixed/floating interest rate swap that has been altered to mimic the performance of a mortgage portfolio. An important feature of such portfolios is the negative convexity that results from the homeowner's prepayment option. In effect, these contracts represent a "pseudo" mortgage bank that funds mortgage assets with LIBOR-based liabilities. The end user of the swap will receive cash flows similar to a pool of fixed-rate mortgages and pay cash flows linked to LIBOR.

This parallel can be appreciated by first considering the dynamics of a commercial bank that obtains its funds in the short-term deposit market and invests in whole mortgages or mortgage-backed pass-throughs paying a fixed rate. If both deposit and mortgage rates rise, the bank experiences a lower net interest margin, assuming a parallel shift in the yield curve. Conversely, if deposit and mortgage rates both fall, the bank bears the burden of increased refinancings and prepayments, meaning that its high-coupon assets simply disappear. Thus, the bank thrives best in a world with a static, upwardly sloped yield curve; it suffers most if rates dramatically rise or fall.

This bank can be described as being inherently "short volatility" in that it benefits if interest rate volatility declines. Of course, the key factor in this analysis is that fixed-rate mortgages are prepayable at the option of the homeowner, not the investor. Consequently, in contrast to typical (noncallable) fixed-income instruments, upside gains in mortgage products are limited as rates fall. A receive-fixed IAR swap is designed to replicate these value changes in a mortgage portfolio funded with deposits. The fixed rate received—the underlying Treasury yield plus the swap spread—represents the long position in mortgages; the floating rate paid (LIBOR) represents the short position in deposits.

The negative convexity on the mortgages is mimicked by varying the notional principal on the swap as conditions in the market change. Unlike a varying-principal swap that follows a predetermined schedule to reduce the notional amount, an IAR swap ties the reduction in principal each period to the change in some market reference rate (not necessarily the one that determines the settlement cash flows). This reference rate is often a constant-maturity Treasury bond yield. For example, a simple structure might be that after a "lockout" period of two years, the notional principal declines by:

- 0 percent if the (ten-year) CMT is unchanged or rises during the period,
- 20 percent if the CMT declines by up to 200 basis points, or
- 100 percent if the CMT declines by more than 200 basis points.

For example, if the CMT yield were to fall from its original level of 8 percent to 7 percent after the lockout period had passed, an IAR swap that started with a notional principal of $50 million would see that amount reduced to $40 million. The other $10 million would be subject to "reinvestment risk" in the sense that the receive-fixed counterparty would have to find an alternative revenue stream under less profitable market conditions.

In general, the receiver of the fixed rate on an IAR swap obtains a considerably higher swap spread than on a plain vanilla swap. This additional amount can be viewed as the premium on a path-dependent option written by the fixed-rate receiver. In options parlance, the fixed-rate receiver is "selling volatility," as indicated by the negative convexity of the IAR swap. In fact, an advantage of the IAR swap relative to actually holding the mortgage securities is that the notional principal reduction in the former is tied exclusively to rate movements while prepayments in the latter can occur for myriad other reasons (e.g., home sales because of job transfers or retirement, or property insurance settlements after a natural disaster) that may be difficult to forecast. Accordingly, end users have tended to be banks and other institutions that want the performance of a mortgage portfolio without having to hold the underlying instruments. Furthermore, some banks have used IARs as a substitute for more traditional banking activities when loan demand has been weak.

Corridor Swaps. Traditional interest rate swaps allow the end user to speculate on the *direction* of interest rate movements. Constant-maturity swaps allow the end user to speculate on changes in the *shape* of the yield curve. Corridor swaps are another example of what has come to be known as "structured" swaps. They allow the end user to speculate on the *volatility* of rate changes. For example, suppose that a fund manager currently holding floating-rate debt securities in his or her portfolio can enter into either of the following three-year, semiannual settlement swaps:

- Traditional: Pay six-month LIBOR, and receive 5.75 percent.
- Corridor: Year 1 Payment: Six-month LIBOR for days when 4 percent ≤ LIBOR ≤ 5 percent, 0 all other days;

  Year 2 Payment: Six-month LIBOR for days when 5 percent ≤ LIBOR ≤ 6 percent, 0 all other days;

Year 3 Payment: Six-month LIBOR for days when 6 percent ≤ LIBOR ≤ 7 percent, 0 all other days; and

Receive 4.50 percent.

Although the traditional swap would allow the manager to lock in a fixed income of 5.75 percent, the corridor arrangement offers the possibility of an enhanced return if LIBOR falls outside of the prescribed range during a substantial portion of the settlement period. For example, if LIBOR is 3.80 percent for the first half of a settlement period during Year 1 and 4.20 percent for the second, the combined yield of a corridor swap and an FRN paying LIBOR flat would be 6.40 percent, computed as 4 percent received on the floater [(0.50 × 3.80 percent) + (0.50 × 4.20 percent)] plus 4.50 percent received on the swap less 2.10 percent paid on the swap [(0.50 × 0 percent) + (0.50 × 4.20 percent)]. If LIBOR was 4.20 percent during the whole period, however, this same combination would yield just the 4.50 percent on the fully swapped coupon, considerably less than the 5.75 percent that could have been realized with the plain vanilla alternative. Consequently, a manager committing to the corridor agreement is attempting to enhance return by taking the view that short-term rate movements will be extreme enough to carry LIBOR outside the designated band.

Extensions of the Swap Concept

Although the preceding forms of contracting are all legitimate innovations, each of them can be viewed as a straightforward modification of the original swap design. Further, they all were described by applications in fixed-income security management. In this section, we discuss three ways in which swap agreements have been adapted to help investors and issuers manage risk in other markets as well.

Options on Swaps ("Swaptions"). One of the most important developments in the swap market of the late 1980s was the growth of the swap entry option, or *swaption*. A swaption gives the holder of the option the right, but not the obligation, to enter into an interest rate swap having a predetermined fixed rate at some later date. As with all options, these agreements are of two types: *receiver* and *payer* swaptions.

A receiver swaption gives the buyer the right, but not the obligation, to enter a swap on prearranged terms (fixed rate, tenor, notional principal, floating rate index, settlement periods, documentation, etc.) as the fixed-rate receiver. The writer of the option, in return for an up-front premium, must enter the swap as the fixed-rate payer upon demand of the buyer. Naturally, the buyer will only exercise the receiver swaption if the market swap rate is less than the strike rate at the maturity of the option; that is, if he or she can receive an above-market fixed rate while paying LIBOR.

A payer swaption gives the buyer the right, but not the obligation, to enter a swap on prearranged terms as the fixed-rate payer. The writer of the option is obligated to receive the fixed rate at the buyer's request. The holder of the payer swaption will only exercise if the market pay-fixed swap rate prevailing at the option exercise date is higher than the strike rate, thereby entitling him or her to pay a below-market fixed rate while receiving LIBOR.

Swaptions are most useful to those firms who, at the present time, are not sure whether they will be exposed to interest rate movements in the future. An example would be a bond portfolio manager who may be forced to liquidate part of his or her holdings in a year's time. In such a situation, the bond manager might like to have the option of fixing the future interest rate at the levels priced into today's forward curve.

Another example of how swaptions are used involves the management of callable debt. Specifically, assume the following scenario, which is illustrated on the time line in Figure 6.4. Three years ago, Company XYZ issued 15-year, fixed-rate callable debt with a coupon rate of 12 percent. Interest rates for XYZ's credit grade

Figure 6.4 Time Line for Callable Debt Management Example

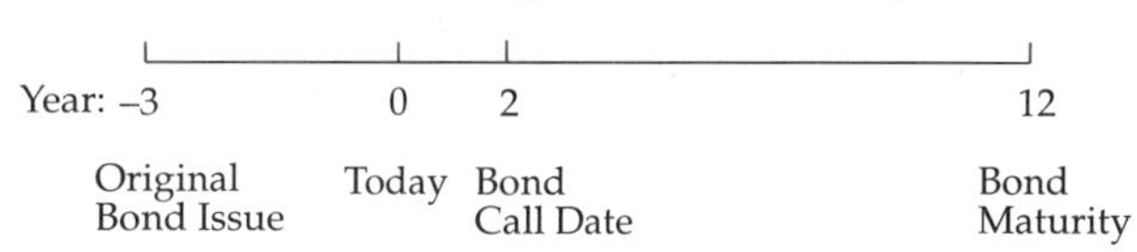

have since fallen to 8 percent, but the outstanding debt issue still has two years before its call deferment period is over. Clearly, the issuing company would call the debt today if it could (it would rather make 8 percent coupon payments than 12 percent payments). The call option it holds on the bond is therefore currently in the money. The company, however, must wait for two more years to exercise the call, during which time interest rates may rise above 12 percent. Furthermore, because the option cannot be separated from the original bond, it can not be sold directly in today's market.

One solution to this dilemma is through the use of swaptions. Consider what would happen if the issuing firm made the following transaction today: Sell a two-year receiver option on a ten-year swap, which gives the holder the right, but not the obligation, to receive the fixed rate of 12 percent. The benefit of this transaction is that the company will receive a premium from selling the swaption at origination. This receipt of cash, which is shown in Figure 6.5, is analogous to what the company would have received if it had been able to sell the call feature embedded in the underlying bond directly in the marketplace.

To see what this transaction will cost the company, consider what will happen in two years when the swaption expires and the bond can be called. If interest rates are 12 percent or greater, neither the bond option nor the swap option will be exercised; they both expire out of the money. The issuing company continues to pay a 12 percent coupon for the next ten years. This is shown in the top panel of Figure 6.6. Conversely, if interest rates are less than 12 percent, both the bond option and swap option will be exercised by their respective holders. To XYZ, this means that it (1) can refinance its original debt with a ten-year FRN (assumed to be at LIBOR) and (2) will be forced to pay a fixed rate of 12 percent as per the terms of the swaption. Thus, the net effect is that the issuing company will continue to pay a 12 percent coupon for the next ten years. The lower panel of Figure 6.6 illustrates this set of transactions.

Figure 6.5 Call-Monetization Cash Flows: Origination

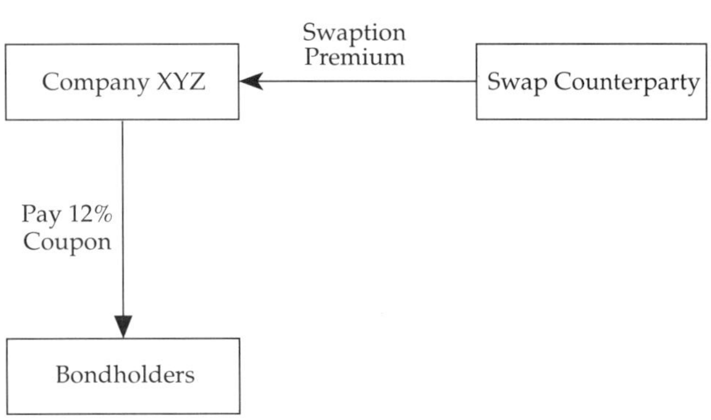

Figure 6.6 Call-Monetization Cash Flows: Swaption Expiration Date

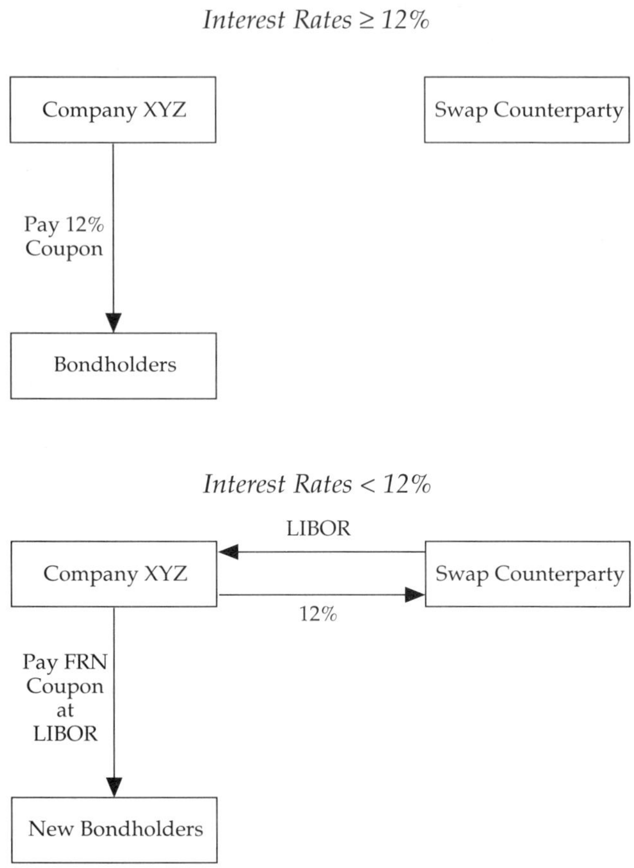

The important point is that by selling the swaption today, the company has committed itself to paying a 12 percent coupon for the remaining life of the original bond. The swaption was sold in exchange for an up-front swaption premium received at Date 0. Thus, even though the bond's call option could not be sold directly, it has been effectively "monetized" via the swaption market. Not surprisingly, this strategy is often referred to as *call monetization*. Notice, however, it can also be used to effectively restructure the coupon rate on the underlying bond by setting the strike rate on the swaption at a level other than 12 percent.

One important caution about using this strategy is that swap rates and bond rates do not necessarily move in exactly the same fashion. This possibility will create basis (or correlation) risk in that a swap market instrument is being used as a substitute, or proxy, for a capital market instrument. For instance, in this example, the worst-case result for the company would have been if the fixed rate on a ten-year swap was below 12 percent in two years but its debt refunding rate in the capital market was above 12 percent. This situation, which could occur if XYZ's credit quality deteriorates over the next two years, would mean that the company would be forced either to enter into a swap it does not want or to liquidate the position at a disadvantage and not be able to refinance its borrowing profitably.

Equity-Index-Linked Swaps. Similar in form to plain vanilla interest rate swaps, equity-index-linked swaps are equivalent to portfolios of forward contracts calling for the exchange of cash flows based on two different investment rates: a *variable debt rate* (e.g., three-month LIBOR) and the *return to an equity index* (e.g., Standard & Poor's 500). The index-linked payment is based either on the total return (i.e., dividends and capital gain or loss) or on the percentage index change for the settlement period *plus* a fixed spread adjustment, which is expressed in basis points and can be negative. The floating-rate payments are typically based on LIBOR flat. Like interest rate and currency swaps, equity swaps are traded in the over-the-counter markets and have maturities out to ten years.

Swaps linked to equity indexes are a major part of a larger, rapidly developing market in equity derivative products. In addition to swaps, other prominent equity derivatives include options and warrants on individual shares or market indexes and index-linked bonds. The two most commonly used—and frequently quoted—indexes in the equity swap market are the Standard & Poor's 500 (United States) and Nikkei 225 (Japan). Other indexes for which equity swaps can be structured include TOPIX (Japan), FTSE 100 (Great Britain), DAX (Germany), CAC 40 (France), TSE 35 (Canada), EOE (Netherlands), and Hang Seng (Hong Kong).

Equity swaps can be structured so that the cash flows are denominated in the same currency or in two different currencies. Typically, the equity-index-based cash flow is denominated in the currency of the index's country of origination, but the swap can be designed so that this payment is hedged into a different currency. These agreements specify a notional principal that is not exchanged at origination but serves the purpose of converting percentage returns into cash flows. This notional principal can be either *variable* or *fixed* during the life of the agreement, but the same notional principal applies to both sides of the transaction.

The equity swap market has developed for several reasons. First, these agreements allow investors to take advantage of overall price movements in a specific country's stock market without having to purchase the equity securities directly. This feature has the advantage of reducing both the transaction costs and tracking error associated with actually assembling a portfolio that mimics the index, as well as allowing the investor to avoid dividend withholding taxes normally associated with cross-border investing. Second, creating a direct equity investment in a foreign country may be difficult for some companies for which that strategy is prohibited by law or operating policy. Third, an investment fund wanting to accumulate foreign index returns denominated in their domestic currencies may not be able, in some cases because of legal prohibitions, to obtain sufficient exchange-traded futures or option contracts to hedge a direct equity investment. The equity swap can be structured so that separate hedging transactions are unnecessary.

The most common application for an equity swap involves a counterparty that receives an index-based payment in exchange for making a floating-rate payment. As an example of how this transaction might arise, consider a pension fund that currently has a substantial portion of its asset portfolio invested in floating-rate notes paying quarterly coupons based on LIBOR. If the manager of this fund would like to change the existing asset allocation by converting some of these debt-based cash flows into equity-based receipts, he or she has two ways to do so. One way is to sell the existing floating-rate notes and purchase a portfolio of equities directly in the market. Alternatively, the manager could enter into an equity swap with an initial notional principal equal to the amount of the existing debt holdings to be converted. From the standpoint of reducing transaction costs, the second alternative is clearly preferable. The mechanics of this arrangement are illustrated in Figure 6.7.

Figure 6.7 Altering an Asset Allocation Position with an Equity Swap

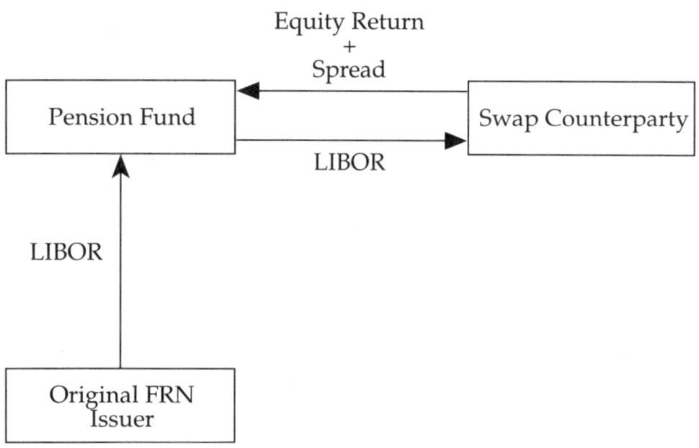

The net return to the fund in this example is simply the return on the equity index plus the spread adjustment. If the floating-rate notes held as an asset yield more than LIBOR, this incremental amount would serve to increase the overall net return. Assuming that both cash flows are denominated in the same currency, the net settlement payment on the swap from the company's standpoint can be calculated as the difference between the variable-rate outflow and the equity-linked inflow, where

$$\text{Payment} = (\text{LIBOR} - \text{Spread}) \times \text{Notional principal} \times \left(\frac{\#\text{ of days}}{360}\right)$$

and

$$\text{Receipt} = \left(\frac{\text{Index}_{new} - \text{Index}_{old}}{\text{Index}_{old}}\right) \times \text{Notional principal}$$

and Index_{new} and Index_{old} represent the index levels occurring on the current and immediate past settlement dates, assuming all dividends are reinvested. Notice that to minimize calculations, the settlement payment is computed using (LIBOR − Spread) rather than adding a separate inflow for the equity spread itself. Indicative quotes for this spread as of late 1992 are listed in Table 6.4 for several different countries. It should be noted, however, that the equity swap quotation methods are not standardized across all dealers and so the quoted values may not be directly comparable.

Table 6.4 Indicative Spreads on One-Year Equity Swaps
(basis points)

Country (Index)	Index Plus
Germany (DAX)	90
France (CAC 40)	60
Switzerland (SMI)	50
United Kingdom (FTSE)	25
United States (S&P 500)	(10)
Japan (Nikkei 225)	(15)
Netherlands (EOE)	(25)
Australia (All Ordinaries)	(30)
Hong Kong (Hang Seng)	(60)

Source: Swiss Bank Corporation.

Another way to see the effect of this swap-based cash flow transformation is shown in Figure 6.8. This illustration makes clear that equity swaps differ from interest rate and currency swaps in one important way. Specifically, because the equity index is not guaranteed to appreciate in value from one settlement period to the next, the party receiving the equity index could have to make a double payment. First, it will have to pay the usual cash flow based on LIBOR. Second, whenever Index_{new} is less than Index_{old}, it will also make an equity-index-based payment to ("receive" a negative payment from) its counterparty. Thus, rather than netting one cash flow against the other, the company will pay both when the value of the equity index declines. Examples of this situation are represented by the third and fifth swapped cash flows in the diagram.

This company now faces two sources of credit risk. First, as the holder of the floating-

Figure 6.8 An Equity-Index-Linked Swap Transaction

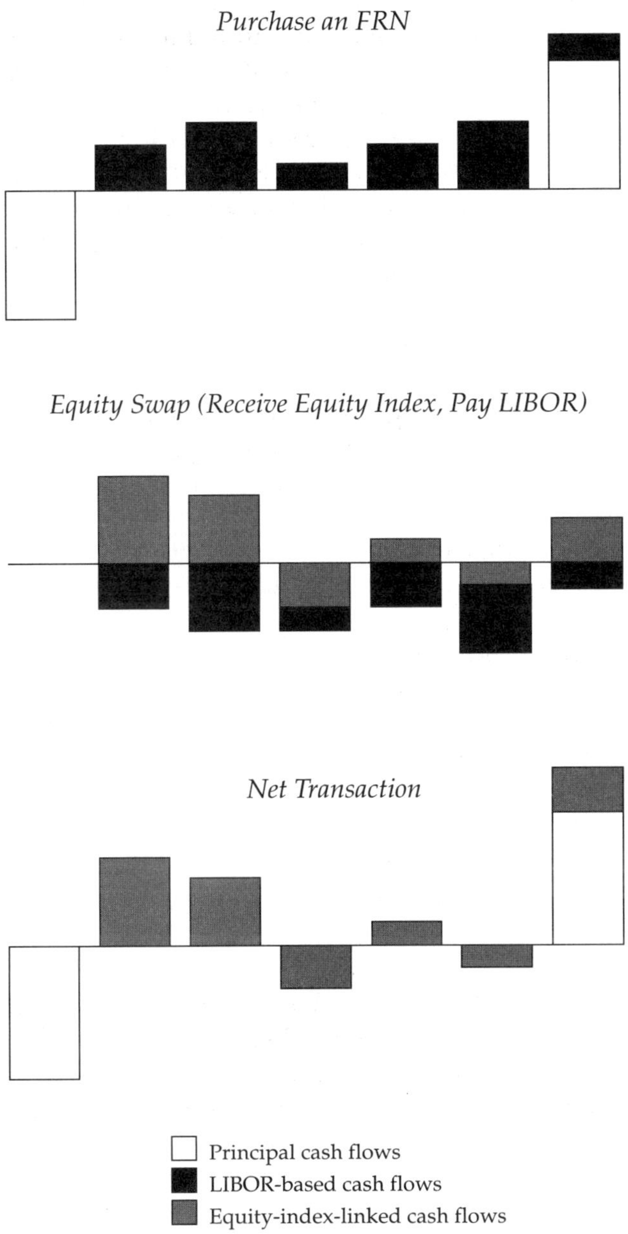

rate asset, it is exposed to the firm that issued the bond. Second, it is now also exposed to the swap counterparty. This second exposure will manifest itself on any settlement date when the index-linked return is greater than LIBOR. From the viewpoint of the "pay-equity-index" side of the deal (the swap counterparty in this example), this exposure can be magnified by the fact that equity returns can be negative. The credit exposure on the swap is limited to a single settlement date, however, because of the manner in which both LIBOR and the equity index are marked to market each period. In this sense, the equity swap is similar to a floating/floating interest rate swap (i.e., a basis swap).

Commodity Swaps. As the preceding equity example just demonstrated, swap contracting can be applied to hedging exposures to economic variables other than interest and exchange rates. In particular, there is a fast-growing market for over-the-counter derivative agreements tailored to mitigate uncertain commodity price movements. Although the producers and end users of any commodity could benefit from the existence of well-developed swap markets, the most active markets to date have been related to *energy* (crude oil, heating oil, unleaded gas, and natural gas), *precious metals* (gold and silver), and *base metals* (aluminum, copper, nickel, zinc, lead, and tin). As in the rate swap markets, the growth of commodity swaps has been primarily attributable to the constraints imposed on hedgers and speculators by the rigid standardization of exchange-traded futures contracts.

A commodity swap effectively fixes the price of a commodity over a certain period of time (the swap tenor) in the same way that an interest rate swap fixes the value of LIBOR. On each settlement date, the two counterparties exchange cash flows based on (1) a fixed commodity price that does not change over the life of the agreement and (2) a variable commodity price that does. The analog to the floating-rate index in a commodity swap is the price of a commodity index, (e.g., the West Texas Intermediate Oil index or the COMEX gold index), which is reset periodically over the life of the swap. The agreement also sets a notional amount of the commodity on which the periodic cash exchanges are based, but no physical delivery ever takes place.

To illustrate how a commodity swap works and who might benefit from its use, suppose Company OIL is a Dallas-based independent producer of oil whose production is limited to 500,000 barrels a month. Because of high production costs, OIL needs to guarantee that it receives an average price of $19.50 a barrel, particularly as the firm attempts to recover its initial investment. Company KEM is a Houston-based firm that uses a monthly average of 500,000 barrels of West Texas Intermediate (WTI) in the production of its petrochemicals. Because of the competitive nature of its business and the highly elastic demand for its products, KEM's operations will lose financial viability if oil prices rise above $20.50 a barrel during the next three years.

Clearly, in this case, OIL and KEM are concerned about falling and rising oil prices, respectively. Thus, they are good candidates for a three-year oil swap with monthly settlement and "notional principal" of 500,000 barrels. Working through a swap dealer, they arrange the transactions illustrated in Figure 6.9. The monthly WTI index value is determined as the average of the daily settlement prices for the WTI futures contract traded on the New York Mercantile Exchange. By their agreements with the swap dealer, OIL is effectively fixing the price of its oil sales at $20.00 a barrel and KEM is fixing the price of its purchase at $20.10. The actual settlement transactions will be as follows:

- If average WTI settlement price is $20.75:
  OIL pays to Dealer: ($20.75 − $20.00) × (500,000) = $375,000, and
  KEM receives from Dealer: ($20.75 − $20.10) × (500,000) = $325,000.
- If average WTI settlement price is $19.40:
  OIL receives from Dealer: ($20.00 − $19.40) × (500,000) = $300,000, and
  KEM pays to Dealer: ($20.10 − $19.40) × (500,000) = $350,000.

Notice that, barring default of one of the counterparties, the swap dealer in this matched transaction has no exposure to WTI prices and simply collects the spread of $50,000 each month. The

Figure 6.9 Illustration of an Oil-Oriented Commodity Swap

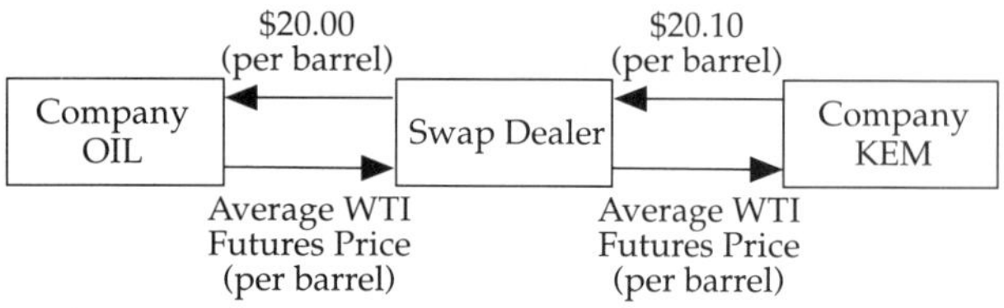

measurement of actual and potential default exposure is comparable to that for rate swaps.

Using commodity swaps to maintain the economic viability of a high-cost project such as oil drilling or gold mining is not merely a matter of convenience. Because reopening oil fields or mines that have been shut down can cost an inordinate amount of money, typically it pays to keep them running at a loss for a limited period of time. Thus, it is often prudent for producers (e.g., Company OIL) to enter into receive-fixed commodity swaps to remove price volatility at those times when the operation is particularly vulnerable.

Commodity swaps can also be used to reverse forward positions previously transacted if the counterparty to those agreements changes its view of the future prices. For example, airlines often use forward contracts to lock in the price of jet fuel two or three years out. If a carrier believes prices will decrease to a level below the contracted price, a swap could neutralize the long forward position, allowing the user to effectively pay the market price.

Summary of Swap Variations and Extensions

The rapid and phenomenal growth of the swap industry could not have occurred if only one basic product were available or if it could be used in only one way. In this chapter, we have described several ways in which the plain vanilla form of swap contracting has been expanded to meet the needs of an increasingly sophisticated and demanding audience. These adaptations range from straightforward variations on the traditional theme to extensions of the concept into entirely new markets. Any such list will always be incomplete and, given the present rate of progress, is likely soon to be obsolete. Nevertheless, we hope to have conveyed a sense that swap agreements are one of the most flexible financial instruments ever created. The importance of swaps in modern financial markets cannot be overstated, and consequently, a thorough understanding of why they exist and how they work is imperative for anyone functioning in those markets. It is our hope that the preceding discussions have provided guidance in this regard.

Exercises

Exercise 6.1: The diff swap illustrated in Figure 6.2 required the swap dealer to pay DEM LIBOR plus 1.85 percent in exchange for sterling LIBOR, with both rates translated into cash flows using the same GBP 10 million notional principal. The tenor of this agreement, which specified quarterly settlements, was two years.

(a) Assuming that the swap dealer has left this position unhedged, what is the implicit view he is taking with respect to rate changes in the United Kingdom and Germany?

(b) Given that the present pound and deutschemark LIBOR differential (i.e., 110 bps = 6.25 percent − 5.15 percent) is less than the 185-basis-point swap spread differential, one immediate problem the dealer faces is that he will be required to make the first net settlement payment. Suppose that bid–ask fixed rates on two-year, sterling-denominated, plain vanilla swaps (against three-month sterling LIBOR) are currently being quoted in the interbank market at 8.00 percent and 8.05 percent, respectively. What combination of transactions would be needed to transform the diff swap into a contract by which the dealer receives a cash flow of the form (constant percent − deutschemark LIBOR) and pays sterling LIBOR? After engineering this modification, comment on whether the dealer's resulting exposure is consistent with the implied view from Part (a) above.

Solution:

(a) The dealer is implicitly assuming that the differential between British and German short-term rates will widen more rapidly, and by a greater amount, than the current market view. Such a result could occur if German rates actually fall as British rates rise, or if sterling LIBOR rises at an accelerated pace relative to deutschemark LIBOR.

(b) The desired transformation could be made by combining a pay-deutschemark LIBOR/receive-sterling LIBOR diff swap position with two receive-8.00 percent fixed/pay-sterling LIBOR swaps (or one for twice the GBP 10 million principal). Figure E-6.1 shows this transaction graphically (assuming the swap fixed rate is also quoted on an actual/365 day count). Notice that the dealer's initial net cash flow on the

Figure E-6.1 Converting the Diff Swap Synthetically

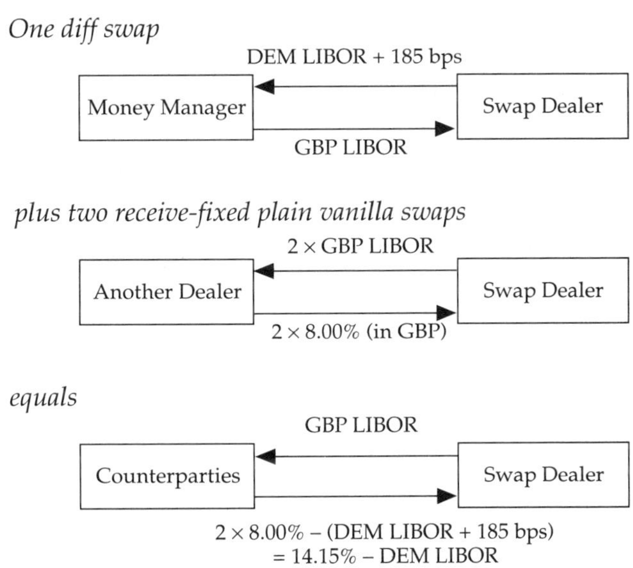

combined transaction is now positive [2.75 percent = (14.15 percent − 5.15 percent) − 6.25 percent]. Although the dealer still benefits from a German or British rate decline, an increase in either rate—regardless of the size of the differential between them—will erode this advantage. Thus, the new position creates a markedly different exposure for the dealer than did the original diff swap.

Exercise 6.2: A recently negotiated, indexed, amortizing rate swap contract has the following terms:

• Maturity	Three years
• Notional principal	USD 50 million
• Fixed rate	6.50% (actual/365 day count)
• Floating rate index	Six-month LIBOR (actual/360 day count)
• Lockout period	One year
• Payment and amortization frequency	Semiannually
• Amortization schedule	If LIBOR < 3.50 percent, 100 percent amortization If LIBOR > 7.50 percent, 0 percent amortization If 3.50 percent ≤ LIBOR ≤ 7.50 percent, amortize 0.25 percent of notional per basis point
• "Clean up" call	When principal has amortized to 15 percent of original principal, swap terminates

Suppose that the LIBOR values corresponding to each future settlement/amortization date are as follows: 0–6 months, 6.00 percent; 6–12 months, 6.75 percent; 12–18 months, 6.25 percent; 18–24 months, 5.50 percent; 24–30 months, 5.00 percent; and 30–36 months, 4.50 percent. Calculate the outstanding notional principal on each settlement date.

Solution: The amortization schedule implied by the designated LIBOR path is presented in Table E-6.1. For instance, the reduction to \$34.38 million on the first amortization date is calculated as \$50 million times [1 − (750 bps − 625 bps) × (0.25 per bp)]. The principal balance of \$17.19 million in the next period is then calculated as \$34.38 times [1 − (750 bps − 550 bps) × (0.0025)]. The swap terminates in the following period when the clean-up call limit of (0.15 × \$50,000,000) = \$7.5 million is reached.

Table E-6.1 Amortization Schedule for IAR Swap

Period (months)	LIBOR (%)	Reduction (%)	Outstanding Notional Principal (\$million)
0–6	6.00	Lockout	50.00
6–12	6.75	Lockout	50.00
12–18	6.25	31.25	34.38
18–24	5.50	50.00	17.19
24–30	5.00	62.50	6.45
30–36	4.50	—	Swap terminated

Exercise 6.3: Suppose that two years ago, in August 1992, a corporation issued seven-year bonds with a fixed coupon rate of 10 percent payable semiannually on February 15 and August 15 of each year. The debt was structured to be callable (at par) after a four-year deferment period and was issued at par value of \$100 million. Now, in

August 1994, the bonds are trading in the market at a price of 106, reflecting the general decline in market interest rates and the corporation's recent upgrade in its credit quality. The corporate treasurer believes that the current interest rate cycle has bottomed. If the bonds were callable today, the firm would realize a considerable savings in annual interest expense. Unfortunately, however, the bonds are still in the call-protection period. The treasurer's fear is that market rates might rise considerably prior to the call date in August 1996.

Assess the pros and cons of the following strategies that could be adopted in August 1994 to manage the corporation's interest rate risk problem. For each strategy, plot the gains and losses associated with the underlying exposure and affiliated hedge against the three-year Treasury yield (T) that prevails in August 1996. In this effort, define the corporation's August 1996 refunding rate as $T + BS$, where BS is the company-specific bond credit spread. The value of the swap position (as of August 1996) will depend on prevailing three-year swap fixed rates, or $T + SS$, where SS stands for the swap spread.

Strategy I: Enter an off-market forward swap as the fixed-rate payer by agreeing to pay 9.50 percent (rather than the at-market rate of 8.50 percent) for a three-year swap, two years forward. Because this fixed rate is above the at-market level, the corporation will receive from its counterparty an up-front payment of $2.25 million. Assume that the corporation's refunding spread remains at its current 100-basis-point level and the three-year swap spread over Treasuries remains at 50 basis points. Then, the annual reduction in interest expense after refunding is [10 percent − (T + 0.50 percent)] if the firm is able to refund, zero if it is not. The gain (or loss) on unwinding the swap is the fixed rate at that time: [(T + 0.50 percent) − 9.50 percent]. Those two effects net to zero, given the assumed spreads. Thus, the corporation has effectively "sold" the embedded call option for $2.25 million.

Strategy II: Buy a payer swaption expiring in two years with a strike rate of 9.50 percent. This transaction would give the corporation the right to enter a $100 million, three-year swap as the fixed-payer, and the counterparty that wrote the option would be obligated to receive the fixed rate. The corporation would exercise the option if the fixed rate on three-year swaps in 1996 is above 9.50 percent and then unwind the swap position at a profit. That gain would offset the loss of not being able to call the bonds and refinance at lower interest expense. (For example, if interest rates in August 1996 are 12 percent, the bond would not be called but the swaption would be worth the present value of a three-year annuity of $2.5 million.) This payer swaption would cost the firm only $1.1 million because the swaption is out of the money; a swaption with a strike rate below 8.50 percent would be in the money.

Strategy III: Sell a receiver swaption expiring in two years at a strike rate of 9.50 percent. This arrangement gives the buyer, presumably a swap dealer, the right to enter a three-year swap in 1996 as the fixed receiver while the corporation pays the fixed rate. The dealer would exercise the option only if the future swap fixed rate is less than 9.50 percent. Presuming that both three-year swap and bond rates are less than 9.50 percent in August 1996, both the corporation and the bank will exercise their options, with the benefit of one offsetting the cost of the other. The premium the corporation receives for selling this in-the-money swaption is $2.5 million. Thus, as in Strategy I, the company has effectively monetized its embedded call option position.

Solution: The August 1996 decisions and payoff diagrams associated with each strategy are as follows:

Strategy I. Enter an off-market forward swap.
Initial cash flow: Receive \$2.25 million
August 1996 decisions:

- Gain on refunding (per settlement period):
  [10 percent − ($T + BS$)] if $T + BS < 10$ percent,
  0 if $T + BS \geq 10$ percent.
- Gain (or loss) on unwinding the swap (per settlement period):
  − [9.50 percent − ($T + SS$)] if $T + SS < 9.50$ percent,
  [($T + SS$) − 9.50 percent] if $T + SS \geq 9.50$ percent.

Assuming that $BS = 1.00$ percent and $SS = 0.50$ percent, these gains and losses in 1996 can be depicted as in the top panel of Figure E-6.2. The net effect is shown in the lower panel.

Figure E-6.2 Callable Debt Management with a Forward Swap

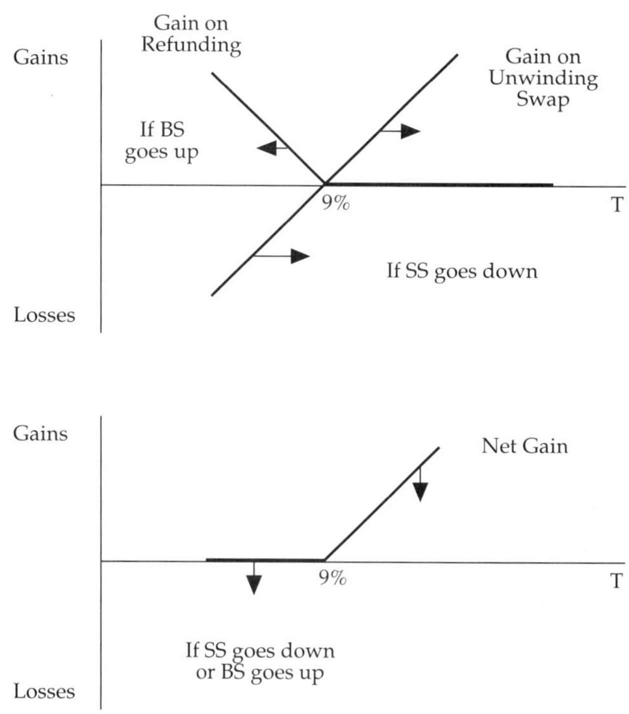

Notice that because the company stands to gain in August 1996 if rates rise, it has not fully monetized the embedded call option. The problem with this solution is that it uses a symmetric-payoff instrument (a forward swap) to hedge an asymmetric-payoff (option) problem.

Strategy II. Buy payer swaption.
Initial cash flow: Pay \$1.10 million
August 1996 decisions:

- Gain on refunding (per settlement period):
  [10 percent − ($T + BS$)] if $T + BS < 10$ percent,
  0 if $T + BS \geq 10$ percent.

- Gain on unwinding the swap (per settlement period):
  $[(T + SS) - 9.50$ percent$]$ if $T + SS > 9.50$ percent,
  0 if $T + SS \leq 9.50$ percent.

With $BS = 1.00$ percent and $SS = 0.50$ percent, these gains and losses are as shown in the top panel of Figure E-6.3. The net gain is shown in the lower panel.

Figure E-6.3 Callable Debt Management with a Payer Swaption

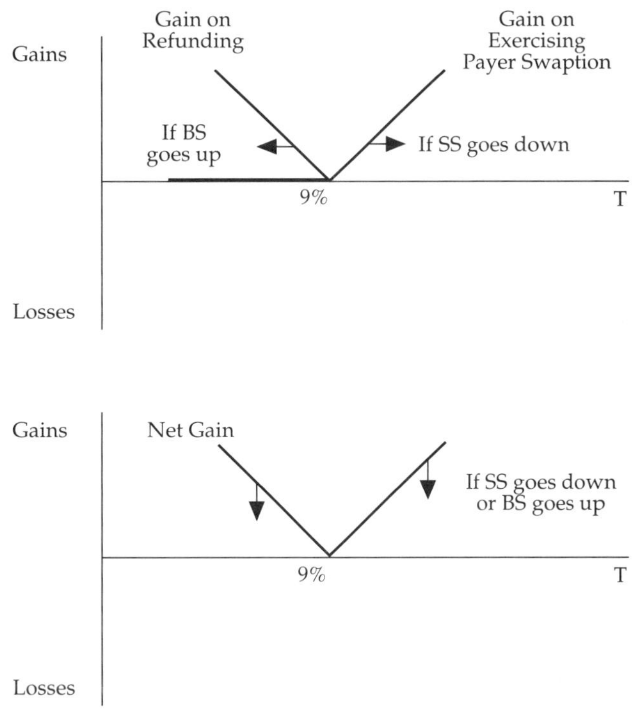

In this case, the company will benefit from Treasury rates being either higher or lower than 9 percent in August 1996. Of course, the treasurer had to spend an additional \$1.10 million to lock in this "straddle," so although the benefit to the embedded refunding option has been preserved, it was done at a significant price.

Strategy III. Sell receiver swaption.
Initial cash flow: Receive \$2.50 million
August 1996 decisions:

- Gain on refunding (per settlement period):
  $[10$ percent $- (T + BS)]$ if $T + BS < 10$ percent,
  0 if $T + BS \geq 10$ percent.
- Loss on unwinding the swap (per settlement period):
  0 if $T + SS \geq 9.50$ percent,
  $[9.50$ percent $- (T + SS)]$ if $T + SS < 9.50$ percent.

With $BS = 1.00$ percent and $SS = 0.50$ percent, these gains and losses and the net effect are as shown in Figure E-6.4.

By selling the receiver swaption, the company has been able to simulate the sale of the embedded call feature of the bond, thus fully monetizing that option. The only remaining uncertainty is the basis risk associated with unanticipated changes in swap and bond spreads.

Figure E-6.4 Callable Debt Management with a Receiver Swaption

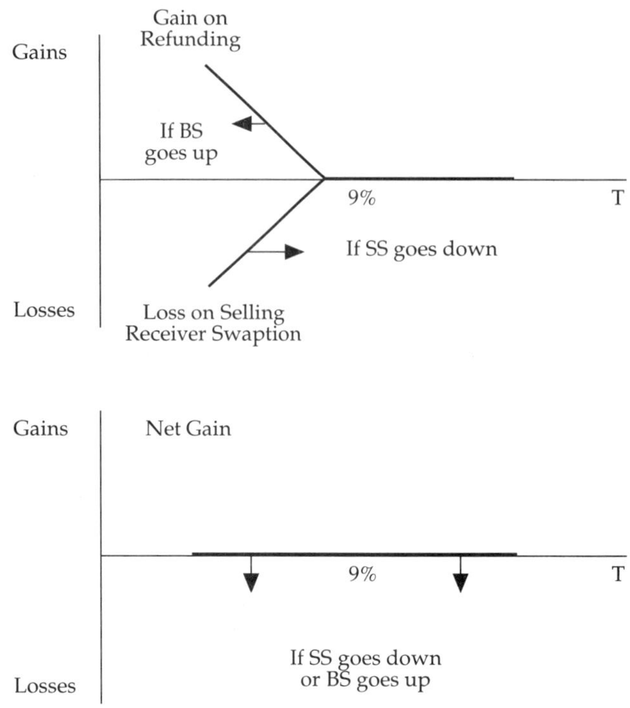

Exercise 6.4: On December 2, the manager of a tactical asset allocation fund that is currently invested entirely in floating-rate debt securities decides to shift a portion of her portfolio to equities. To effect this change, she has chosen to enter into the "receive equity index" side of a one-year equity swap based on movements in the S&P 500 index plus a spread of 10 basis points. The swap is to have quarterly settlement payments, and the floating-rate side of the agreement is pegged to three-month LIBOR denominated in U.S. dollars. At the origination of the swap, the value of the S&P 500 index was 463.11 and three-month LIBOR was 3.50 percent. The notional principal of the swap is fixed for the life of the agreement at $50 million, which matches the amount of debt holdings in the fund that she would like to convert to equity.

(a) Calculate the net cash receipt or payment—from the fund manager's perspective—on each future settlement date, assuming the values for the S&P 500 index (with all dividends reinvested) and LIBOR are as follows:

Settlement Date	*Number of Days*	*S&P Level*	*LIBOR Level*
December 2 (initial year)	—	463.11	3.50%
March 2 (following year)	90	477.51	3.25
June 2	92	464.74	3.75
September 2	92	480.86	4.00
December 2	91	482.59	—

(b) Explain why the fund manager might want the notional principal on this swap to vary over time and what the most logical pattern for this variation would be.

Solution:

(a) With these estimates, the settlement payments can be calculated as follows:

March 2:

Floating-rate payment =
(0.0350 − 0.0010) × ($50,000,000) × (90/360) = $425,000

Equity-index receipt =
[(477.51 − 463.11)/463.11] × ($50,000,000) = $1,554,706.

So the *net receipt* the fund expects would be ($1,554,706 − $425,000) = $1,129,706.

June 2:

Floating-rate payment =
(0.0325 − 0.0010) × ($50,000,000) × (92/360) = $402,500

Equity-index receipt =
[(464.74 − 477.51)/477.51] × ($50,000,000) = −$1,337,145.

So the *net payment* the fund owes would be ($1,337,145 + $402,500) = $1,739,645.

September 2:

Floating-rate payment =
(0.0375 − 0.0010) × ($50,000,000) × (92/360) = $466,389

Equity-index receipt =
[(480.86 − 464.74)/464.74] × ($50,000,000) = $1,734,303.

So the *net receipt* the fund expects would be ($1,734,303 − $466,389) = $1,267,914.

December 2:

Floating-rate payment =
(0.0400 − 0.0010) × ($50,000,000) × (91/360) = $492,917

Equity-index receipt =
[(482.59 − 480.86)/480.86] × ($50,000,000) = $179,886.

So the *net payment* the fund owes would be ($492,917 − $179,886) = $313,031.

(b) It is also quite common for equity swaps to be based on a notional principal amount that varies directly with the level of the underlying index. If, for instance, the swap participants had agreed to let the initial notional principal of $50 million vary over time, it would have been adjusted up on March 2 to $51.555 million. This adjustment is calculated as ($50 million {1 + [(477.51 − 463.11)/463.11]}). That is, each settlement date, the notional principal is adjusted up (down) by the percentage of capital appreciation (depreciation) in the starting level of the index. This adjustment process, which is equivalent to adding the gross equity settlement payment to the initial notional principal, simulates the return that investors with direct stock positions would obtain inasmuch as their actual equity exposure would rise or fall with market conditions. In contrast, a fixed notional principal in an equity swap is equivalent to an asset allocation strategy by which the equity exposure is kept constant.

Appendix: Calculation of the Macaulay Duration Statistic

Duration is a summary statistic about the price risk of a financial asset or liability. It combines both the coupon and maturity effects of a change in yield on the market value of the security. Technically, duration is a measure of the *price elasticity* of the security with respect to its yield, measuring the percentage change in price for a given percentage change in its periodic yield. That is,

$$\text{Duration} \approx -\frac{\Delta\text{Price}/\text{Price}}{\Delta(1 + \text{Yield})/(1 + \text{Yield})}.$$

Consider a 12 percent, annual payment, five-year bond that is priced at 107.581574 (percent of par value) to yield 10 percent. If the yield were to fall by 1 basis point to 9.99 percent, the price would rise to 107.621428. The duration of the bond can be approximated as

$$\text{Duration} \approx -\frac{(107.621428 - 107.581574)/107.581574}{-0.0001/1.1000} = 4.075.$$

Although duration in this context has no dimension (it is merely a percentage change divided by another percentage change), it usually is interpreted in units of time. This five-year bond would have a duration of about 4.075 years. Notice that this measure is an approximation of the true relationship between a bond's price and its yield to maturity. For a fixed-income security without embedded options, that connection is *convex*; duration provides a linear approximation of what really is a nonlinear relationship. Moreover, duration is a somewhat biased approximation in that it overestimates price decreases when yields rise and it underestimates price increases when yields fall. This relationship is illustrated in Figure A-1.

Many applications of duration come from rearranging the elasticity expression

$$\frac{\Delta\text{Price}}{\text{Price}} \approx -\text{Duration} \times \frac{\Delta(1 + \text{Yield})}{(1 + \text{Yield})}.$$

The percentage price change is a measure of the riskiness of a financial asset. For a given change in yield, duration provides an estimate of the percentage price move-

Figure A-1 Price–Yield Relationship for Fixed-Income Bonds without Embedded Options

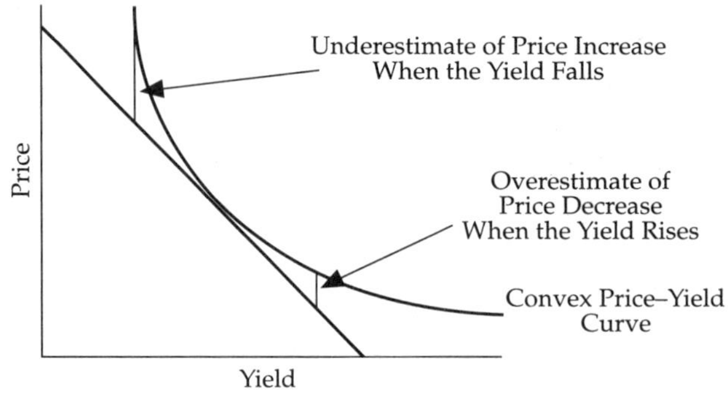

ment. Clearly, the larger the duration, the greater the price change. Another rearrangement focuses on the absolute change in the yield, not the percentage change; that is,

$$\frac{\Delta\text{Price}}{\text{Price}} \approx -\frac{\text{Duration}}{(1+\text{Yield})} \times \Delta\text{Yield}.$$

Duration divided by 1 plus the yield per period is known as *modified duration.*

Yet another rearrangement draws attention to the absolute change in the asset's price.

$$\Delta\text{Price} \approx -\left[\frac{\text{Duration}}{(1+\text{Yield})} \times \text{Price}\right] \times \Delta\text{Yield}.$$

The term in brackets, the modified duration times the market value of the security, is known as *dollar duration.*

Another special case is when the change in price is measured for a change in yield limited to 1 basis point. If ΔYield is equal to 0.0001, then ΔPrice is known as the *basis point value* (BPV) of the bond:

$$\text{BPV} \approx -\left[\frac{\text{Duration}}{(1+\text{Yield})} \times \text{Price}\right] \times 0.0001.$$

Duration was first developed and named by Frederick Macaulay in 1938. His duration statistic, which continues to bear his name, is calculated as a weighted average time to maturity, where the weights are the shares of total value represented by each cash flow. This can be written as:

$$\left\{1 \times \left[\frac{\text{Coupon}/(1+\text{Yield})}{\text{Price}}\right]\right\} + \left\{2 \times \left[\frac{\text{Coupon}/(1+\text{Yield})^2}{\text{Price}}\right]\right\}$$
$$+ \ldots + \left\{\#PDS \times \left[\frac{(\text{Coupon}+\text{Par})/(1+\text{Yield})^{\#PDS}}{\text{Price}}\right]\right\}.$$

Notice that the numerators of the terms in brackets are the present values of the cash flows. The numerator in the final term combines the last coupon and the redemption of the par value. Each cash flow is discounted by the periodic yield to maturity. The denominator in each term is the market price of the security. Therefore, the terms in brackets are the shares of total present value for each cash flow. Finally, note that the present value share of each cash flow is multiplied by the date the payment is received, from the first to the final payment. The total number of periods is indicated by *#PDS*.

Consider again the five-year, 12 percent bond yielding 10 percent. Suppose its par value is $1,000. The price and duration statistic can be calculated as shown in Table A-1. Notice that the Macaulay duration statistic, shown to be 4.074, is virtually the same as found above by estimating the price elasticity to yield changes. This five-year coupon bond can now be thought of as a portfolio of five zero-coupon bonds, one for each payment date. The duration of the coupon bond at 4.0740 years is the weighted average maturity of the portfolio, where the weights are the respective shares of market value (e.g., the one-year zero is 10.14 percent of the value of the portfolio, the five-year zero is 64.64 percent). Duration also can be interpreted as the *zero-coupon equivalent maturity*: A five-year coupon bond having a duration of 4.0740 years is "equivalent" in terms of price risk to a zero-coupon bond having a maturity of 4.0740 years.

Table A-1 Calculation of the Macaulay Duration Statistic

Year	Cash Flow	PV at 10%	(PV/Price)	[Year(PV/Price)]
1	120	109.09	0.1014	0.1014
2	120	99.17	0.0922	0.1844
3	120	90.16	0.0838	0.2514
4	120	81.96	0.0762	0.3047
5	1,120	695.43	0.6464	3.2321
		Price = 1,075.82		Duration = 4.0740

A general formula for calculating the Macaulay duration statistic can be derived from taking the sums of the finite geometric series and rearranging terms. This formula can be written as

$$\text{Duration} = \frac{1 + \text{Yield}}{\text{Yield}} - \frac{1 + \text{Yield} + \{\#PDS \times [(\text{Coupon/Par}) - \text{Yield}]\}}{\{(\text{Coupon/Par}) \times [(1 + \text{Yield})^{\#PDS} - 1]\} + \text{Yield}}.$$

In the numerical example above, yield = 0.10, #PDS = 5, and the coupon rate, given as (coupon/par), = 0.12. The Macaulay duration can be solved as

$$\text{Duration} = \frac{1 + 0.10}{0.10} - \frac{1 + 0.10 + [5 \times (0.12 - 0.10)]}{\{0.12 \times [(1 + 0.10)^5 - 1]\} + 0.10} = 4.0740.$$

The Macaulay duration formula is applicable only to fixed-income securities. For instance, one cannot directly calculate the duration of an FRN because the future cash flows are not known with certainty. Using the idea that duration is a measure of price elasticity, however, analysts often use the concept of *implied duration*. The implied duration of an FRN that resets its coupon every six months (e.g., at LIBOR + 0.25 percent) is taken to be the time remaining in the coupon reset period.

Immediately before the next coupon rate is set, the implied duration is zero. The market price of the FRN will be par value no matter what the level of LIBOR. Note that this result assumes no constraining maximum or minimum coupon rate and no change in the credit risk of the issuer or in the marketability of the issue itself. Immediately after the rate is set, the implied duration is six months because, like any zero-coupon security, the next cash flow is certain. The implied duration will then decline in a linear fashion as the next reset date nears. This pattern is shown in Figure A-2.

Figure A-2 Implied Duration for a Floating-Rate Note

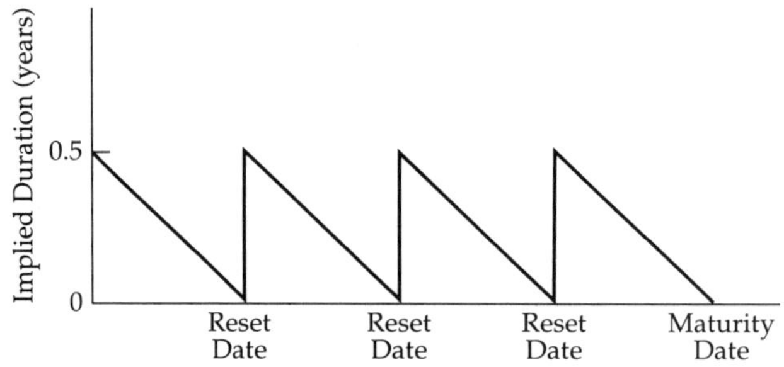

Selected Swap References

Collections

Beidleman, Carl R., ed. 1991. *Interest Rate Swaps.* Homewood, Ill.: Business One Irwin.

______. 1992. *Cross Currency Swaps.* Homewood, Ill.: Business One Irwin.

General References

Brown, Brandon. 1989. *The Economics of the Swap Market.* London: Routledge.

Dattatreya, Ravi E., Raj E.S. Venkatesh, and Vijaya Venkatesh. 1994. *Interest Rate & Currency Swaps.* Chicago: Probus Publishing.

Dattatreya, Ravi E., and Kensuke Hotta. 1994. *Advanced Interest Rate and Currency Swaps.* Chicago: Probus Publishing.

Eckl, S., J.N. Robinson, and D.C. Thomas. 1991. *Financial Engineering: A Handbook of Derivative Products.* Cambridge, Mass.: Basil Blackwell.

Gastineau, Gary L. 1992. *Dictionary of Financial Risk Management.* Chicago: Probus Publishing.

Kapner, Kenneth, and John Marshall. 1991. *The Swaps Handbook.* New York: New York Institute of Finance.

Kawaller, Ira. 1992. *Financial Futures and Options.* Chicago: Probus Publishing.

Hull, John. 1993. *Options, Futures, and Other Derivative Securities,* 2nd ed. Englewood Cliffs, N.J.: Prentice Hall.

Marshall, John, and Kenneth Kapner. 1992. *The Swaps Market,* 2nd ed. Miami, Fla.: Kolb Publishing.

Price, John A.M., and Schuyler K. Henderson. 1984. *Currency and Interest Rate Swaps.* London: Butterworths.

Smith, Clifford W., Jr., Charles W. Smithson, and D. Sykes Wilford. 1990. *Managing Financial Risk.* New York: Harper & Row.

Walmsley, Julian. 1988. *The New Financial Instruments.* New York: John Wiley & Sons.

Background and Overview

Arak, Marcelle, Arturo Estrella, Laurie Goodman, and Andrew Silver. 1988. "Interest Rate Swaps: An Alternative Explanation." *Financial Management* 17:12–18.

Bicksler, James, and Andrew H. Chen. 1986. "An Economic Analysis of Interest Rate Swaps." *The Journal of Finance* 41:645–56.

Campbell, Tim S., and William A. Kracaw. 1991. "Intermediation and the Market for Interest Rate Swaps." *Journal of Financial Intermediation* 1:362–84.

Falloon, William. 1988. "The ABC's of Swaps." *Intermarket* 5:25–42.

Loeys, Jan G. 1985. "Interest Rate Swaps: A New Tool for Managing Risk," Federal Reserve Bank of Philadelphia *Business Review,* 17–25.

Smith, Clifford W., Jr., Charles W. Smithson, and Lee M. Wakeman. 1986. "The Evolving Market for Swaps." *Midland Corporate Finance Journal* 3:20–32.

______. 1988. "The Market for Interest Rate Swaps." *Financial Management* 17:34–44.

Sood, Arvinder. 1988. "The Long and Short of Interest Rate Swap Spreads." *Risk* April:24–26.

Wall, Larry D., and John J. Pringle. 1988. "Interest Rate Swaps: A Review of the Issues." *Economic Review* 73:22–40.

______. 1989. "Alternative Explanations of Interest Rate Swaps: A Theoretical and Empirical Analysis." *Financial Management* 18:59–73.

Wishon, Keith, and Lorin Chevalier. 1985. "Interest Rate Swaps—Your Rate or Mine?" *Journal of Accountancy,* 63–84.

Applications

Arnold, Tanya. 1984. "How to Do Interest Rate Swaps." *Harvard Business Review* 62:96–101.

Brown, Keith C., and Donald J. Smith. 1989. "Swap Driven Deals." *Intermarket* 6:15–18.

Einzig, Robert, and Bruce Lange. 1990. "Swaps at Transamerica: Applications and Analysis." *Journal of Applied Corporate Finance* 2:48–58.

Felgran, Steven D. 1987. "Interest Rate Swaps: Use, Risk, and Prices." Federal Reserve Bank of Boston *New England Economic Review,* 22–32.

Goodman, Laurie S. 1990. "The Uses of Interest Rate Swaps in Managing Corporate Liabilities." *Journal of Applied Corporate Finance* 2:35–47.

Kawaller, Ira G. 1989. "Interest Rate Swaps versus Eurodollar Strips." *Financial Analysts Journal* 45:55–61.

Kopprasch, Robert W. 1993. "Using Swaps in the Fixed-Income Portfolio." In *Derivative Strategies for Managing Portfolio Risk,* 27–32. Charlottesville, Va.: Association for Investment Management and Research.

Kuprianov, Anatoli. 1994. "The Role of Interest Rate Swaps in Corporate Finance." Federal Reserve Bank of Richmond *Economic Quarterly* 80:49–68.

Madura, J., and C. Williams. 1987. "Hedging Mortgages with Interest Rate Swaps vs. Caps: How to Choose." *Real Estate Finance* 3:90–96.

Park, Y.S. 1984. "Currency Swaps as a Long-Term International Financing Technique." *Journal of International Business Studies* 15:47–54.

Szabo, Andrew J. 1988. "Interest Rate Swaps: A Powerful Tool in Real Estate Finance." *Real Estate Review* 17:37–43.

Titman, Sheridan. 1992. "Interest Rate Swaps and Corporate Financing Choices." *The Journal of Finance* 47:1503–16.

Valuation and Empirical Analysis

Abken, Peter A. 1992. "Valuation of Default-Risky Interest Rate Swaps." *Advances in Futures and Options Research* 6:93–116.

Bansal, Vipul K., M.E. Ellis, and John F. Marshall. 1993. "The Pricing of Short-Dated and Forward Interest Rate Swaps." *Financial Analysts Journal* 49:82–87.

Bansal, Vipul K., James L. Bicksler, Andrew H. Chen, and John F. Marshall. 1993. "Gains from Synthetic Financing with Interest Rate Swaps: Fact or Fancy?" *Journal of Applied Corporate Finance* 6:91–94.

Brown, Keith C., W.V. Harlow, and D. Smith. 1994. "An Empirical Analysis of Interest Rate Swap Spreads." *The Journal of Fixed Income* 3:61–78.

Khoury, Sarkis J. 1990. "The Nature of Interest Swaps and the Pricing of Their Risks." *Journal of Accounting, Auditing and Finance* 5:459–73.

Kim, Sung-Hwa, and Gary D. Koppenhaver. 1993. "An Empirical Analysis of Bank Interest Rate Swaps." *Journal of Financial Services Research* 7:57–72.

McNulty, James E. 1990. "The Pricing of Interest Rate Swaps." *Journal of Financial Services Research* 4:53–63.

Rendleman, Richard L. 1993. "How Risks are Shared in Interest Rate Swaps." *Journal of Financial Services Research* 7:5–34.

Simpson, John L. 1993. "Credit Risk and the Pricing of Interest Rate Swaps." Working paper, Federal Reserve Bank of New York.

Sun, Tong-sheng, Suresh Sundaresan, and Ching Wang. 1993. "Interest Rate Swaps: An Empirical Investigation." *Journal of Financial Economics* 34:77–99.

Sundaresan, Suresh. 1989. "Valuation of Swaps." Working paper, Columbia University.

Turnbull, Stuart. 1987. "Swaps: A Zero Sum Game?" *Financial Management* 16:15–21.

Wall, Larry D. 1989. "Interest Rate Swaps in an Agency Theoretic Model with Uncertain Interest Rates." *Journal of Banking and Finance* 13:261–70.

Whittaker, J. Greg. 1987. "Pricing Interest Rate Swaps in an Options Pricing Framework." Working paper, Federal Reserve Bank of Kansas City.

Yaksick, Rudy. 1992. "Swaps, Caps, and Floors: Some Parity and Price Identities." *Journal of Financial Engineering* 1:105–15.

Credit Risk Issues

Aggarwal, Raj. 1991. "Assessing Risks in Interest-Rate Swaps: The Role of Legal and Institutional Uncertainties." *Journal of Cash Management* 11:15–18.

Brown, Keith C. 1993. "Understanding the Risks in Over-the-Counter Derivative Structures," 20–25. In *Derivative*

Strategies for Managing Portfolio Risk. Charlottesville, Va.: Association for Investment Management and Research.

Brown, Keith C., and Donald J. Smith. 1993. "Credit Risk and Innovations in the Design of Interest Rate Swaps." *Financial Management* 22:94–105.

Cooper, Ian A., and Antonio S. Mello. 1991. "The Default Risk of Swaps." *The Journal of Finance* 46:597–620.

Hull, John. 1989. "An Analysis of the Credit Risks in Interest Rate Swaps and Currency Swaps." *Recent Developments in International Banking and Finance* 3:109–30.

Muffet, Mark. 1987. "Modeling Credit Exposure on Swaps," 473–96. In *Conference on Bank Structure and Competition*. Federal Reserve Bank of Chicago.

Neal, Kathleen, and Katerina Simons. 1988. "Interest Rate Swaps, Currency Swaps, and Credit Risk." *Issues in Bank Regulation*, 26–29.

Simons, Katrina. 1989. "Measuring Credit Risk in Interest Rate Swaps." Federal Reserve Bank of Boston *New England Economic Review,* 29–38.

Smith, Clifford W., Jr., Charles W. Smithson, and Lee M. Wakeman. 1987. "Credit Risk and the Scope of Regulation of Swaps." In *Conference on Bank Structure and Competition*, 166–85. Federal Reserve Bank of Chicago.

Smith, Donald J. 1988/1989. "Interest Rate Movements and the Credit Risk of Interest Rate Swaps." *Commercial Lending Review* 4:39–52.

Solnik, Bruno. 1990. "Swap Pricing and Default Risk: A Note." *Journal of International Financial Management and Accounting* 2:79–91.

Sorensen, Eric H., and Thierry F. Bollier. 1994. "Pricing Swap Default Risk." *Financial Analysts Journal* 50:23–33.

Usmen, Nilufer. 1994. "Currency Swaps, Financial Arbitrage, and Default Risk." *Financial Management* 23:43–57.

Wall, Larry D., and Kwun-wing C. Fung. 1987. "Evaluating the Credit Exposure of Interest Rate Swap Portfolios." Working paper, Federal Reserve Bank of Atlanta.

Documentation, Regulation, and Tax Issues

Arak, Marcelle. 1992. "The Effect of the New Risk-Based Capital Requirements on the Market for Swaps." *Journal of Financial Services Research* 6:25–36.

Genova, Diane, and Don Thompson. 1988. "A Guide to Standard Swap Documentation." *Commercial Lending Review* 3:44–49.

Greenberg, Suzanne F., and Christopher R. Kelly. 1989. "Swaps and Gaps: Clarifying U.S. Tax Rules." *International Financial Law Review* (U.K.) 8:7–10.

Riley, W.B., and G.S. Smith. 1987. "Interest Rate Swaps: Disclosure and Recognition." *CPA Journal* 57:64–70.

Tucker, Scot. 1991. "Interest Rate Swaps and the 1990 Amendments to United States Bankruptcy Code: A Measure of Certainty within Swap Contracts." *Utah Law Review*, 581–615.

Whittaker, J. Greg. 1987. "Interest Rate Swaps: Risk and Regulation." Federal Reserve Bank of Kansas City *Economic Review* 72:3–13.

Related Discussions

Bansal, Vipul K., M.E. Ellis, and John F. Marshall. 1992. "The Spot Swap Yield Curve: Derivation and Use." *Advances in Futures and Options Research* 6:279–90.

Brooks, Robert, and D.K. Malhotra. 1992. "Components of the Bid Ask Spread of Default-Risky Interest Rate Swaps." *Advances in Futures and Options Research* 7:237–49.

Brown, Keith C., and Donald J. Smith. 1988. "Recent Innovations in Interest Rate Risk Management and the Reintermediation of Commercial Banking." *Financial Management* 17:45–58.

Chen, Andrew H., and Marcia H. Millon. 1989. "The Secondary Market and Dynamic Swap Management." *Recent Developments in International Banking and Finance* 3:131–48.

Smith, Clifford W., Jr., Charles W. Smithson, and D. Sykes Wilford. 1989. "Building Blocks: Forwards, Futures, Swaps, Options and Hybrids." *Intermarket* 6:32–37.

Smith, Donald J. 1989. "The Arithmetic of Financial Engineering." *Journal of Applied Corporate Finance* 1:49–58.

Swap Variations and Advanced Strategies

Abken, Peter. 1991. "Beyond Plain Vanilla: A Taxonomy of Swaps." Federal Reserve Bank of Atlanta *Economic Review* 75:12–29.

Allen, Julie A., and Janet L. Showers. 1991. "Equity-Index-Linked Derivatives: An Investor's Guide." Working paper, Salomon Brothers.

Brown, Keith C., and Robert F. Semmens. 1994. "Perspectives on Integration in the Oil Industry: Innovations from the Financial Market." In Kate Gillespie, ed., *Oil in the New World Order.* Gainesville, Fla.: University of Florida Press.

Brown, Keith C., and Donald J. Smith. 1990. "Forward Swaps, Swap Options and the Management of Callable Debt." *Journal of Applied Corporate Finance* 2:59–71.

Fernald, Julia D. 1993/1994. "The Pricing and Hedging of Index Amortizing Rate Swaps." Federal Reserve Bank of New York *Quarterly Review* 18:71–74.

Galaif, Lisa N. 1993/1994. "Index Amortizing Rate Swaps." Federal Reserve Bank of New York *Quarterly Review* 18:63–70.

Gastineau, Gary L. 1993. "Using Swaps in Equity Portfolios." In *Derivative Strategies for Managing Portfolio Risk,* 74–77. Charlottesville, Va.: Association for Investment Management and Research.

______. "Rate Differential Swaps and Deferred Strike Options." *The Journal of Derivatives* 2:59–62.

Litzenberger, Robert H. 1992. "Swaps: Plain and Fancy." *The Journal of Finance* 47:831–50.

Marshall, John F., Vipul K. Bansal, Anthony F. Herbst, and Alan L. Tucker. 1992. "Hedging Business Cycle Risk with Macro Swaps and Options." *Journal of Applied Corporate Finance* 4:103–108.

Marshall, John F., Eric H. Sorensen, and Alan L. Tucker. 1992. "Equity Derivatives: The Plain Vanilla Equity Swap and Its Variants." *Journal of Financial Engineering* 1:219–41.

Glossary of Swap Terminology

Arbitrage: The opportunity to exploit price differentials on two otherwise identical sets of cash flows. In arbitrage-free financial markets, any two transactions with the same risks and expected cash flows should have the same price.

Arrears Swap: A swap agreement in which the floating rate is both set and paid at the end of the settlement period. In contrast, the usual arrangement is to set the rate in advance and pay it in arrears.

Asset Swap: A standard swap contract that is used to convert the interest rate or currency exposure of any security held as an asset.

Assignment: The transfer of an existing swap contract from one counterparty to another. Because of credit quality differentials between the existing and potential participants, assignment requires either consent of the remaining counterparty or legal action.

Basis Point (bp): An amount equal to 0.01 percentage point. For example, a change in rates from 5.00 percent to 5.25 percent would be an increase of 25 basis points.

Basis-Point Value: The change in the market value of an investment holding caused by a 1-basis-point change in interest rates. This change is often approximated by multiplying a position's dollar duration statistic by 0.0001.

Basis Risk: The residual risk resulting from hedging an underlying economic exposure with a hedge vehicle that is less-than-perfectly correlated. Basis risk in swap transactions can exist because of reference rate, notional principal, or settlement date mismatches. Basis risk is also known as *tracking error* or *correlation risk*.

Basis Swap: An interest rate swap in which both sides are linked to reference rates that reset on each settlement date.

Bid–Offer Spread: The fixed rate at which a dealer will take either the pay- or the receive-fixed side of a swap transaction. The offer rate is also called the *ask* rate.

Broker: A financial institution that facilitates a swap transaction between two counterparties but does not itself become a counterparty to the agreement. The broker's compensation comes in the form of a swap arrangement fee.

Cap Agreement: A contract that on each settlement date pays its holder the greater of the difference between the reference rate and the strike rate or zero. A cap is equivalent to a series of call options on the reference rate or put options on the underlying security.

Collar Agreement: The combination of a long (short) cap agreement and a short (long) floor agreement for which the cap and floor strike rates are usually selected to be out of the money. An interest rate swap can be viewed as a zero-cost collar in which the cap and floor strike rates are identical. Also called a *range forward* in foreign exchange (FX) deals.

Commodity Swap: A swap transaction in which one of the cash flows is tied to a fixed price for a commodity and the other is based on a fluctuating commodity index level. The most common commodity swaps involve base metals, precious metals, and energy.

Constant-Maturity Swap: A form of basis swap in which one side is referenced to a short-term rate such as LIBOR and the other is based on the long-term constant-maturity Treasury bond yield. By resetting the two sides of the agreement to different points on the yield curve, this contract is often used to exploit changes in the shape of the term structure of interest rates. Also known as a *yield curve swap*.

Constant-Maturity Treasury (CMT): An interest rate index that is based on a hypothetical Treasury security with a fixed maturity. Most often used as the floating-rate side of a constant-maturity basis swap or the reference rate in an indexed amortizing rate swap.

Convexity: A statistic summarizing how the duration of a fixed-income security changes when yields change. Convexity can be viewed as the approximate difference between the actual price response to a given interest rate change and the response predicted by the duration-based formula. A security with positive convexity will benefit more (suffer less) than predicted from rate declines (increases). Negative convexity instruments such as mortgage-linked securities having prepayment options will show the opposite effect.

Correlation: A statistical measure summarizing the joint volatility of two variables such as the prices or yields on different financial instruments. A positive correlation coefficient indicates that two security returns tend to move in the same direction. Negative correlation, which is the basis for hedging, exists when the two return series tend to move in opposite directions.

Corridor Swap: An interest rate swap in which the payment obligation accrues only on those days during the settlement period when the reference rate is within a predetermined range, or corridor. This arrangement is structured to help a counterparty exploit a view on the volatility of interest rates.

Counterparty: A participant in a swap transaction. It is often useful to distinguish between counterparties that are corporate end users and the market makers whose function is to facilitate trade.

Cross-Default: A swap contract provision specifying that default by a counterparty on any other financial transaction triggers default on the swap. This condition is intended to eliminate a distressed firm's ability to strategically time a swap's default.

Currency Swap: A swap transaction in which the cash flows are denominated in different currencies. This type of contract often dictates a physical exchange of principal on the origination and maturity dates. It can be designed so that both rates are fixed, both are floating, or one is floating and the other fixed. A deal structure that does not require the re-exchange of principal at maturity is called a *currency annuity swap*.

Day Count: The convention used for prorating an interest rate movement expressed on an annual basis to the percentage of the year represented by the settlement period. The three most common day-count conventions are actual/360, actual/365, and 30/360.

Dealer: A financial institution that facilitates swap transactions by acting as a direct counterparty. A dealer's compensation comes as trading profit from paying a low fixed rate (i.e., the bid rate) and receiving a high fixed rate (i.e., the offer rate).

Default Exposure: The loss that would be incurred by an individual or corporation on a swap transaction if its counterparty defaults. Measurement of default exposure is usually divided into the actual loss that would be realized if the counterparty defaults today (i.e., *mark-to-market* exposure) and the worst-case potential exposure (i.e., *fractional* exposure) if the counterparty defaults at some point in the future.

Dollar Duration: A statistic approximating the dollar change in the price of a fixed-income security for a given percentage change in 1 plus the periodic yield. Dollar duration is calculated by rearranging the basic *Macaulay duration* equation linking percentage price and percentage yield movements.

Duration: A statistic summarizing the approximate relationship between the price of a fixed-income security and interest rates. *Macaulay duration* links the percentage change in a bond's price with the inverse of the percentage change in 1 plus the periodic yield; *modified duration* is the Macaulay statistic divided by 1 plus the periodic yield.

Equity Swap: A swap transaction in which one cash flow is tied to the return to an equity portfolio position, often an index such as the Standard & Poor's 500, while the other is based on a floating-debt yield such as LIBOR.

Financial Engineering: An idiomatic expression most often associated with the action of packaging or repackaging a set of cash flows in order to satisfy the disparate needs of different end users or to create a risk–return trade-off that is otherwise unavailable. A simple example would be combining a floating-rate note with an interest rate swap to convert a variable stream of debt payments into a fixed-rate obligation.

Floating-Rate Note (FRN): Also known as floaters, these instruments are short- to intermediate-term bonds with coupon payments linked to a variable reference rate, most often LIBOR. Common coupon reset formulas include *traditional* floaters, for which the cash flow varies directly with LIBOR movements; *reverse FRNs*, which specify a coupon equal to a constant percentage less LIBOR; and *bear floaters*, with coupons equal to a multiple of LIBOR less a constant percentage.

Floor Agreement: A contract that on each settlement date pays its holder the greater of the difference between the strike rate and the reference rate or zero. A floor is equivalent to a series of put options on the reference rate or call options on the underlying security.

Forward Curve: The sequence of future yields corresponding to the floating reference rates on a swap. Forward curves can be observed directly from the rates built into *forward rate agreements* and Eurodollar futures prices, inferred from cash market prices, or estimated by interpolation from the Treasury yield curve.

Forward Rate Agreement (FRA): A transaction in which two counterparties agree to a single exchange of cash flows based on a fixed and a floating rate, respectively. FRAs can be viewed as one-date interest rate swaps.

Forward Swap: Also known as a *deferred-start swap*, this agreement is one for which the terms are negotiated now but not scheduled to begin until a later date.

Fractional Exposure: The potential default exposure on an uncollateralized derivative transaction. This exposure is often calculated by measuring the mark-to-market exposure of a swap, cap, or floor at every future settlement date using each of several projected interest rate paths and then selecting the worst-case scenario.

Gap Analysis: The process of establishing interest rate and currency exposure mismatches among the assets and liabilities on a balance sheet. *Duration gap* is one form of this analysis using the present value sensitivities of the various accounts.

Hedge: A financial transaction designed to reduce, either fully or partially, the market risk associated with a particular security or balance sheet account. This reduction in risk is accomplished by adopting a hedge position, often by using a derivative such as a swap that is negatively correlated with the underlying exposure.

Hedge Ratio: The amount of the hedge position required to offset the market risk in an underlying position. Depending on the nature of the instruments involved, hedge ratios can be expressed in either numbers of contracts or the total dollar value needed.

Implied Forward Rate: The reinvestment rate built into the yields of financial instruments that differ only in time to maturity. For example, one- and two-year zero-coupon yields of 5 percent and 6 percent, respectively, imply a one-year yield, one year forward of 7 percent; that is, 6 percent a year for two years is equivalent to 5 percent for the first rolled into 7 percent for the second.

Implied Volatility: A volatility measure derived by setting the market price of a derivative security (such as a swaption) equal to its fair value, as indicated by a theoretical valuation model. Implied volatility statistics are often used as surrogate measures in determining whether a derivative security is mispriced.

In the Money: A derivative security that is profitable for the holder to exercise at current market conditions is said to be in the money. For example, an in-the-money cap agreement is one for which the level of the reference rate is greater than the strike rate.

Indexed Amortizing Rate Swap: A swap in which the notional principal varies according to changes in a market reference rate, often the constant-maturity Treasury index or LIBOR. Used to mimic the negative convexity in mortgage securities, the notional principal is typically scheduled to decline as market rates fall.

Interest Rate Swap: A generic agreement calling for the periodic exchange of cash flows, one based on an interest rate that remains fixed for the tenor of the contract and the other linked to a variable-rate index. Cash payments are determined by a notional principal and are usually made on a net settlement basis.

Intermediation: The act of repackaging the cash flows between the ultimate long and short positions in a financial transaction. In the swap market, intermediation usually involves hedging one contract with any of several different instruments, including other swaps, forward rate agreements, futures, and option contracts. This process is sometimes called running a *dynamic book.*

International Swap and Derivatives Association (ISDA): A trade group whose major contribution has been the creation of the Master Swap Agreement, which has become the standard for documentation in the industry.

London Interbank Offered Rate (LIBOR): The primary short-term rate used in Euromarket security and swap transactions. LIBOR can be expressed in several currencies, including U.S. dollars, British sterling, German marks, Swiss francs, and Japanese yen.

Long Position: The holder, or buyer, of an investment position. Being long in a plain vanilla swap refers to the counterparty in the pay-fixed position.

Matched Book: A situation in which a market maker has arranged exactly offsetting swap transactions so that he or she has no net market risk.

Mark-to-Market (MTM) Exposure: The actual loss incurred on an existing swap (or a long position in a cap or floor) if the counterparty defaults today, measured as the cost of negotiating a replacement for the defaulted transaction. For instance, if a company paying fixed on an 8 percent, three-year swap had its counterparty default at a time when new swaps require 9 percent payments, the MTM exposure would be the present value of a three-year annuity equal to the 1 percent rate differential times the notional principal.

Mark-to-Market Swap: An interest rate swap in which the mark-to-market (i.e., actual) default exposure is exchanged in cash on each settlement date, along with the usual net settlement payment. The fixed rate on the swap is then reset to reflect prevailing market conditions.

Market Maker: In a swap context, any dealer or intermediary who provides regular bid and offer quotes and stands ready to book either a pay-fixed or receive-fixed transaction.

Market Risk: The exposure that results from holding an unhedged swap as market conditions change. For instance, the fixed-rate receiver will see the value of its existing swap position decline as new fixed rates on comparable replacement swaps increase.

Master Swap Agreement: Created and maintained by ISDA, the set of documents outlining the standard terms and conditions governing all swap transactions between two counterparties.

Net Settlement: A condition of a swap agreement that simplifies the settlement process by having the counterparty that owes the larger amount pay the net of the larger and smaller gross obligations.

Netting Agreement: A provision in a swap contract that allows for the offset of settlement payments and receipts on all contracts between the same two counterparties. Although not fully established in all legal venues, this provision is intended to limit default exposure to a counterparty.

Notional Principal: The principal value of a swap transaction, which is not exchanged but is used as a scale factor to translate interest rate differentials into cash settlement payments.

Off-Market Swap: An interest rate swap in which the fixed rate is purposefully set away from the market-clearing level. This requires a payment from the receiver of the above-market (or payer of the below-market) rate to the other counterparty.

Out of the Money: A derivative security that is out of the money cannot be exercised by its holder at a profit under current market conditions. For instance, an out-of-the-money floor agreement is one for which the level of the reference yield is greater than the strike rate.

Parallel Loans: An arrangement that precedes a swap transaction whereby two counterparties create simultaneous loans with one another. These loans are typically made in different currencies and often have different fixed/floating rate exposures.

Plain Vanilla: A term used to describe the most basic form of a single-currency, constant-notional-principal interest rate swap in which fixed-rate cash flows are exchanged for floating-rate payments.

Quality-Spread Differential: The difference between the borrowing advantage that a superior-credit company has over a weak-credit firm in different maturity classes. The standard credit arbitrage explanation for interest rate swaps relies on the existence of a nonzero quality-spread differential between the fixed- and floating-rate markets.

Rate-Differential Swap: Also known as a *diff swap*, this contract is a form of basis swap in which the two cash flows are referenced to short-term rates established in different countries but denominated in the same base currency. In general, derivative structures in which a rate settles in a currency different from the original denomination are called *quantos*.

Reference Rate: The interest rate index defining the floating-rate side of a swap, cap, floor, or swap option agreement. LIBOR is the pre-eminent reference rate in swap-related transactions.

Risk Premium: The difference between the yield set for a risky transaction and the risk-free rate of corresponding maturity. The risk premium is known as a *credit spread* in the bond market and *swap spread* in swap transactions.

Settlement Date: The point in time on which swap cash flows are documented and exchanged. Quarterly or semiannual settlement dates are typical for swap agreements.

Short Position: The seller of an investment position. Being short in a plain vanilla swap refers to the counterparty in the receive-fixed position.

Strike Rate: The rate at which a cap, floor, or swap option can be exercised. It is analogous to the fixed rate in a swap agreement.

Structured Finance: An approach to creating financial transactions that attempts to tailor an instrument to the specific needs of the eventual end user. These deals often require an intermediary to combine stock and bond positions with derivative securities to construct a set of cash flows that either have the desired properties or create an arbitrage opportunity.

Swap Option: Also called *swaptions*, these contracts give the holder the right, but not the obligation, to enter into an interest rate or currency swap at prearranged terms. A *receiver* swaption gives the holder the right to enter the swap as the fixed-rate receiver; a *payer* swaption permits entry as the fixed-rate payer. Swaptions can also be designed to allow a counterparty to exit from an existing swap.

Swap Spread: The difference between the fixed rate on a swap and the Treasury yield of equivalent maturity. Most often used as a convenience in quoting U.S. dollar-denominated interest rate swaps.

TED Spread: The Treasury bill futures price less the Eurodollar futures price for contracts of comparable maturities and a common delivery date.

TED Spread Swap: A basis swap structured so that the respective cash flows are referenced to LIBOR and the Treasury bill yield. This contract is designed to take advantage of changes in the credit spread at the short-term end of the yield curve.

Tenor: The maturity of a swap transaction.

Varying Notional Principal Swap: A swap transaction in which the notional principal changes with each settlement, usually according to a prearranged schedule. *Amortizing* swaps have decreasing notional principal levels, and *accreting* swaps have increasing levels. An agreement that first accretes and then amortizes is called a *roller coaster* swap.

Volatility: A statistical representation of the changes in price or yield of a given security or balance sheet account over time. Often used to gauge the level of market risk inherent in an underlying position before structuring a hedge portfolio, volatility is indicated by such quantitative measures as *standard deviation* or *beta*.

Yield Curve: A graphical depiction of the current yields to maturity versus time for a set of financial instruments that are alike in all respects (e.g., liquidity, taxation, default risk) except for maturity. Also known as the *term structure of interest rates* when referring to yields on zero-coupon, default-free securities.

Zero-Coupon Swap: A swap in which the fixed-rate receiver gets a single settlement payment at maturity and the fixed-rate payer receives periodic settlements based on movements in a floating-rate index.